Test Bank for

THE
AMERICAN
PROMISE

A HISTORY OF THE UNITED STATES

Volume I: To 1877

Second Edition

D1406871

Test Bank for

THE AMERICAN PROMISE

A HISTORY OF THE UNITED STATES

Volume I: To 1877

Second Edition

VALERIE HINTON
Richland College

NORMAN C. MCLEOD JR.
Dixie State College

BEDFORD / ST. MARTIN'S
Boston • New York

Copyright © 2002 by Bedford/St. Martin's

All rights reserved.
Manufactured in the United States of America.

6   5   4   3   2   1
f   e   d   c   b   a

For information, contact: Bedford/St. Martin's, 75 Arlington Street, Boston, MA 02116
(617-399-4000)
www.bedfordstmartins.com

ISBN: 0–312–39409–8

Instructors who have adopted *The American Promise: A History of the United States,* Second Edition, as a textbook for a course are authorized to duplicate portions of this test bank for their students.

PREFACE

Thoroughly revised for the second edition of *The American Promise* and developed with the assistance of the author team to meet teachers' varying needs, the *Test Bank* helps instructors assess students' understanding of historical material by balancing questions that test basic comprehension with questions that encourage and promote students' critical-thinking skills. Because facts are much more significant when considered within their historical context, special attention has been given to structuring questions that assess students' grasp of the broader significance of specific political, social, economic, and cultural events and developments.

Content and Organization

For each chapter in the textbook, the *Test Bank* includes fifty **multiple-choice** questions focused on important details and concepts. The correct answer for each question, the heading and page numbers for the corresponding textbook section, and a ranking of easy, medium, or difficult are provided in the **Answer Key** at the back of the book, allowing instructors to give the desired amount of coverage to each chapter topic and to design tests that challenge their students appropriately. A **terminology** exercise asks students to match significant names, places, events, and ideas with a definition or example. This exercise offers instructors further opportunity to adjust the difficulty level of their tests: used with the list of definitions provided, as a matching section, the terminology exercise is ranked as easy to medium; used without the list of definitions, with students being asked to define or give an example of each term themselves, the exercise is ranked as medium to difficult. A **chronology** exercise designed to emphasize causal relationships asks students to put key events in chronological order. Answers for the terminology and chronology exercises are provided in the Answer Key as well. Next, ten **short-answer** and four **essay** questions — rated as easy, medium, or difficult, with references to corresponding sections in *The American Promise* — require students to interpret and discuss historical data and major ideas using material from the chapter. Lastly, a map exercise tests students' ability to garner basic information from maps as well as relate that information to historical events or developments discussed in the chapter.

Computerized Test Bank and Quizzing on the Online Study Guide

The *Test Bank for THE AMERICAN PROMISE* is also available on CD-ROM for Windows and Macintosh formats. Easy-to-use software provides the test items in the print version and gives instructors the option of editing those questions or creating their own questions. Instructors can generate print versions of tests and quizzes, and tests can be administered over a network. A grade-management function helps keep track of student progress.

In addition, the Online Study Guide for *The American Promise* provides multiple-choice tests as well as structured and easily accessed help. A total of three multiple-choice tests per chapter helps students grasp their command of the material, and a Recommended Study Plan suggests specific exercises that cover the subject areas students still need to master. Additional exercises encourage students to think about chapter themes as well as help them develop skills of analysis. Please contact your local Bedford/St. Martin's sales representative to request a computerized test bank, and visit **www.bedfordstmartins.com/tap** to learn more about this unique online study guide.

CONTENTS

PROLOGUE: ANCIENT AMERICA
Before 1492

Multiple Choice   Choose the letter of the best answer.

1. Prior to the find at Folsom, New Mexico, in the 1920s, many archaeologists believed that the first people of North America
   a. arrived relatively recently, probably no more than four thousand years ago.
   b. hunted giant bison before they became extinct around A.D. 1100.
   c. were skilled Viking sailors.
   d. arrived from Polynesia by navigating the South Pacific.

2. The following statement does not accurately describe the work of an historian:
   a. Historians seek artifacts over written documents to determine the attitudes of a people.
   b. Historians study artifacts, but they focus more of their attention on written documents left by people in the past.
   c. Historians and archaeologists usually employ different methods to obtain information.
   d. Historians study personal as well as public writings.

3. The basic reason for the early, prolonged absence of humans in the Western Hemisphere is that
   a. the warm climate of Africa attracted most of the earth's population.
   b. large herds of mammoths made migration to the Americas too dangerous.
   c. North and South America had become detached from the gigantic continent of Pangaea.
   d. food was too plentiful for northern European tribes to seek a different home.

4. The Wisconsin glaciation created conditions that permitted
   a. a warming of the waters of the Bering Strait, thereby raising the sea level 350 feet and allowing easy navigation over submerged icebergs.
   b. a very narrow land bridge to surface for a short time to permit some migrating hunters to leave Asian Siberia and enter American Alaska.
   c. the creation of Beringia, which supported herds of mammoth, bison, and horses.
   d. a freezing of the waters of the Bering Strait, which supported over-the-ice migration of hunters into American Alaska.

5. Although the exact time people first migrated to North America is debated by experts, the first migrants probably arrived
   a. around 25,000 years ago.
   b. around 15,000 years ago.
   c. over 1.5 million years ago.
   d. less than 5,000 years ago.

6. Most of the artifacts that have survived from the Paleo-Indian era suggest that
   a. the people specialized in hunting big mammals.
   b. the people developed permanent settlements along the Canadian Rockies.
   c. the people used bows and arrows to kill small animals.
   d. the people rejected a diet of plants.

7. About 11,000 years ago, the Paleo-Indians faced a major crisis:
   a. the people had difficulty living in a cooling climate.
   b. the large animals they hunted had difficulty adapting to a warming climate.
   c. an overconcentration on hunting small animals eliminated much of the food sources of the large mammals.
   d. water became scarce as the climate cooled.

8. The apparent uniformity of the big-game-oriented Clovis culture was replaced by great cultural diversity in the last eleven millennia because
   a. people devoted more energy to developing stationary agriculture, which led to more diverse farming cultures.
   b. people devoted more energy to domesticating animals to replace the large mammals, which led to greater specialization of tribal roles.
   c. people devoted more energy to developing trade networks, which led to more bartering and exchange of ideas.
   d. people devoted more energy to foraging, which pushed them into other natural environments that led to more profound environmental adaptations.

9. The term *Archaic* describes the
   a. hunting and gathering cultures that descended from Paleo-Indians, as well as the period in time from 8000 B.C. to approximately 2000–1000 B.C.
   b. agricultural cultures that preceded the Paleo-Indians before 11,000 B.C.
   c. hunting and gathering cultures that descended from Paleo-Indians, as well as the period in time from A.D. 800–1500.
   d. agricultural cultures that descended from Paleo-Indians after A.D. 800.

10. The following is an accurate description of Archaic Indians:
    a. They depended on agriculture for food.
    b. Most established permanent, though small, villages.
    c. They developed a technique for pulverizing seeds into edible form.
    d. They domesticated animals as a food source.

11. Archaic Indians who hunted the bison herds of the Great Plains were
    a. skilled horsemen.
    b. nomads who moved constantly to maintain contact with their prey.
    c. solitary hunters.
    d. noble hunters who avoided stampeding the herds.

12. The Archaic Indians in the Great Basin inhabited a region of
    a. moderate temperature variations and long growing seasons.
    b. few game animals and waterfowl.
    c. predominantly desert topography with little plant or animal life.
    d. great environmental diversity, including marshes, deserts, and mountains.

13. The most important source of food for Archaic peoples in the Great Basin was
    a. bison.
    b. fish.
    c. plants.
    d. waterfowl.

14. The Archaic Indians of the Great Basin maintained their basic hunter-gatherer way of life until long after A.D. 1492 by
    a. diversifying their food sources and migrating to favorable locations.
    b. carefully charting and following the migrations of a particular game animal.
    c. concentrating their settlements near the rainy foothills of mountains.
    d. relying primarily on a diet of small game meat.

15. The primary reason native peoples in California remained hunters and gatherers for hundreds of years after Europeans arrived in the western hemisphere was that
    a. California was the least populated area in all of ancient America, and little competition existed for food sources.
    b. both the land and ocean provided an abundant food supply.
    c. the native people developed specialized diets that included only fish and marine life.
    d. the small number of tribes in the region freely shared acorn-gathering territory.

16. Archaeological evidence indicates that the California Chumash culture was characterized by
    a. a highly nomadic existence.
    b. a relatively conflict-free society.
    c. a notable proportion of violent deaths.
    d. a population living on the edge of starvation.

17. Much of the conflict among Archaic Northwestern tribes seems to have arisen from
    a. attempts to defend good fishing sites.
    b. a scarcity of salmon and other fish.
    c. the pressure to find a constant supply of fresh food.
    d. clan rivalries.

18. The Archaic Northwest peoples
    a. erected small tents of buffalo skins adorned with highly intricate quillwork.
    b. carved out pueblo dwellings in the side of mountains, adorned with sand paintings.
    c. constructed large, multifamily cedar houses adorned with totems.
    d. created small, single-family structures from glacial ice adorned with ironwork.

19. The cultures of the Archaic peoples of the Eastern Woodland were shaped by their
    a. mountainous environment.
    b. forest environment.
    c. desert environment.
    d. seacoast environment.

20. Until approximately four thousand years ago, the basic survival strategies of Woodland Indians consisted of
    a. hunting deer and gathering nuts and seeds.
    b. following the great herds of bison and harvesting wild-growing corn.
    c. herding sheep and fishing for salmon.
    d. building large, permanent settlements and growing a variety of crops.

21. Around 2000 B.C., the following two important changes occurred among Woodland cultures:
    a. they abandoned their hunting-gathering lifestyle and built permanent settlements devoted to raising corn.
    b. they abandoned their hunting-gathering lifestyle and began domesticating animals for food sources.
    c. they began focusing less on hunting and more on plant gathering because their traditional animal food sources were becoming scarce.
    d. they incorporated limited forms of plant growing and pottery making into their hunting-gathering lifestyle.

22. Archaic cultures in the Southwest adopted agriculture in response to
    a. a climate characterized by predictable amounts of rainfall.
    b. fertile, moist soil that yielded surplus quantities of wild plant food.
    c. environmental conditions that encouraged reliable harvests of wild plant seeds for future planting.
    d. environmental conditions that made the supply of wild plant food very unreliable.

23. Corn became a food crop for Southwestern cultures
    a. around A.D. 1620.
    b. around A.D. 1492.
    c. around 1500 B.C.
    d. around 4000 B.C.

24. Ancient Southwestern Indians became experts in
    a. water conservation.
    b. soil conservation.
    c. wild-game conservation.
    d. waterfowl conservation.

25. Multistory cliff dwellings and pueblos are residential structures associated with the
    a. Mogollon culture.
    b. Adena people.
    c. Anasazi communities.
    d. Hopewell excavations.

26. Burial mounds and chiefdoms are associated with
    a. Southwestern cultures.
    b. Woodland cultures.
    c. Pacific Northwest cultures.
    d. Great Basin cultures.

27. The analysis of grave goods in burial mounds at Hopewell sites shows that in at least this chiefdom,
    a. there was a limited trade network restricted to Indians of Illinois and Ohio.
    b. the people lacked artisan skills.
    c. hunters had an elevated status.
    d. lavish personal effects were rejected.

28. Eastern Woodland peoples around the time of Columbus's arrival in 1492 clustered into three major groups:
    a. the Algonquian, Iroquoian, and Muskogean people.
    b. the Pawnee, Mandan, and Comanche tribes.
    c. the Apache, Navajo, and Hopi tribes.
    d. the Sioux, Cheyenne, and Blackfeet people.

29. The League of Five Nations, which remained powerful well into the eighteenth century, was formed as
    a. an alliance among Spain, England, France, Netherlands, and Portugal in A.D. 1500 to promote New World exploration.
    b. a confederation of the Aztec tribes for the purpose of establishing a trade network.
    c. an alliance among the Algonquin tribes for the purposes of perpetuating their nomadic existence.
    d. a confederation of the Iroquoian tribes for the purposes of war and diplomacy.

30. The Athapascan tribes — mainly Apache and Navajo — were
    a. peaceful nomadic tribes who preyed on buffalo.
    b. skillful warriors who preyed on the sedentary pueblo Indians.
    c. successful farmers who grew both corn and sunflowers.
    d. descendants of the Anasazi cultures who lived in settled agricultural communities.

31. At the time of Columbus's arrival in the New World, the population of Native Americans in North America was approximately
    a. 500,000.
    b. 1 million.
    c. 4 million.
    d. 15 million.

32. The greatest similarity among the many tribes that inhabited North America at the dawn of European colonization was that
    a. they employed some form of written language.
    b. they no longer depended upon hunting and gathering for a major portion of their food.
    c. they used domesticated animals for hunting and agricultural production.
    d. their distinct cultures had developed as adaptations to their local natural environments.

33. In A.D. 1492, the empire of the Mexica
    a. stretched from Brazil to Mexico and encompassed 5 million people.
    b. encompassed 25 million people and became enriched by redistributing the wealth of the conquered.
    c. encompassed 2.5 million people and had a rich culture due to the region's abundant rainfall and natural resources.
    d. traded peacefully with neighboring groups, which allowed the Mexica to develop a rich culture that included writing, waterworks, gardens, and zoos.

34. The human sacrifices practiced by the Mexica are said to have been on a scale unequaled in human history; to the Mexica, human sacrifice was
    a. an intuitive remedy to a protein deficiency.
    b. a ritual modeled after their one god, Quetzalcoatl, who methodically sacrificed all the other gods as he created the universe.
    c. a normal and reasonable activity to demonstrate their religious devotion.
    d. a ritual necessary to make crops grow fruitfully.

35. Spanish conquerors exploited the weaknesses of the Mexican empire, which included
    a. subject peoples who did not see the Mexica rulers as either legitimate or fair.
    b. an overreliance on trade with neighboring cultures.
    c. a brewing democratic reform movement.
    d. diverse tribal factions that were often in conflict with one another.

Terminology Matching   Select the word or phrase from the Terms section that best matches the definition or example provided in the Definitions section. Some terms may be used more than once; some may not be used at all.

TERMS

a. archaeologists

b. Archaic

c. artifacts

d. Beringia

e. Bering Strait

f. chiefdoms

g. Chumash

h. Clovis point

i. culture

j. Eastern Woodland cultures

k. Folsom points

l. giant bison

m. Great Basin cultures

n. historians

o. *Homo erectus*

p. *Homo sapiens*

q. Mexica

r. Pacific Coast cultures

s. Paleo-Indians

t. paleontologists

u. prehistory

v. ritualistic cannibalism

w. Southwestern cultures

x. symbolic cannibalism

y. totems

z. Wisconsin glaciation

DEFINITIONS

1. A practice associated with human sacrifice in the Mexica culture in which everyone ate small flour and blood cakes shaped into human forms. _____

2. These artifacts, found in the 1920s along with bones of giant bison, provided new archaeological evidence that human beings had been alive in North America at least 10,000 years ago. _____

3. A distinctively shaped spearhead used by Paleo-Indians to kill big animals found in excavations throughout North and Central America that provides evidence of a shared common ancestry and way of life among nomadic hunters between 9500 and 9000 B.C. _____

4. A group of scholars who obtain information about people of the past by focusing their study on physical objects such as bones, pots, baskets, graves, and buildings. _____

5. A group of scholars who obtain information about people of the past by focusing their study on written records. _____

6. A somewhat misleading term often used to label the long era in which humans existed before the invention of writing. _____

7. Objects remaining from ancient cultures that can be studied as clues to the activities and ideas of the humans who created them. _____

8. Early human beings who evolved in Africa about 1.5 million years ago. _____

9. A one-thousand-mile-wide region, often called a "land bridge," that existed between Asian Siberia and American Alaska during most of the last great global cold spell. _____

10. Scientific term applied to the last great global cold spell in which the sea level dropped as much as 350 feet below its current level, during the era between 78,000 B.C. and 8000 B.C. _____

11. A body of water about sixty miles wide that today separates easternmost Siberia from westernmost Alaska and is a key element in a commonly accepted theory of how the first people migrated into North America. _____

12. An archaeological term referring to the first people and their descendants who migrated into North America around 15,000 years ago. _____

13. A term used by archaeologists that describes the important era in the history of ancient America that followed the Paleo-Indian big-game hunters and preceded the development of agriculture; also denotes a hunter-gatherer way of life that persisted throughout most of North America well into the era of European colonization. _____

14. A term used to describe what is commonly called the "way of life" of a group of people, including — but not limited to — their methods of providing food and shelter, family relationships, social groupings, and religious ideas. _____

15. Elaborately carved images of animals, supernatural beings, or ancestors adorning tribal houses in the Northwest beginning around A.D. 500. _____

16. These Indians inhabited the region between the Rocky Mountains and the Sierra Nevada and used piñon nuts as a dietary staple. _____

17. This grouping of Indian cultures is distinguished by a diversity of about five hundred separate tribes who spoke some ninety languages and who remained hunters and gatherers for hundreds of years after Europeans arrived in the Western Hemisphere because of the abundance of land and ocean resources in their environment. _____

18. One of the many California cultures, they emerged near Santa Barbara around 3000 B.C., established relatively permanent villages, left evidence of many violent deaths, and relied on acorns as a major food source. _____

19. Some Indian cultures in this group had free time to develop sophisticated woodworking skills, partly because they caught large quantities of salmon, halibut, and other fish, which they dried for a continuous food source. _____

20. Deer were the most important prey of these Indian cultures that adapted to a forest environment east of the Mississippi River. _____

21. A term archaeologists apply to social and political hierarchies associated with mound-building cultures. _____

22. The Anasazi were part of this group of Indian cultures, which is characterized by large, multi-story cliff dwellings and pueblo construction. _____

23. By 1500, this cultural group ruled an empire that stretched from coast to coast across central Mexico and included almost 25 million people. _____

24. These ancient Americans probably began cultivating corn in response to a dry climate and unpredictable fluctuations in rainfall that made wild plants an unreliable food source. _____

25. The Hopewell mound building people were part of this cultural group, which had established a large trade network ranging from Wyoming to Florida. _____

Chronology   Place the events in chronological order.

SET ONE

A. Corn cultivation begins in North America.

B. Corn cultivation begins in Central and South America.

C. Paleo-Indians in North and Central America use Clovis points.

D. Bows and arrows appear in North America.

First _____

Second _____

Third _____

Fourth _____

SET TWO

A. Anasazi peoples build cliff dwellings.

B. Mexican empire is established.

C. Eastern Woodland cultures start to build burial mounds.

D. Hopewell culture emerges in Ohio and Mississippi valleys.

First _____

Second _____

Third _____

Fourth _____

Short Answer   Write a paragraph in response to each question.

1. Explain the following statement in reference to Archaic Americans: The absence of written sources means that ancient human beings remain anonymous.

2. Identify the biological and linguistic evidence that archaeologists use to support their conclusions that the first migrants to North America were of Asian origin.

3. Describe the two major adaptations the Paleo-Indians made in their way of life as the mammoths and other large game they hunted became extinct.

4. Explain how the adoption of bows and arrows affected Great Plains hunters who formerly used spears.

5. Identify the climate change that is speculated to have caused the disappearance of the Anasazi culture around A.D. 1130, and explain why this phenomenon would have had such a significant impact on this culture.

6. Around 500 B.C., Woodland peoples in the vast Mississippi valley began to construct burial mounds and other earthworks that suggest the existence of social and political hierarchies that archaeologists term chiefdoms. Define *chiefdoms*, and briefly explain how the mounds and the goods found in them constitute evidence of chiefdoms.

7. The four million Native Americans in North America in 1492 differed in where they lived and how their cultures had adapted to their local natural environments, but they also had many similarities. Describe how these cultures were similar to one another and how they differed from the culture of Europe at the time.

8. Describe the size of the Mexican Empire at the time of its discovery by the Europeans in 1492, and explain how it got to be so large in physical size and population.

Essay   Respond to each of the following questions in an essay of three to four paragraphs. Your responses should include specific evidence and your interpretation of the significance of historical events and concepts.

1. The archaeological discoveries in the excavation of the Folsom Bone Pit in New Mexico during the 1920s have been characterized as having revolutionized knowledge about the first Americans. Write an essay in which you explain how these discoveries helped scholars get a better sense of the migration of the first people to North America, provide an overview of the origins of these people and the geological conditions that facilitated their migration, and speculate on how this migration resulted in the astounding variety of Native American cultures that existed at the dawn of European exploration of the New World.

2. When the first European explorers in the late fifteenth century encountered the culture of Meso-America, they were astounded at the complexity of its society and the wealth of its empire. In an essay, explain the conditions that existed within this culture that made possible their achievements. Include a discussion of the power structure that permeated and controlled this society.

Map Questions   Answer the questions below using Map P.3, Native North Americans about 1500 (p. P-18).

READING THE MAP Name the tribes associated with (1) the Eastern Woodlands region of America, (2) the area between the Mississippi River and the Appalachian Mountains, and (3) the Northeast region of America.

CONNECTIONS According to the tentative conclusions of archaeologists and other experts, in which region(s) of America did corn cultivation begin, and where did it spread? How did this technology spread from one region of the country to another? Did any other technologies migrate from one tribe and region of the country to another?

EUROPEANS AND THE NEW WORLD

1492–1600

Multiple Choice   Choose the letter of the best answer.

1. The government of which country sponsored Christopher Columbus's 1492 exploration?
   a. Italy
   b. France
   c. Spain
   d. Portugal

2. When Columbus first sighted land in 1492, he believed he had discovered a new route to
   a. India and China.
   b. Africa and the Mid-East.
   c. the Americas.
   d. the Mediterranean.

3. Columbus's first impression of the Tainos was that
   a. they would be good slaves.
   b. they possessed strong religious values.
   c. they would be good and intelligent servants.
   d. they could pass as ordinary European peasants.

4. The Tainos shared the following traits with the Europeans:
   a. they farmed, were accomplished seafarers, and held religious beliefs.
   b. they farmed, fished, and held religious beliefs.
   c. they fished, used navigational instruments, and worshiped the spirits of ancestors.
   d. they fished, farmed, and valued gold currency.

5. The impact of Columbus's exploration of the Western Hemisphere differed from the impact of previous explorers because
   a. earlier explorers sought only fish and lumber and left all else alone.
   b. earlier explorers sought only information about the world.
   c. after Columbus, many other explorers set sail, funded by countries that sought resources from colonies.
   d. after Columbus, explorers came to capture slaves as replacements for workers who had died during the bubonic plague epidemic in Europe.

6. While it was unfortunate that the bubonic plague killed about a third of Europe's population, it was beneficial in that it
    a. eased food shortages and weakened the feudal system.
    b. eased pressure on food resources and created greater opportunities for advancement.
    c. created a food surplus which stimulated exploration for new marketplaces.
    d. created a more even distribution of food and weakened the authority of the Catholic Church.

7. Factors which encouraged exploration and territorial expansion included
    a. technological advances in navigational instruments and the hopes of monarchs to gain control of marketplaces.
    b. technological advances in navigational instruments and movable type.
    c. the stability of fifteenth-century European life and the opening of trade between all countries.
    d. the shift in power among European countries and longer life expectancies.

8. The first European nation to break the Italian merchants' control of the Far Eastern trade in the fifteenth century was
    a. England.
    b. Spain.
    c. France.
    d. Portugal.

9. Portugal was an unlikely nation to lead Europe into the Age of Exploration because
    a. it was primarily populated by impoverished, illiterate peasants whose monarchy was destabilized by economic warfare.
    b. it was a small, landlocked nation which, prior to the 1500s, had little interest in expanding its borders.
    c. it was a small nation populated by poor peasants and had a monarch who had spent much wealth on wars to expel Muslims.
    d. its monarchy was controlled by the Catholic Church, which resisted the idea of exploration.

10. Portugal's early interest in exploration and expansion stemmed from a desire to
    a. expel Muslims from Europe and control the African trade for wheat and gold.
    b. to control the gold and slave trade of Africa.
    c. to shift the balance of power in Europe from France to itself.
    d. to shift the balance of power in Europe from England to itself.

11. By the 1460s, Portuguese used African slaves to work sugar plantations on the Cape Verde Islands and became the first nation to
    a. use slaves.
    b. use African slaves.
    c. associate plantation labor and African slavery.
    d. realize the profitability of slavery.

12. Which country first navigated a sea route from Europe to Asia?
    a. Italy
    b. Spain
    c. France
    d. Portugal

13. A sea route to Asia impacted Europe in important ways, greatly influencing exploration and
    a. causing Europeans to immigrate to the East.
    b. destroying the Catholic Church's control over the Italian city states.
    c. destroying the monopoly Italian merchants had on the Asian marketplaces.
    d. lowering the prices of perishable products in Europe.

14. The writings of Ptolemy, an ancient geographer, were the basis of most fifteenth-century Europeans' knowledge of the earth. Ptolemy believed
    a. that the earth was flat and that monsters lived at its edge.
    b. in the rotation of the sun around the earth.
    c. that the earth was a small sphere which rotated around the sun.
    d. that the earth was a sphere too large to circumnavigate before dying of thirst and starvation.

15. One could rationally assume that Christopher Columbus's perception of the earth was primarily influenced by
    a. writings of Ptolemy, his father-in-law, and Portugal's Prince Henry.
    b. his father, writings of Ptolemy, and Spanish navigators.
    c. his father, Aristotle, and the Italian merchants he grew up with.
    d. his personal observations, his father, and teachings of Ptolemy.

16. When Columbus first arrived in the New World, he thought he was in
    a. St. Augustine.
    b. Cuba.
    c. the West Indies.
    d. the East Indies.

17. For a generation after 1492, Columbus's discovery
    a. disappointed the Spanish crown.
    b. had little impact on the European perception of the world.
    c. delighted the Spanish monarchy with the amount of gold, silver, and slaves which flowed from the New World.
    d. created great hostility between French and Spanish explorers.

18. If you were a statesman in the early to mid-1500s and followed the news of Columbus, you might argue that his most important contribution was
    a. forcing the European world to admit that the earth was not flat.
    b. his discovery of a western passage to Asia.
    c. proving that it was possible to sail from Europe to the western Atlantic and return to Europe.
    d. introducing slavery into Mediterranean trade.

19. In the 1500s, Spain turned to which decision-making body to legitimize its control of the New World?
    a. the Catholic Pope
    b. the Spanish Inquisition
    c. the Mediterranean Council
    d. the Council of Tordesillas

20. The Treaty of Tordesillas between Spain and Portugal in 1494
    a. drew an imaginary line down the Atlantic Ocean, and that which was west belonged to Spain and that which was east belonged to Portugal.
    b. protected Spain's holdings in the New World, protected Portugal's holdings in Africa, and removed the financially exhaustive competition to reach Asia.
    c. resolved their differences with the Catholic Church concerning territorial ownership and the division of wealth brought back from these territories.
    d. finally removed the Muslims from the European Continent.

21. John Cabot was sponsored by the English monarch to search for a westward passage to India. Which area did he manage to reach and claim for England?
    a. Canada
    b. Newfoundland
    c. Brazil
    d. Cuba

22. The Portuguese explorer Pedro Álvars Cabral accidentally made landfall at
    a. Mexico.
    b. Guatemala.
    c. Peru.
    d. Brazil.

23. If you were Martin Waldseemüller in the early 1500s, then you were among the very first to understand
    a. that earth was a sphere and not flat.
    b. that a round globe rather than a flat map depicted the earth with greater accuracy.
    c. that the Treaty of Tordesillas shifted power from Italy to Spain and Portugal.
    d. that the discoveries of Columbus, Balboa, and Vespucci proved there was a continent which existed west of Europe and east of Asia.

24. Magellan's circumnavigation of the world left no doubt that America was separated from Asia by an enormous ocean. His voyage
    a. resulted in the founding of the first Portuguese colony in the New World.
    b. convinced Europeans that a westward passage to the East was not a feasible route.
    c. made the Italian merchants rejoice in that their control of the Asian trade would no longer be challenged.
    d. validated the findings of Columbus and Cabral.

25. While Magellan died knowing that he had discovered a route to the East, this explorer died believing he had found the ocean route to Asia and disbelieving a continent lay between Europe and Asia.
    a. John Cabot
    b. Ponce de Leon
    c. Columbus
    d. Balboa

26. The transatlantic exchange of goods, people, and ideas between the New World and Europe is referred to as the
    a. Pan Atlantic Exchange.
    b. Columbian Exchange.
    c. Renaissance.
    d. Atlantic Trade.

27. Why do you think Italian city-states refrained from sponsoring explorations?
    a. The city-states were shortsighted and would not sponsor explorations.
    b. The merchants of these city-states were too poor to finance explorations.
    c. The Catholic Church dominated the Italian principalities and discouraged exploration.
    d. The Italians possessed sufficient wealth and could obtain more wealth from their lucrative overland trade with the East and northern Africa.

28. Hernán Cortés's dominance over Mexico was most significant because
    a. it served as a model for future colonization, and it disrupted the balance of power in Europe by making Spain the wealthiest nation.
    b. it destroyed the Mayan heritage and made Spain the most powerful nation in America.
    c. it destroyed the Aztec heritage and diverted Spain's attention from enemies in Europe.
    d. it gave Spain gold and diverted Spain's attention from enemies in Europe.

29. Hernán Cortés was eventually able to defeat the Mexicans in 1521 by
    a. enlisting the help of a Mayan chief and his followers.
    b. enlisting the help of the Yucatan and of Catholic priests.
    c. enlisting the help of the Aztec peoples.
    d. enlisting the help of tens of thousands of Indian allies who favored the destruction of the Aztecs.

30. The largest treasure found in the New World before 1540 was held by the
    a. Aztecs.
    b. Incas.
    c. Zuni.
    d. Tlaxcalans.

31. The most important treasure the Spanish plundered from their New World holdings was
    a. tobacco.
    b. gold.
    c. land.
    d. Indian labor.

32. During the 1600s, the New World was primarily dominated by
    a. Spain, because it was the first country to secure the St. Lawrence and Mississippi rivers and thus to control the interior of the continent.
    b. Spain, because it had more colonial possessions than other European countries.
    c. England, because Spain and Portugal had diverted their attention to the trade with Asia.
    d. England, because of the Catholic Church's missionary work there.

33. The Spanish introduced *encomienda* as a way to
    a. reward conquistadors who claimed territory in the New World.
    b. provide housing for the Indians who labored in the silver mines.
    c. divide the wealth of the New World between the monarchy and the Catholic Church.
    d. punish wrongdoers.

34. The distribution of conquered towns, the right to rule the Indians and the land around them, and the right to exact a tribute and labor from the Indians was called
    a. the *repartimiento.*
    b. indenture.
    c. *encomienda.*
    d. *encomendero.*

35. When Catholic priests such as Fray Bartholomé de Las Casas complained to the Spanish government about the brutal treatment of Indians, royal officials
    a. ignored the problems because money was still flowing into Spain and because they thought priests were "too soft."
    b. saw the behavior in terms of a greater fear — that the Spanish bureaucracy was losing control over the conquistadors.
    c. sent delegates to investigate and punish those guilty.
    d. encouraged the Catholic Church to suppress complaints from the priests and friars.

36. The system of coerced labor in New Spain grew directly out of Spaniards' assumption that
    a. coercion was the only way Indians would work.
    b. Indians were so smart that, if not watched, they would sabotage mines.
    c. Spaniards were superior to Indians.
    d. they needed to rule harshly to maintain control over the Indians.

37. In 1549, the Spanish government issued the *repartimiento,* limiting the amount of labor Indians could be forced to do,
    a. to reduce the autonomy and power of the old conquistadors.
    b. to increase the longevity of the Indians in order to sustain a large labor force to work in the silver mines.
    c. to allow Indians more time with missionaries.
    d. as a response to the Catholic priests' concern over the treatment of Indians.

38. If you were among the royal bureaucracy of Spain in the 1500s, you might view
    a. the colonists as improving the living conditions and likelihood of survival in the colonies.
    b. the colonists and Indians as sustaining the power and wealth of Spain.
    c. the colonists as unruly parasites on the treasury of Spain.
    d. the New World as of great scientific value but hardly worth the amount of time, energy, and money the Spanish government had invested in it.

39. Between 1492 and 1592, about 225,000 Spaniards settled in the colonies. These colonists were made up primarily of
    a. the displaced younger sons of Spanish nobility who were left poor by primogeniture.
    b. the young men of common folk who brought their families to gain land and wealth in the New World.
    c. artisans, laborers, and sailors of Jewish or Islamic faith who escaped the Spanish Inquisition.
    d. poor young men of common folk who were artisans, laborers, soldiers, and sailors.

40. The gender and number of Spanish settlers shaped two fundamental features of the society of New Spain:
    a. Spaniards married Spaniards and Indians married Indians, and the two social structures lived side by side.
    b. a fluid family and class structure based on Indian norms emerged.
    c. a fluid family and class structure based on Spanish norms emerged.
    d. Spanish men frequently married Indian women, and a hierarchical class structure based upon ethnicity emerged.

41. If you were born in the Spanish New World to parents who had come from Spain, you would be put in the social class of
    a. *mestizos.*
    b. *creoles.*
    c. *peninsulares.*
    d. Cajuns.

42. If you were born to a Spanish man and an Indian woman in the Spanish New World, you would be considered part of the social class of
    a. Cajuns.
    b. *creoles.*
    c. *mestizos.*
    d. *peninsulares.*

43. The Spanish monarchy administered New Spain by taxing and monopolizing essential goods. The result was that
    a. the Spanish New World economically thrived, and immigrants rushed to take advantage of incentives which gave them more land and more political power than they had in Spain.
    b. corporations quickly moved into New Spain to make a profit, and immigrants quickly responded to the incentives to leave Spain.
    c. competition was stifled under rigidly controlled economic development, and incentives failed to encourage immigration and development.
    d. the Indians and colonists ignored Spain and worked to establish their own separate institutions and traditions.

44. After fifty years of contact with Europeans in the New World,
    a. nine out of ten Indians had died, primarily from the harshness of colonial policies and diseases inadvertently transmitted by Europeans.
    b. five out of ten Indians in New Spain had died from smallpox, measles, and other microorganisms Cortés purposefully used to destroy the natives.
    c. nine out of ten Indians in New Spain had died, primarily from harsh working conditions and torture when they refused to convert to Catholicism.
    d. five out of ten Indians in New Spain had died, primarily from war and coerced labor.

45. The deaths of millions of Indians affected Spain
    a. little. The Spanish believed Indians to be inferior anyway and their deaths to be no great loss.
    b. greatly. By this death toll, the Spaniards accidentally realized the value of germ warfare and used it in the future.
    c. greatly. The lack of natives created a labor shortage that led to the purchase of African slaves.
    d. little. Spain had exhausted all natural resources in the areas it had colonized.

46. The first permanent European settlement within what became the United States was
    a. Plymouth, Massachusetts.
    b. Santa Fe, New Mexico.
    c. New Orleans, Louisiana.
    d. St. Augustine, Florida.

47. The grandson of Isabella and Ferdinand of Spain became King Charles I in 1516. He and his successor used the wealth of New Spain
    a to challenge the Portuguese and Italian influence in Asia.
    b. to consolidate the largest empire in Europe and to fight religious wars with Protestants and Muslims.
    c. to support the exploration and colonization of interior Africa.
    d. to purchase luxury items and hire mercenaries for war.

48. In 1517, Martin Luther publicized his criticism of the Catholic Church. The theological differences between Luther and the Catholic Church centered around
    a. how salvation could be gained.
    b. the role of saints.
    c. whether or not reading the Bible was important.
    d. who could become a priest.

49. In the 1500s, the British and the French
    a. tried to duplicate Spain's New World discoveries and successes but were diverted by religious wars.
    b. sent explorers into the New World but were unable to sustain thriving colonies.
    c. successfully colonized in North America only where the Spanish were not already present.
    d. saw no benefit to colonization as long they could successfully raid Spanish treasure ships.

50. The Cathay Company sent Martin Frobisher to the New World in order to
    a. fish off the coast of Newfoundland.
    b. take New Spain.
    c. explore the Southeast.
    d. open trade with China.

Terminology Matching   Select the word or phrase from the Terms section that best matches the definition or example provided in the Definitions section. Some terms may be used more than once; some may not be used at all.

TERMS

a. astrolabe

b. bubonic plague

c. caravel

d. Columbian exchange

e. Columbus

f. *encomendero*

g. *encomienda*

h. English

i. Italians

j. Magellan

k. Mexica

l. Northwest Passage

m. Portuguese

n. *portulanos*

o. Reconquest

p. *repartimiento*

q. smallpox

r. Spanish

s. syphilis

t. Tainos

DEFINITIONS

1. Indigenous inhabitants of San Salvador first encountered by Columbus. _____

2. These merchants dominated overland trade routes to Persia, Asia Minor, India, and Africa from the twelfth through fifteenth centuries. _____

3. This killed a third of the European population during the mid-fourteenth century. _____

4. Scientific advancement that helped explorers determine latitude. _____

5. Detailed drawings of shoreline and compass settings for sailing from one point to another. _____

6. This led to Portuguese exploration down the coast of Africa. _____

7. This sturdy ship, known as the workhorse of exploration, was developed by the Portuguese. _____

8. These explorers were the first to develop plantations using African slaves. _____

9. This explorer rejected conventional Ptolemaic wisdom and was convinced that Asia lay 2,500 miles from the westernmost boundary of the known world. _____

10. This term applies to a sought-after route to the Indies across the North Atlantic. _____

11. These explorers accidentally discovered Brazil. _____

12. After this explorer's voyage to the Philippines via the New World and around the southern tip of South America, most Europeans who sailed west sought out destinations in the New World, not Asia. _____

13. This term refers to the exchange of goods and ideas between Europe and the New World. _____

14. Transferred between natives and Europeans, these caused many deaths on both sides of the Atlantic. _____

15. This name is what the Aztecs called themselves. _____

16. This term applies to "the man who owns the town" and is associated with exploitation of indigenous peoples. _____

17. This system reduced the number of days an individual Indian could be forced to work in a Spanish silver mine to forty-five days per year. _____

18. This group was responsible for the technology that enabled Columbus to sail to the Caribbean. _____

19. This group introduced African slaves to Mexico to supplement the dwindling numbers of Indians. _____

20. This group of explorers was not able to establish any surviving settlements within North America during the sixteenth century. _____

Chronology   Place the events in chronological order.

SET ONE

A. Magellan circumnavigates the world.

B. Portugal gains access to Africa.

C. Christopher Columbus makes his first voyage to the Western Hemisphere.

D. Martin Waldseemüller publishes a map that shows the New World separate from Asia.

First _____

Second _____

Third _____

Fourth _____

SET TWO

A. Significant colonization efforts by France

B. Significant colonization efforts by Spain

C. Significant colonization efforts by England

First _____

Second _____

Third _____

Short Answer   Write a paragraph in response to each question.

1. Describe trade patterns and routes in the Mediterranean from the twelfth century to the early sixteenth century. Be sure to mention what countries dominated trade at different times.

2. Briefly explain the Reconquest and its significance to European exploration.

3. Identify and discuss the events that led to the relationship between African slaves and plantation labor on the Cape Verde islands.

4. What impact did Columbus's journeys have on Europeans' understanding of the geography of the world?

5. Identify three key factors that Cortés employed to enable him to conquer the Mexica and gain control of the capital of the Mexican empire.

6. Cite two reasons Spain became the dominant colonial power in the Americas during the sixteenth century.

7. Two Spanish groups became critical of the *encomienda* system and were influential in abolishing its early form in 1569. Identify both groups, cite their major criticism, and explain the results of their criticism.

8. Briefly explain results of the gender imbalance of Spanish immigrants in the New World during the sixteenth century.

9. Why did the Spanish monarchy insist on having northern outposts in Florida and New Mexico?

10. Explain the model of exploration that sixteenth-century Spain set for France and England, and discuss these two countries' attempts at exploration in the New World.

Essay   Respond to each of the following questions in an essay of three to four paragraphs. Your responses should include specific evidence and your interpretation of the significance of historical events and concepts.

1. A series of events and conditions existed in the Old World at the dawn of the fifteenth century that made New World exploration not only possible but also desirable. Write an essay in which you identify these events and conditions, as well as explain how each helped set the stage for exploration.

2. Although the Portuguese seemed ideally qualified to discover America, the opportunity fell to an Italian explorer supported by the Spanish monarchy. In an essay, discuss how the Portuguese became the leaders in exploration during the fifteenth century, as well as their reasons for not sponsoring Columbus's expedition to the New World. Include in your discussion the significant accomplishments of the Portuguese relating to exploration.

3. Despite Columbus's lack of success in locating the Asian mainland by sailing west, by initiating the Columbian exchange, his arrival in the Caribbean had profound and lasting impact on both the Old and New Worlds. Write an essay in which you (a) explain the meaning of Columbian exchange, (b) discuss the significant ways the Old and New Worlds experienced both gains and losses because of the exchange, and (c) develop a position regarding whether there was a clear winner in this exchange. Defend your position with specific evidence and examples.

4. During the sixteenth century, Spain became the most powerful country in both Europe and the Americas. Write an essay in which you explain how Spain rose to this position of power, and describe how the Spanish transformed the New World.

Map Questions   Answer the questions below using Map 1.2, European Explorations in Sixteenth-Century America (p. 10).

READING THE MAP What were the first five voyages of exploration shown on the map? What countries sponsored them?

CONNECTIONS Explain why, with the exception of John Cabot, the English and French explorations were later than Spanish explorations. Who do you think fared better by the Treaty of Tordesillas?

THE SOUTHERN COLONIES IN THE SEVENTEENTH CENTURY

2

1601–1700

Multiple Choice   Choose the letter of the best answer.

1. The story of Pocahontas saving Captain John Smith from her father's death sentence was told to inform the reader
   a. of Pocahontas's great love of John Smith.
   b. of the origins of the "Noble Savage."
   c. of how inadequately Englishmen understood Indian rituals.
   d. that Powhatan never truly understood the English.

2. When Pocahontas intervened to save John Smith, she most likely was participating in an Algonquian ceremony that
   a. expressed Powhatan's supremacy and his ritualistic adoption of a subordinate chief.
   b. demonstrated the power of females in the Algonquian matriarchal society.
   c. was to culminate in a human sacrifice.
   d. expressed the power of Powhatan's ability to control life and death and to appease the Algonquian gods.

3. One of the key events which convinced King James I by 1600 that England should and could colonize in the New World was
   a. the Treaty of Tordesillas.
   b. the English Reformation.
   c. England's defeat of the Spanish Armada.
   d. the last voyage of John Cabot.

4. Richard Hakluyt, a strong proponent of colonization, argued that English colonies would
   a. enhance England's ability to maintain a balance of power in Europe and throughout the Mediterranean world.
   b. provide a market for English goods and a place for the unemployed.
   c. provide raw materials for England and a strategic political outpost.
   d. provide a dumping ground for England's surplus goods and disenfranchised younger sons of the nobility.

5. King James's land grant to the Virginia Company of over six million acres and everything they might contain was in essence
   a. a royal license to poach on Spanish claims and on Indian lands.
   b. an attempt to ally with France to weaken Spain's control over Europe.
   c. an attempt to challenge the Catholic Church's authority to legitimatize territorial conquests.
   d. a declaration of war against Powhatan and the Roanoke Indians.

6. Only 38 of the 144 Englishmen who made the first voyage to what would became Jamestown, Virginia, survived the first year. This high mortality rate is explained primarily by
   a. malnutrition, disease, and the failure to let go of traditional notions of class and labor.
   b. malnutrition and sporadic fights with the Indians.
   c. disease, cannibalism, and ignorance of farming methods.
   d. bad drinking water, cannibalism, and starvation.

7. The majority of the original settlers who came to Jamestown and the Virginia colony were
   a. gentlemen and their servants.
   b. soldiers.
   c. artisans and laborers.
   d. planters and ex-convicts.

8. The Virginia colony in 1607 could have better survived had the colonists
   a. fought the Indians using guerilla warfare.
   b. been willing to learn how to farm.
   c. brought more equipment with them from England.
   d. exploited the Indians more effectively.

9. Compared to the Spanish colonists in the New World in the sixteenth century, the English of the Virginia Company
   a. expressed less concern for the conversion of the Indians to Christianity.
   b. intermarried with the Indians more frequently.
   c. expressed less interest in finding great wealth.
   d. were more likely to slaughter the Indians.

10. Because of the success of the Virginia colony, Powhatan's people
    a. were hit hard by disease.
    b. were Christianized.
    c. moved far away.
    d. allied with the neighboring tribes and the Spanish.

11. Powhatan and his people were suspicious of English intentions because the colonists
    a. bullied Indians to make them follow English norms.
    b. converted Indians to Christianity.
    c. intermarried with Indian women.
    d. adopted Indian children.

12. King James revoked the Virginia Company charter and made it a royal colony in 1624. Factors contributing to this decision included
    a. John Smith's reports of hostility with Indians.
    b. John Smith's execution of two of the younger sons of English aristocrats.
    c. Powhatan's uprising and an investigative report showing that disease and mismanagement were responsible for high mortality rates.
    d. John Smith's arbitrary actions and the need to stop colonists from skimming the "royal fifth" from the tobacco profits.

13. Under royal government in Virginia, all free adult men could vote for
    a. members of Parliament.
    b. taxation measures.
    c. the colony's governor.
    d. local burgesses.

14. The crop that turned Virginia into a stable colony was
    a. corn.
    b. tobacco.
    c. rice.
    d. cotton.

15. If you wanted to be a highly profitable tobacco farmer in the 1600s in Virginia, the biggest obstacle you were likely to face was
    a. a lack of affordable land.
    b. a lack of workers.
    c. getting the crop to grow.
    d. being able to afford the technology needed to grow tobacco.

16. Most hired workers
    a. earned in one year in Chesapeake tobacco fields what they earned in two or three years of labor in England.
    b. refused to work as indentured servants because the rewards were too small.
    c. preferred work in rice fields in Carolina because labor there was easier.
    d. in the Chesapeake returned to England as soon as possible to escape the harsh working conditions.

17. Headrights were initiated by the Virginia Company and continued by the royal government as an incentive to encourage settlement in the Virginia colony. A headright
    a. permitted the head of a family the right to vote in the House of Burgesses.
    b. granted the right of primogeniture to immigrants as well as the right to purchase land at steep discounts.
    c. granted the head of non-English immigrant families the rights of English citizenship.
    d. granted fifty acres of land to settlers who paid their own transportation to the colony.

18. A servant labor system in the British colonies was created by
    a. the New World's labor shortage and the poverty of Englishmen who were willing to work.
    b. the poverty of the English people who sought to escape debtor's prison or religious persecution.
    c. racism and the lower cost of an African slave relative to that of an indentured servant.
    d. following the model of Spain's labor system.

19. Seventeenth-century Chesapeake society was essentially a society of
    a. planters and slaves.
    b. workers, 80 percent of whom were indentured servants.
    c. families who relied heavily on their slaves.
    d. free adult males.

20. After serving his or her indenture, an employer was required to give a servant
    a. freedom dues.
    b. free land.
    c. a share of the master's crop.
    d. nothing.

21. Indentured servants tended to be
    a. poor young men born in the colony.
    b. poor young men born in England.
    c. young men and older women from England.
    d. natives and prisoners from England.

22. Some planters saw indentured servants as
    a. slaves, who they frequently abused.
    b. equals and taught them valuable skills.
    c. property that they sometimes sold.
    d. temporary workers, who they saw as cheap investments.

23. Indentured women
    a. were as rare as skilled workers and could set the price of their labor.
    b. often ran off with free men to start farms of their own.
    c. were given more rights than were their male counterparts, to entice them to the colony.
    d. were not permitted to marry until their servitude was complete.

24. Indentured servants could have their servitude extended by years if they
    a. stole, became pregnant, or ran away.
    b. became ill.
    c. did not work as hard as their masters wanted.
    d. did not have children.

25. Indentured servants saw themselves
    a. as without rights and with little likelihood of ever receiving their "freedom dues."
    b. as slaves.
    c. free people who were temporarily servants.
    d. virtual prisoners without hope of release.

26. The authors of *The American Promise* claim tobacco propelled the evolution of Chesapeake society. They claim tobacco agriculture shaped
    a. a relatively classless society governed by religious doctrine.
    b. an equal society and a pattern of settlement different from that in England.
    c. a pattern of settlement and class structure very similar to that of rural England.
    d. a relatively classless society that acted more on economic factors than on religious beliefs.

27. Masters in the Chesapeake were so hungry for labor that they
    a. did not hesitate to devise legal ways to keep servants under their control.
    b. convinced England to send convicts over for long-term servitude.
    c. captured Indians and forced them to work.
    d. bought up small farmers' land, forcing the farmers to work for them.

28. The dispersion of settlements in the Chesapeake can be explained by the
    a. ethnicity of the immigrants and the acreage necessary to plant tobacco.
    b. the marketing system of farmers and the acreage needed to make a profit.
    c. acreage needed to make a profit on tobacco and the ethnic rivalry of the population.
    d. the limit on the amount of land a farmer could lay deed to and a poor transportation system.

29. Lord Baltimore received six and a half million acres in the Chesapeake region and created the colony of Maryland as a refuge for Catholics;
    a. however, the majority of settlers there were Protestants, few of whom were as wealthy as the Catholics, and conflict existed between the groups.
    b. indeed, the majority of settlers were Catholics who created a religious society that farmed tobacco.
    c. though more Protestants than Catholics populated the colony, the two groups coexisted peacefully.
    d. however, Catholics were in favor in England, so few left for Maryland.

30. The term *yeoman planter* refers to a
    a. poor farmer who wears the yoke of an ox and pulls his own plow.
    b. farmer who owns a small plot of land which is worked primarily by himself and his family.
    c. farmer who rents his land.
    d. wealthy farmer who owns only a few slaves.

31. The decline in the price of tobacco in the third quarter of the seventeenth century contributed to the
    a. end of the rough equality within the Chesapeake population.
    b. stability of the rough equality within the Chesapeake population.
    c. increase in the number of servants surviving their indenture.
    d. bankruptcy of the Virginia Company of London.

32. By the 1670s, the Chesapeake social structure was polarized. This social structure was based on the following criteria:
    a. ownership of land and the amount possessed, income, and status of freedom.
    b. income and ownership of servants and slaves.
    c. race, income, and birthright.
    d. race, ownership of land, income, and whether one was Catholic or Protestant.

33. If one wanted to argue that there was less political equality in Virginia in 1670 than in the early years of the colony, one might use the following evidence:
    a. Only free males could vote at that date, and governors frequently served their terms of office back in England.
    b. The Anglican Church was made the state church and received public tax dollars, and the tax structure was inequitable among the classes.
    c. Only male landowners and homeowners could vote, and at one point there were no elections for the House of Burgesses for fifteen years.
    d. The king and royal government used their mercantilist assumptions to control the House of Burgesses and deny free elections.

34. Mercantilism is
    a. an economic policy that places the welfare of the imperial power above the welfare of the colonies.
    b. an economic policy which favors business of agriculture.
    c. a socioeconomic policy that puts merchants and bankers in decision-making positions.
    d. a socioeconomic policy which declares that parity between merchants and farmers must exist in order to maximize profits.

35. The most obvious inequality in the social structure in the Chesapeake was between servants and masters. The colonial government
    a. worked to enforce this distinction but recognized servants' rights to fair and just treatment.
    b. worked to ease the tension between the two groups by letting former servants serve in the governor's council.
    c. neglected to handle the problem until it led to a servant rebellion.
    d. enforced this distinction by failing to prosecute fairly those masters who brutalized their servants.

36. The relationships between the king's royal government and the colony and between master and servant were similar in that
    a. rulers and masters expected to rule and be obeyed, and colonies and servants expected to be ruled and punished for disobeying.
    b. rulers and masters expected to rule and be obeyed, while colonies and servants always dreamed of being independent.
    c. rulers and masters expected to rule and be obeyed, and colonies and servants expected to earn their independence through profit and hard work.
    d. rulers and masters expected to eventually lose control of colonies and servants.

37. Bacon's Rebellion erupted in 1676 as a dispute over Indian policy, and it ended as a conflict between
    a. the planter elite and small farmers.
    b. indentured servants and their masters.
    c. Indians and the Virginia militia.
    d. small farmers and newly freed servants.

38. Nathaniel Bacon distressed the royal government and elite planters of Virginia because his demands
    a. caused the traditional establishment to lose power to newcomers and small farmers.
    b. were unfair to Indians and set slaves free.
    c. permitted newly freed indentured servants to have Indian lands, which lowered the price of land and hurt landlords' investments.
    d. challenged the king and Parliament's right to rule.

39. After Bacon's death,
    a. Governor Berkeley and his loyalists returned to power.
    b. royal officials removed Berkeley and nullified Bacon's Laws.
    c. indentured servitude as an institution had been destroyed.
    d. tension lessened between the servant and slave classes.

40. The social and political distance that existed between planters and small farmers decreased between 1660 and 1700. Factors involved in this change include the
    a. opening of frontier lands and an increase in the number of indentured servants in the colony.
    b. decline in the number of indentured servants in the colony and a greater dependency on slave labor.
    c. diversification of commercial activity and the increase in free workers.
    d. immigration of peoples of the "middling" class and the diversification of commercial activity.

41. From where was the slave labor system that was introduced to the Chesapeake "exported"?
    a. the gold coast of Africa
    b. Spanish colonies
    c. Barbados
    d. the East Indies

42. Which British colony brought in the greatest profit in 1700?
    a. Virginia
    b. Newfoundland
    c. Barbados
    d. Carolinas

43. The only seventeenth-century English colony to be settled principally by colonists from other colonies rather than from England was
    a. Georgia.
    b. Carolina.
    c. Pennsylvania.
    d. Maryland.

44. The first profitable export crop grown in Carolina was
    a. tobacco.
    b. cotton.
    c. indigo.
    d. rice.

45. It is important to study the economy and slave labor system of the Caribbean sugar islands because it helps us better understand
    a. the first major settlement of slaves and slave owners in Carolina.
    b. the resistance to slavery by abolitionists.
    c. why the Chesapeake did not pursue sugar agriculture.
    d. the relationship between West Indians and Africans.

46. Until the 1670s, almost all Chesapeake colonists were English. By 1700,
    a. one out of ten people in the region was West Indian.
    b. one out of five people in the region was West Indian.
    c. one out of eight people in the region was African.
    d. one out of two people in the region was African.

47. The shift from an indentured servant labor force to a slave labor force occurred for many reasons; one was that
    a. many indentured servants decided to return to England.
    b. slavery provided a perpetual labor force.
    c. indentures all ended at the same time.
    d. Bacon's Rebellion scared planters away from working with indentured servants.

48. For planters, a slave labor system had important advantages over a servant labor system, such as that
    a. slaves cost less than indentures.
    b. slaves could be controlled politically.
    c. slaves never ran away.
    d. slaves naturally worked harder.

49. Slavery in the Chesapeake region
    a. was cheap to implement compared to sponsoring indentured servants.
    b. lessened the political tension among the planter elite, small farmers, and free, landless servants.
    c. silenced indentured servants' demands for higher wages, because they now had to compete with slave labor.
    d. allowed small farmers to become part of the planter elite.

50. Compared to slavery in Barbados, slavery in the Chesapeake
   a. seemed less harsh because slaves lived longer and could visit other plantations.
   b. was more confining because slaves often worked alongside white servants and in general were more subject to surveillance by white people.
   c. was less harsh because slaves lived longer and had some rights in regard to living conditions.
   d. faced more opposition from colonists.

Terminology Matching   Select the word or phrase from the Terms section that best matches the definition or example provided in the Definitions section. Some terms may be used more than once; some may not be used at all.

TERMS

a. Catholicism

b. corn

c. cotton

d. farmers

e. freedom dues

f. gentlemen

g. headright

h. House of Burgesses

i. indenture

j. indentured servants

k. laborers

l. Opechancanough

m. Powhatan

n. Protestantism

o. rice

p. slavery

q. sugar

r. tobacco

s. Werowance

t. yeoman

DEFINITIONS

1. Supreme chief of the Algonquian people when the Virginia Company first arrived in America. _____

2. Chief of the Algonquian people who organized a major assault on English settlers in 1622. _____

3. A crop grown by native Americans for centuries that created a profitable export economy for the Chesapeake area settlers in the 1600s. _____

4. A centuries-old Native American crop that requires a special technology to grow, process, and consume. _____

5. The prime necessity supplied by the Algonquians to Jamestown for the first ten years of its existence. _____

6. Name of the legislative body in the Virginia colony. _____

7. This socioeconomic group made up the largest percentage of Englishmen immigrating to Virginia in the early years of the colony. _____

8. This term refers to fifty acres of free land granted by the Virginia Company to settlers who paid their own transportation to Chesapeake. _____

9. About 80 percent of immigrants to the Chesapeake during the seventeenth century were among this socioeconomic group. _____

10. This refers to a work contract that traded passage to the New World for five to seven years of free labor. _____

11. Most settlers in the Chesapeake region professed to this branch of Christianity. _____

12. Most of the earliest settlers in the Maryland colony professed to this branch of Christianity. _____

13. This term applies to a farmer who owned a small plot of land sufficient to support his family and tilled largely by family members and a few servants. _____

14. This crop was grown using slave labor on plantations in Barbados. _____

15. This particular crop flourished in South Carolina in the mid-1690s after colonists developed successful methods of cultivation. _____

16. This term applies to the requirement that an employer supply a servant with three barrels of corn and a suit of clothes. _____

Chronology   Place the events in chronological order.

A. Bacon's Rebellion

B. introduction of slaves from the West Indies to the Chesapeake

C. founding of Jamestown

D. retraction of the Virginia Company's charter and the establishment of Virginia as a royal colony

First _____

Second _____

Third _____

Fourth _____

Short Answer   Write a paragraph in response to each question.

1. Identify two ways in which the features of the government of Virginia, which was first established under the Virginia Company, changed when King James I revoked its corporate charter in 1624 and made Virginia a royal colony.

2. Until 1650, a rough frontier equality existed among free families in Chesapeake. Around 1650, Chesapeake society splintered into two social groups who mistrusted each other. Identify the social groups and the causes of this polarity.

3. List the stipulations of the Navigation Acts of 1660 and 1663 and explain the purpose of these acts.

4. Defend the following statement with specific evidence: Hierarchy and inequality permeated all levels of government and politics, from the relation between king and colonies to that between master and servant, but certain expectations existed during the seventeenth century that moderated the severity of these relationships.

5. Briefly identify the major reason for Bacon's Rebellion in 1676. Include Bacon's principal demand of Governor Berkeley, Berkeley's response, and the result of Berkeley's response.

6. Briefly explain why Bacon's Rebellion caused the king to become concerned enough to order an investigation into the turmoil in Chesapeake, and state the actions taken as a result of the investigation.

7. Defend the following statement with specific evidence: The servant labor system perpetuated the gender imbalance in seventeenth-century Virginia.

8. Provide the rationale behind the following statement: Both economically and socially, seventeenth-century South Carolina was a frontier outpost of the West Indian sugar economy.

9. List the major reasons tobacco planters converted their plantations from servant labor to slave labor beginning around 1670.

10. On what basis could a student of history conclude that the slave labor system reduced the tensions between poor white farmers and prosperous planters in the Chesapeake region after 1670?

Essay   Respond to each of the following questions in an essay of three to four paragraphs. Your responses should include specific evidence and your interpretation of the significance of historical events and concepts.

1. In 1607, the early English colonists who arrived at Jamestown found themselves subordinate to and under the initial protection of the Algonquians and their leader Powhatan. This relationship changed by 1622. Write an essay in which you explain (a) why the native Americans were initially important to the survival of the Chesapeake newcomers, (b) what benefits the newcomers derived from their association with the Algonquians, and (c) how and why their relationship had changed by 1622.

2. King James I of England granted a charter to the Virginia Company of London to establish a colony in the New World. In a very real sense, this was an illegitimate grant on the part of James I. Write an essay in which you (a) provide a rationale for the statement that James's grant was illegitimate, (b) discuss the general stipulations of the charter of the Virginia Company, (c) identify and discuss the benefits a corporate colony was supposed to provide to the monarchy and the Virginia Company, and (d) explain why King James I revoked the charter in 1624 and made Virginia a royal colony.

3. The labor system that existed in Virginia until the 1670s profoundly influenced nearly every feature of Chesapeake society. Write an essay in which you (a) identify the source of labor and explain the major characteristics of this labor system, (b) explain the conditions which caused this system to flourish, and (c) discuss the effects of this system on Chesapeake society up to the 1670s.

4. Because of their determination to profit from tobacco farming, Chesapeake colonists did not reproduce the rural landscape of their homeland in England, and their patterns of community life were not as they had been accustomed to in England. Write an essay in which you describe life in seventeenth-century Chesapeake in the first thirty to forty years of settlement by discussing settlement patterns and the daily lives of colonists, including social and religious aspects.

Map Questions   Answer the questions below using Map 2.1, The Chesapeake Colonies in the Seventeenth Century (p. 48).

READING THE MAP Look at this map and describe the geographic features that seem to determine where the settlement and growth of towns took place.

CONNECTIONS Discuss how navigable rivers could influence the dispersion of farms. When you look at Chesapeake Bay and its coastline, speculate on why the first generations of Virginia colonists grew tobacco while the first generations of Maryland colonists grew rice.

THE NORTHERN COLONIES IN THE SEVENTEENTH CENTURY

3

1601–1700

Multiple Choice   Choose the letter of the best answer.

1. Anne Hutchinson's emphasis on the "covenant of grace" stirred religious controversy in early Massachusetts because
   a. she said only her followers would achieve salvation.
   b. it was feared she was disrupting the good order of the colony.
   c. she encouraged other women to take an active part in religious governance.
   d. she said the Puritan leaders should be excommunicated.

2. King Henry VIII saw in the Protestant Reformation the opportunity to
   a. renounce his Catholic faith so that he could achieve salvation.
   b. make himself the head of the church and its properties in England.
   c. organize a large army and march on the Vatican.
   d. end religious disputes and unrest in England.

3. Sixteenth-century English Puritanism
   a. was a well-organized, centrally administered religious reform movement.
   b. took few ideas from Martin Luther and John Calvin.
   c. was a set of broadly interpreted ideas and religious principles held by those seeking to purify the Church of England and to remove from it what they considered the offensive features of Catholicism.
   d. interpreted Protestantism as a call for increased influence of the clergy in the lives of average parishioners.

4. When King Charles I dissolved Parliament in 1629, many Puritans
   a. were ecstatic, as now the English government could no longer vote against their religion.
   b. believed that the king meant to use his royal prerogatives actively to favor their faith.
   c. saw this as the first positive sign that church and state were to be separated.
   d. despaired at having lost their political voice and began preparing to leave England.

5. Puritans who described themselves as separatists believed that
   a. the Church of England was beyond redemption and sought to separate themselves from it permanently.
   b. a trial separation from the Church of England would give them time to sort out what they most needed to change about their religious lives.
   c. a strict reading of the Bible required separate religious services for men and women.
   d. their religious convictions should remain separate from those found on the European continent.

6. Samoset and Squanto were
   a. leaders of hostile Narragansett Indians threatening to wipe out the young Plymouth colony.
   b. leaders of hostile Wampanoag Indians threatening to destroy Massachusetts Bay.
   c. friendly Wampanoag Indians who helped Puritans settling Connecticut survive their first year.
   d. Wampanoag Indians who befriended the Plymouth settlers and helped ensure the survival of the young colony.

7. The charter of the Massachusetts Bay Company was unique because it
   a. allowed women investors to vote along with men in the concerns of the colony.
   b. contained a feature that allowed the government of the company to be located in the colony rather than in England.
   c. encouraged those emigrating to Massachusetts to abandon the traditional English class structure.
   d. obligated the English government to reimburse investors for any financial losses they might suffer during the first five years of settlement.

8. The Puritans who founded Massachusetts Bay
   a. were glad to be able to settle near like-minded coreligionists down the coast at Plymouth.
   b. struggled to survive and relied on their Plymouth compatriots for help.
   c. had not broken completely with the Church of England and had no use for the separatist beliefs of some of their fellow Englishmen who earlier had founded the Plymouth colony.
   d. invited Plymouth settlers to move north to their colony.

9. According to John Winthrop's sermon aboard the *Arbella*, the Puritans had "entered into a covenant" with God, meaning that
   a. they had agreed to leave England in return for God's assurance that they would at the very least survive in the American wilderness.
   b. they had been chosen to do God's special work of building a holy community as an example to others, and failure meant suffering God's wrath.
   c. they were to transfer the beliefs of the Church of England to the western shores of the Atlantic in return for ten generations of peace and prosperity.
   d. they had been chosen to set up a missionary franchise in America with the exclusive charge to convert native Americans to Christianity.

10. Early settlers in Massachusetts Bay experienced fewer difficulties with native Americans than had colonists in the Chesapeake primarily because
    a. the Indians in Massachusetts fled to the interior when they saw the army the Puritans brought with them.
    b. native Americans in New England were eager to convert to Christianity.
    c. an epidemic had wiped out thousands of Indians in the region before the English settlers arrived.
    d. most of the Indians in the area had relocated to help the colonists at Plymouth.

11. John Cotton, Richard Mather, and Thomas Hooker were
    a. governors of Massachusetts Bay.
    b. lawyers who made names for themselves by defending those accused of witchcraft.
    c. early Puritans who left Massachusetts after joining the Society of Friends.
    d. eminent Puritan ministers in Massachusetts.

12. In his *Indian Dialogues* (1671), author and minister John Eliot put what he believed were useful, albeit fictitious, words in the mouth of the Wampanoag sachem Metacomet describing the Indian chief's misgivings about Christianity. According to Eliot, Metacomet's major concern was that
    a. praying Indians would view him as second to God.
    b. the Christian colonists would want tribute from the Indians.
    c. he would lose all power and authority over his people if they converted to Christianity.
    d. his people would force him to leave the community if they adopted Christianity.

13. For the most part, the Puritans who settled Massachusetts Bay
    a. were farmers or tradesmen who came from the middle ranks of English society.
    b. sprang from the same social origins as those settling Virginia and Maryland.
    c. were well represented by noblemen who had had enough of life in England.
    d. were members of the landed gentry seeking new outlets in the economy of the New World.

14. When John Winthrop described each Puritan family as a "little commonwealth," he meant that
    a. like any good government, the family structure should be democratic.
    b. each family was hierarchical in structure (children were subordinate to their parents and other elders, women were subordinate to their husbands, and so forth), as God had intended.
    c. each family was governed by the laws of England and that each family member should take great care to obey those laws.
    d. families should govern themselves strictly in order to survive, as few family units successfully made the trip to Massachusetts.

15. When Puritans referred to "the church," they meant
    a. the building where people met for religious observances.
    b. the Anglican religious structure they sought to escape.
    c. only the large, ornate edifice in Boston symbolizing the original "errand in the wilderness."
    d. the men and women who had entered a solemn covenant with one another and with God.

16. The Puritan doctrine of predestination
    a. held that before the creation of the world, God had decided who would achieve salvation, that nothing one did could alter one's fate, and that very few deserved or would achieve eternal life.
    b. held that before the creation of the world, God had decided who would achieve salvation, that nothing one did could alter one's fate, and that because of God's love for humankind most would know eternal life.
    c. held that before the creation of the world, God had decided who would achieve salvation, and that God would communicate clearly with each soul he had decided to save.
    d. held that before the creation of the world, God had decided who would achieve salvation, that nothing one did could alter one's fate, and that God might change his mind at any time.

17. One reason Puritans required all town residents to attend church services was to
    a. keep an eye on suspicious members of the community in an effort to reduce crime.
    b. make sure the collection plates were full, as money collected in church funded crucial community building projects.
    c. make sure that the "elect" or "visible saints" who remained ignorant of God's truth appeared in the meeting house to be exposed to that truth.
    d. gather all adult community members in a convenient place to hear public service announcements.

18. Puritan communities in the first half of the seventeenth century could be characterized by
    a. strict segregation of males and females in worship.
    b. a high degree of conformity in community members' views on morality, order, and propriety.
    c. conformity to a work ethic that demanded that children as young as eight work alongside their parents.
    d. huge celebrations on holy holidays such as Christmas or Easter.

19. Churches played no role in the civil government of New England communities because
    a. the majority of Puritans wanted to ensure that minor religions retained their autonomy and freedom.
    b. Puritans did not want to emulate the Church of England, which they considered a puppet of the king rather than an independent body that served the Lord.
    c. Puritans held that religious beliefs should never influence government.
    d. Puritans believed it to be sacrilegious to conduct the affairs of government in the same structure used to worship God.

20. The New England town meeting
    a. brought together a town's inhabitants and freemen in an exercise of voting and popular political participation unprecedented elsewhere in the seventeenth century.
    b. was basically a male bonding experience that allowed the men of the community to gather for militia drill and a day of revelry.
    c. is a nearly mythical concept in early American history and was never very important.
    d. was the first political format in early America to allow women and blacks a significant political voice.

21. Because of the seventeenth-century New England land distribution policy, towns
    a. were few and far between, with most people living on isolated small farms.
    b. were connected by well-engineered roads that encouraged trade.
    c. featured homes that surrounded pastures so the grazing animals would be protected.
    d. tended to consist of centrally located family homes and gardens surrounded by agricultural land, common land, and land set aside for new settlers and descendants.

22. Roger Williams was
    a. the governor of Massachusetts from 1640 to 1652.
    b. a vocal dissenter in early Massachusetts who challenged the religious and political leadership of the colony's powerful men.
    c. the chief minister in Boston to which all other Puritan clergymen reported.
    d. the first Massachusetts settler to lead a Puritan exodus to New York.

23. In 1636, Connecticut began to be settled by
    a. more than eight hundred Massachusetts settlers who were led out of the colony by Roger Williams.
    b. families from the earlier Plymouth colony who objected to the religious restrictions there.
    c. more than eight hundred Massachusetts settlers who were led out of the colony by Thomas Hooker.
    d. newly arrived immigrants from an area in England experiencing a famine.

24. In the seventeenth century, Puritan churches
    a. were remarkably homogeneous in belief.
    b. had a policy of tolerating dissent as long as a dissenter came to church regularly.
    c. experienced a growing number of divisions over issues of doctrine and church government.
    d. realized they had to work together to counter the hostile forces in the new land.

25. Puritans in England in the mid-seventeenth century
    a. disappeared as a religious group.
    b. decided that some elements of Catholicism would serve them well.
    c. organized an army and proceeded to attack continental Europe.
    d. won a civil war, proclaimed a republic, and ruled the nation from 1649 to 1660.

26. The seventeenth-century New England economy mainly consisted of
    a. diversified agriculture producing staples for the world market.
    b. subsistence farming mixed with fishing and timber harvesting for markets in Europe and the West Indies.
    c. reexporting commodities shipped from England.
    d. little more than subsistence farming with some produce for the local market.

27. New England's population continued to grow steadily during the seventeenth century primarily due to
    a. the continuing flood of immigrants from England.
    b. an influx of settlers from colonies farther south.
    c. a new source of immigrants from continental Europe.
    d. a relatively high birth rate coupled with a climate that helped many children survive and live into adulthood.

28. By the 1680s, New England's population had grown large and had splintered to the point that
    a. most people who had formerly considered themselves Puritans now called themselves Calvinists.
    b. some towns did not have enough churches to accommodate all congregants.
    c. although only 15 percent of adult males were church members, heated debates between factions were common.
    d. Puritan leaders repealed all statutes making church attendance compulsory.

29. The Halfway Covenant was
    a. a measure designed to alleviate a labor glut in Massachusetts by instituting a half day's pay for a half day's work.
    b. a measure instituted by Puritan leaders in 1662 allowing the unconverted children of visible saints to become halfway church members, a measure meant to keep communities as godly as possible.
    c. a legal agreement between merchants and shippers dividing the cost of lost cargoes between the two.
    d. a rule adopted in Massachusetts allowing the unconverted to worship in the colony's meeting houses, but only in the back half of the buildings.

30. Members of the Society of Friends, or Quakers, believed that
    a. God spoke directly to each individual through an "inner light" and that only a few individuals possessed the talent to interpret God's voice sufficiently to be a clergyman.
    b. God spoke directly to each individual through an "inner light" that directed them to worship only on Wednesdays and Saturdays.
    c. there was no such thing as God; rather, each human being was his or her own "god."
    d. God spoke directly to each individual through an "inner light" and that neither a minister nor the Bible was necessary to discover God's word.

31. Puritans viewed Quakers as
    a. welcome members of New England communities who contributed much to life there.
    b. dangerous to Puritan doctrines of faith and social order to the point that Puritans executed a few Quakers.
    c. wrongly persecuted fellow Christians with whom they negotiated to organize a colony in Maine.
    d. valuable religious and intellectual competitors whose presence in New England served to uphold basic Puritan beliefs.

32. Accusing people of witchcraft in seventeenth-century New England seems to have been
    a. a way to explain the continual disorder in some communities by blaming difficulties on older, relatively defenseless women assumed to be in league with Satan.
    b. a way to explain the continual disorder in some communities by blaming difficulties on older, relatively defenseless men assumed to be in league with Satan.
    c. a way to explain the continual disorder in some communities by blaming difficulties on young, prosperous women who elicited jealously among less well-to-do colonists.
    d. a creatively perpetrated hoax, as few people really believed in witches.

33. In seventeenth-century New England, accusing someone of witchcraft often became a useful way to
    a. perform the valuable public service of ridding the community of pesky witches.
    b. cast oneself as a victim and blame one's misfortune on evil forces beyond the control of mere mortals.
    c. demonstrate important leadership and administrative abilities.
    d. prosper economically, as convicted witches forfeited all their worldly possessions to those identifying them as devilish menaces to New England.

34. During most of the seventeenth century, New Netherland was
    a. an English colony seized from the Dutch in 1620.
    b. a Dutch colony whose land was discovered in explorations made by Peter Stuyvesant in the 1630s.
    c. a Dutch colony whose land was discovered in explorations made by Henry Hudson in 1609.
    d. the fastest-growing colony in the New World due to its popularity with European immigrants.

35. The colony of New Netherland was marked by a
    a. small, remarkably diverse population.
    b. small, remarkable homogeneous population.
    c. large population consisting almost exclusively of people from France and Spain.
    d. large, remarkably diverse population.

36. In 1664, when Charles II became king of England, New Netherland
    a. formed a representative government and lowered property taxes in the colony.
    b. became New York when the king took it from the Dutch and presented it to his brother James, the Duke of York, as part of a larger grant of land.
    c. became New Jersey when the king purchased it from the Netherlands as part of a deal stipulating that the Dutch exit the New World forever.
    d. established a stronger colonial government that proved able to thwart England's bid to overrun the colony.

37. When the English assumed control of New Netherland, they continued the Dutch policy of religious toleration because
    a. King Charles II's liberal religious views influenced the policies there.
    b. New York became a proving ground for England's own newly enacted policies regarding religious toleration.
    c. the heterogeneity of New Netherland made imposing a uniform religion not only difficult but nearly impossible.
    d. colonists there agreed to provide twice as many recruits for the English army as other colonies provided.

38. The creation of New York led indirectly to the founding of two other middle colonies,
    a. New Jersey and Maryland.
    b. Pennsylvania and Maryland.
    c. Delaware and Pennsylvania.
    d. New Jersey and Pennsylvania.

39. The Quaker maxim "In souls there is no sex" helps explain
    a. the degree to which Quakers allowed women to assume positions of religious leadership in the seventeenth century.
    b. the Quaker belief that men and women would be saved in equal numbers.
    c. the fact that Quakers generally frowned upon the customary gender structure of their own day and time.
    d. why Quaker women held many important political offices in seventeenth-century Pennsylvania.

40. The Indian policy in seventeenth-century Pennsylvania
    a. was similar to Indian policies of the other English colonies of the time.
    b. involved letting the Indians keep their lands if they converted as Quakers.
    c. was more repressive then the Indian policies in the other English colonies of the time.
    d. involved purchasing Indians' land, respecting their claims, and dealing with them fairly.

41. Among other things, religious toleration in Quaker-dominated Pennsylvania meant that colonists there
    a. did not have to put up with Catholics.
    b. could attend any church but were required to worship every week.
    c. did not have to pay taxes to maintain a state-supported church.
    d. tended to be less religious than in other colonies.

42. As proprietor of Pennsylvania, William Penn
    a. could do whatever he wanted with and in the colony.
    b. had extensive powers subject only to review by Parliament, and he sometimes chose to exercise his powers quite ruthlessly.
    c. had extensive powers subject only to review by the king, but he chose to appoint a governor who could veto legislation of the colonial council.
    d. was severely restricted in his actions by the ruling council of Pennsylvania.

43. The Navigation Acts of the 1650s and 1660s were designed to regulate colonial trade in order to
    a. line the pockets of those sitting in the House of Lords.
    b. yield revenues for the crown and English merchants and protect the colonies' trade from England's competitors and enemies.
    c. help colonists in North America make enough money to free themselves from dependence on British merchandising schemes.
    d. ensure that all European nations had equal access to goods produced in America, an early stab at global free trade.

44. By the end of the seventeenth century, colonial commerce was characterized by
    a. an increasing independence from its former ties with the British Empire.
    b. stagnation because the colonies were forbidden by England from importing anything but English-made goods.
    c. strong ties to England due to royal supervision of merchants and shippers, the protection of the British navy, and a healthy flow of imports and exports between the colonies and England.
    d. a status of equality with England as the colonies and the mother country cooperated and made joint decisions on trade matters.

45. King Charles II took a personal interest in getting greater control over New England because
    a. he had invested heavily in several ventures there and was losing money.
    b. his father, Charles I, had been executed by Puritans in England.
    c. he objected to the way colonists were treating Indians.
    d. many New Englanders were lobbying the king to establish a more visible presence for the Church of England in their communities.

46. The outcome of King Philip's War (1676) left New England settlers with
    a. a deep and abiding respect for Native Americans.
    b. the task of rebuilding Boston, which the Nipmucks and Narragansetts had leveled.
    c. a large war debt, a devastated frontier, and an enduring hatred of Indians.
    d. a society so devastated by death and destruction that fresh infusions of English settlers were required to repopulate many areas.

47. In 1686, England created the Dominion of New England, a new government consolidation that
    a. placed all northern colonies under the rule of a local council located in Boston.
    b. invalidated all colonial charters in the region except the one held by Massachusetts.
    c. actually relocated part of Parliament to America as a way to represent colonists more effectively.
    d. placed all colonies north of Maryland under the direct control of England and invalidated all land titles.

48. In 1688, the Glorious Revolution in England influenced American colonists to
    a. rise up against royal authority (and the concept of the Dominion of New England) in Massachusetts, New York, and Maryland.
    b. pledge new support for the concept of the Dominion of New England.
    c. show their support for the religious convictions of King James II.
    d. organize military groups to sail to England to help overthrow William of Orange.

49. King William's War, an attack by Great Lakes and Canadian French forces on villages in New England and New York, demonstrated to the American colonists that
    a. they needed to populate the western territory as soon as possible to drive out the French.
    b. the French did not have their heart in hanging on to their New World possessions.
    c. English military protection from hostile neighbors was still very valuable.
    d. they could hold their own in military matters.

50. The northern colonies established in British North America in the seventeenth century demonstrated that
    a. most of the high ideals that colonists carried with them remained completely intact and were fully realized.
    b. Europeans would have a difficult time establishing viable settlements on the North American continent.
    c. faced with the need to grow, develop, and adapt to a new and hostile environment, the English in North America were up to the task.
    d. English habits and culture would face a difficult time surviving in the New World.

Terminology Matching   Select the word or phrase from the Terms section that best matches the definition or example provided in the Definitions section. Some terms may be used more than once; some may not be used at all.

TERMS

a. Antinomians
b. Cromwell, Oliver
c. Elizabeth I
d. Halfway Covenant
e. Henry VIII
f. Hutchinson, Anne
g. Mary I
h. Massachusetts Bay
i. New York
j. older men (forty-plus)
k. older women (forty-plus)
l. Pennsylvania

m. Pilgrims
n. Plymouth colony
o. praying towns
p. Puritans
q. Quakers
r. Squanto
s. Supremacy Act
t. town meetings
u. Williams, Roger
v. young men
w. young women

DEFINITIONS

1. Devout Puritan who lectured before large crowds in Boston about the sermons of John Cotton and whom John Winthrop referred to as an "Antinomian." _____

2. Label used by Puritans for persons who opposed the law. _____

3. English king who seized the vast properties of the Catholic Church in England in 1534. _____

4. A sect of Protestants who sought to reform the Church of England by eliminating what they considered to be offensive features of Catholicism and who adhered to the doctrine of Luther, Calvin, and others on the European continent. _____

5. English monarch who in 1553 attempted to return England to a pre-Reformation Catholic Church by outlawing Protestantism and persecuting those who refused to conform. _____

6. English monarch who tried to consolidate the English Reformation midway between the extremes of Catholicism and Puritanism and who was responsible for Protestantism being considered a defining feature of English national identity by 1603. _____

7. This outlawed the Catholic Church in England and proclaimed the king "the only supreme head on earth of the Church of England." _____

8. This colony was founded by a sect of Puritans who espoused a heresy known as "separatism." _____

9. This colony was founded by a sect of Puritans who aspired to reform the corrupt Church of England by setting an example of godliness in the New World. _____

10. This person was described by the governor of Plymouth colony as "a special instrument sent of God" who showed the colonists how to plant corn, find fish, and to procure other commodities, enabling the survival of the floundering settlement in 1620. _____

11. A sect of Protestants who believed that God chose only a few human beings, known as visible saints, to receive eternal life. _____

12. A sect of Protestants who believed that God made his love equally available to all persons. _____

13. A political forum established in New England that permitted a level of popular participation that was unprecedented elsewhere during the seventeenth century. _____

14. This critic of Puritan leadership in Massachusetts helped found the colony of Rhode Island and was known for advocating a strict separation of the church from civil influence. _____

15. This person led the Puritan Revolution in England in 1642 and, after executing Charles I in 1649, proclaimed England a Puritan Republic. _____

16. This compromise agreement stated that unconverted children of visible saints could baptize their offspring but could not participate in communion or have the voting privileges of church membership. _____

17. This originated as a proprietary colony of the Dutch West India Company. _____

18. This colony was guided by a leader who formulated an Indian policy characterized by fair treatment, which contrasted sharply with the hostile policies of other English colonies. _____

19. These were places where native Americans agreed to live in conformity with English ways. _____

20. This group represented the majority of those who were accused of witchcraft during the Salem witch trials. _____

Chronology   Place the events in chronological order.

SET ONE

A. John Winthrop leads Puritan settlers to Massachusetts Bay.

B. English Pilgrims (separatists) found Plymouth colony and elect William Bradford governor.

C. James II overthrown by the Glorious Revolution; William III becomes king.

D. English seize New Netherland from the Dutch and rename it New York.

E. Monarchy restored in England; Charles II becomes king.

First _____

Second _____

Third _____

Fourth _____

Fifth _____

SET TWO

A. Indians and colonists clash in King Philip's War.

B. Many Puritan congregations adopt Halfway Covenant.

C. Royal officials create Dominion of New England.

D. Staple Act requires all colonial imports to come from England.

E. Witch trials flourish at Salem, Massachusetts.

First _____

Second _____

Third _____

Fourth _____

Fifth _____

Short Answer   Write a paragraph in response to each question.

1. Define the term *proprietary colony* and identify the advantages proprietary colonies offered to a European monarch.

2. The Navigation Acts of 1650, 1651, and 1660 regulated trade in the English colonies. Describe the two basic stipulations of these acts and identify a major colonial product that was affected by these acts.

3. Briefly describe the cause and results of King Philip's War, and identify "King Philip" and his role in the war.

4. When Massachusetts became a royal colony in 1691, a new charter changed the qualification for voting in colony-wide elections. What was the prerequisite before 1691, and what was the prerequisite after 1691? What did this change signify?

5. Explain the following statement regarding the epidemic of witchcraft accusations that broke out in Salem, Massachusetts, in 1691 and 1692: "Witches made it somewhat easier for New Englanders to consider themselves saints rather than sinners."

6. Provide historical evidence to support the following statement: "By the end of the seventeenth century in New England, the zeal of Puritanism had cooled."

7. Briefly explain the need for Pilgrims to draft the Mayflower Compact on the day they arrived at Plymouth.

8. Modern-day speechwriters, including those of presidents Ronald Reagan and George Herbert Walker Bush, have evoked the metaphor of "a shining city upon the hill." Students of seventeenth-century American history recognize the origins of this phrase in one of the most famous sermons in American history, delivered to Puritans aboard the ship *Arbella*. Who delivered this sermon, and what point did he want to make by using the phrase "city upon a hill"?

9. Compare the colony at Massachusetts Bay with that founded at Chesapeake Bay.

10. The Quakers found themselves in conflict with the English government and Puritans in America. Briefly list the basic tenets of the Quaker concept of God and the manner in which these tenets shaped their worship services. Include a sentence that states how this offended Puritans.

Essay   Respond to each of the following questions in an essay of three to four paragraphs. Your responses should include specific evidence and your interpretation of the significance of historical events and concepts.

1. The English Reformation, in the short run, allowed Henry VIII to achieve one of his political goals; however, in the long run, it fostered certain kinds of problems that he had hoped to avoid. Write an essay in which you discuss Henry VIII's political responses to the Protestant Reformation that was taking place on the European continent; explain how his political actions were inconsistent with his theology and religious practices, identify the political goals that guided his responses, and describe the long-term results of Henry's actions.

2. The Puritan faith community shaped the New England colonies in virtually every way during much of the seventeenth century. Write an essay in which you discuss the ideas and religious principles that characterize Puritanism and explore the significant differences between the Puritan sect led by William Bradford, who founded Plymouth colony, and the group of Puritans led by John Winthrop, who founded Massachusetts Bay colony.

3. The Dutch colonial outpost of New Netherland contrasted significantly with the English colonies of New England. Write an essay in which you compare the origins, social environment, and governmental structure of New Netherland with that of the Puritan colonies.

4. Within twenty years of its founding, Philadelphia, the capital city of the colony of Pennsylvania, became one of the most important centers of commerce in British North America. Write an essay in which you evaluate the role played by William Penn in the evolution of Pennsylvania from "a holy experiment" into a prosperous North American colony.

Map Questions   Answer the questions below using Map 3.1, New England Colonies in the Seventeenth Century (p. 77).

READING THE MAP

1. The towns indicated on the map were settled around an important geographical feature. What is that basic feature? Do any towns on the map deviate from this characteristic?

2. What is the geographical position of Massachusetts relative to other New England colonies? Which colonies are north of Massachusetts? Which are south of Massachusetts?

CONNECTIONS

1. Explain what the founding dates of the colonies surrounding Massachusetts appear to reveal about the ability of the Bay colony's leaders to maintain their original vision of a godly community.

2. Describe New England's overall geographical situation and how it led to unprecedented health and longevity for settlers there.

COLONIAL AMERICA IN THE EIGHTEENTH CENTURY

4

1701–1770

Multiple Choice   Choose the letter of the best answer.

1. The most important change in eighteenth-century colonial America was
   a. a phenomenal population growth.
   b. an increase in the British population due to famine in England.
   c. more land development.
   d. a decrease in the Indian population.

2. In eighteenth-century America, the main sources of population growth and diversity were
   a. Eastern European and Palatine German immigrants.
   b. Irish and Italian immigrants.
   c. Russian and English immigrants.
   d. immigration and natural increase.

3. In the eighteenth century, the majority of immigrants coming to America were
   a. English or African.
   b. from German principalities.
   c. Scots-Irish or African.
   d. Scottish.

4. The colonial economy in the eighteenth century was unique because
   a. a few colonists held most of the wealth, whereas most people were very poor.
   b. of the modest economic welfare of most of the free population.
   c. almost all colonists considered themselves wealthy.
   d. the standard of living in the colonies rose by one-tenth of a percent.

5. While the New England population grew sixfold during the eighteenth century, it lagged behind the growth in the other colonies because
   a. most immigrants chose other colonies due to the inhospitable Puritan orthodoxy and relatively high ratio of people to land.
   b. wealth could be gained quicker in other colonies.
   c. the weather was too cold in New England.
   d. merchants of New England did not encourage more colonists to settle there.

6. Because of the colonial New England practice of "partible inheritance" in land distribution, by the eighteenth century lands could no longer be subdivided, as the plots had become too small for a family to make a living. *Partible inheritance* means that
   a. lands were subdivided about equally among all the children in a family.
   b. lands were subdivided about equally among all the sons in a family.
   c. lands were subdivided between the eldest and youngest males of the family.
   d. lands were subdivided among the wife and three oldest children in a family.

7. By 1770, New Englanders had only one-fourth as much wealth as free colonists in the South, in part because
   a. scarcity of land made it impossible for farmers to produce cash crops in the quantities necessary to become wealthy.
   b. the growing season was too short.
   c. the craggy, rocky soil would not grow cash crops.
   d. a lack of rainfall kept farm goods from growing.

8. The eighteenth-century New England economy could be characterized as
   a. being dominated by farmers with large landholdings.
   b. a diversified worldwide commercial economy.
   c. being dominated by a network of trade with the expanding settler population.
   d. a primarily agricultural society that imported most of its material goods from England.

9. The commercial economy of New England was dominated by
   a. artisans.
   b. farmers.
   c. printers.
   d. merchants.

10. As compared with the poor in England, eighteenth-century New Englanders
    a. were much poorer and lacked the bare essentials.
    b. were equally poor and needy.
    c. lived more comfortably.
    d. did not have a class of poor, as wealth was quite equally distributed.

11. Why were there so few slaves in New England during the eighteenth century?
    a. New England's family farming was not suited for slave labor.
    b. New Englanders didn't have the money to buy slaves.
    c. The slave trade was prohibited in New England.
    d. Slaveholding violated Puritan beliefs.

12. By 1770, the middle colonies had a uniquely diverse immigrant population; the largest number of immigrants were
    a. Dutch.
    b. Catholic.
    c. German and Scots-Irish.
    d. Yankee.

13. Most of the Scots-Irish who came to the colonies were farm laborers or tenant farmers who were leaving behind
    a. lush green farmland seized by the British.
    b. droughts, crop failures, high food prices, or high rents.
    c. small farms that had been in their families for decades.
    d. farm lands that were flooded from the great rains of Ireland.

14. Many Germans without passage money arrived in Philadelphia as "redemptioners," which were
     a. people who obtained money for passage from a friend or relative in the colonies or by selling themselves as servants once they arrived.
     b. people who redeemed their possessions with a ship's captain for passage to the colonies.
     c. people who agreed to work aboard ship for free passage to the colonies.
     d. skilled artisans who agreed to work a year in the colonies for passage.

15. In the middle colonies of the eighteenth century, slaves
     a. were not much needed on the wheat farms, which operated mostly with family labor.
     b. grew tremendously in number due to burgeoning tobacco farms.
     c. were frowned upon and treated more like redemptioners where they were used.
     d. were mostly of Indian descent.

16. An early Pennsylvania policy encouraging settlement was
     a. to give away land to adult white males.
     b. to pay settlers to farm Indian lands.
     c. a very low property tax.
     d. to negotiate with Indian tribes to purchase land, which reduced frontier clashes.

17. Why did New York's Hudson River Valley attract fewer immigrants than its southern neighbor, Pennsylvania?
     a. Owners of huge New York estates preferred to rent rather than sell their land.
     b. Pennsylvania was perceived to be safer.
     c. Indian clashes were more likely in New York than in Pennsylvania.
     d. all of the above

18. Economic growth in the middle colonies, particularly in Pennsylvania, came from
     a. the timber industry.
     b. wheat production.
     c. fishing.
     d. ship building.

19. A result of the comparatively high standard of living in rural Pennsylvania and the surrounding middle colonies between 1720 and 1770 was that
     a. the per capita consumption of imported goods from England more than doubled.
     b. colonists began buying more land.
     c. colonists increased the size of their families.
     d. daughters of colonists were sent to schools in England.

20. The dominant group in eighteenth-century Philadelphia society in terms of wealth and political power was
     a. fishermen.
     b. Quaker merchants.
     c. wheat farmers.
     d. artisans.

21. *Poor Richard's Almanack* mirrored the beliefs of its Pennsylvania readers in its glorification of
     a. Quaker values.
     b. the small farmer.
     c. work and wealth.
     d. the slave as a "noble savage."

22. The defining feature of the southern colonies in the eighteenth century was
    a. slavery.
    b. parasitic diseases due to the heat.
    c. cotton farms.
    d. sugarcane farming.

23. From 1700 to 1770, the black population in the South increased almost three times faster than the white population of that area; by 1770, blacks made up
    a. 20 percent of the southern population.
    b. 40 percent of the southern population.
    c. 75 percent of the southern population.
    d. 90 percent of the southern population.

24. The huge increase in the slave population in the South during the second half of the eighteenth century can be attributed to
    a. slave immigration.
    b. natural increase and the Atlantic slave trade.
    c. slaves leaving New England to come South.
    d. natural increase.

25. Southern planters tended to buy newly arrived Africans in small groups because
    a. planters were afraid of insurrection.
    b. escalating prices meant that they had to buy slaves on credit, and small groups of slaves ensured that newcomers could be trained by the planters' seasoned slaves.
    c. they bought groups of slaves jointly with another plantation owner.
    d. they had to be very selective to get the best buys.

26. South Carolina planters favored slaves from the central African Congo and Angola regions because
    a. linguistic and cultural similarities allowed them to communicate with other African slaves from the same region, thereby easing newcomers' acculturation to slave life.
    b. they were more common and thus less expensive.
    c. they were larger and stronger.
    d. they came from a region in Africa that was similar in climate to South Carolina and thus stayed healthier and were able to work more.

27. The purpose of "seasoning" slaves was to
    a. acclimate them to the physical and cultural environment of the southern colonies.
    b. break them so they would obey their masters.
    c. slowly introduce them to the slaves already on the plantations so that the slaves from differing cultures would get along.
    d. teach them English.

28. A "creole" or "country-born" slave was one who
    a. was used to the ways of southern slavery after a seasoning process.
    b. was born into slavery in the colonies.
    c. had been held in slavery for ten years.
    d. spoke the Creole dialect.

29. Why did Thomas Jefferson think that a "[slave] child raised every 2 years is of more profit than the crop of the best laboring [slave] man"?
    a. Children worked harder and complained less than adult slaves.
    b. Through natural increase his slave holdings would grow to larger numbers and thus include more laboring individuals.
    c. Children ate less than a laboring slave man did.
    d. The mortality rate of adult male slaves was high.

30. Southern masters preferred black slaves over white indentured servants because
    a. masters had to pay indentured servants a small sum each year.
    b. indentured servants would not work as many hours as slaves.
    c. indentured servants were surly and talked back.
    d. slaves served for life and could be beaten into submission.

31. The Stono rebellion proved that slaves
    a. were dangerous in large, organized numbers.
    b. could not overturn slavery nor win in the fight for freedom.
    c. would continue to rebel until they received their freedom.
    d. could not organize themselves against their smart, armed masters.

32. The Stono rebellion resulted in South Carolina laws passed to govern slavery; for example,
    a. trusted slaves were chosen to monitor other slaves on the plantation.
    b. white men were to serve on patrols to check for suspicious activity among slaves.
    c. planters were allowed to buy only newly imported slaves, in the hope that such slaves would be more obedient.
    d. slaves were to be in their hut by sundown and accounted for by their master.

33. Newly imported African slaves usually arrived alone; how did they develop kinship relationships in the existing slave communities?
    a. Established slave families often adopted new arrivals as kin, recognizing them as aunts or uncles.
    b. New arrivals used sign language, since they did not speak the same dialect.
    c. Seasoned slaves taught new arrivals the ways of the plantation and shared food with them.
    d. The master or plantation owner assigned new arrivals to seasoned slaves in kinship units.

34. As the eighteenth century progressed, tobacco, rice, and indigo made the southern colonies
    a. as rich as the New England merchants.
    b. the richest in North America.
    c. dependent upon the West Indies for trade.
    d. a colonial appendage of the middle and New England colonies.

35. While the eighteenth-century southern gentry privately looked down upon poor whites, they publicly acknowledged them as
    a. necessary to the growth of Southern economy.
    b. their equals by virtue of belonging to the "superior" white race.
    c. a contemptible group of lost souls.
    d. having the opportunity to become gentry someday.

36. In the eighteenth century, the southern slaveholding gentry dominated
    a. the Supreme Court.
    b. the Atlantic coastal towns.
    c. both the politics and the economy of the South.
    d. the U.S. Congress.

37. Members of the eighteenth-century southern gentry typically
    a. attended the Presbyterian church each week.
    b. felt they deserved a life of idleness.
    c. gambled, wore the finest clothes, and bought fine wines and books from Europe.
    d. were skilled with weaponry.

38. Though the three regions of British North America became more distinct in the later part of the eighteenth century, they still shared several unifying experiences, such as
    a. agricultural roots, a lessening reliance upon religion, and a realization of their British colonial identity.
    b. steadily declining opportunities to buy land and a related increase in industrial development.
    c. growing concern over the slavery issue and the increasing importance of evangelical religion.
    d. very similar colonial governments and a growing concern over the slavery issue.

39. An increased supply of items such as tobacco and sugar in eighteenth-century colonial America led to
    a. increased obesity and a subsequent sedentary lifestyle.
    b. a drop in prices, prompting slaveholders to decrease the number of slaves they bought.
    c. a new market for luxury goods, as ordinary people proved that if they could, they would buy things they desired rather than merely needed.
    d. increased exports to England and increased trading with Indians to the west.

40. A communication medium that brought the colonies closer together as it evolved was
    a. newspapers.
    b. printed pamphlets.
    c. lending libraries.
    d. philosophical societies.

41. The increasing presence of English goods in the colonial market in the eighteenth century
    a. caused the colonists to rebel and concentrate on home manufacture of goods.
    b. improved the colonial standard of living while increasing resentment toward the British.
    c. spurred competition with goods imported from continental Europe.
    d. tied the colonists to the British economy while making them feel more British.

42. The largest group of non-Christians in eighteenth-century North America was made up of
    a. Hurons.
    b. slaves.
    c. southerners.
    d. indentured servants.

43. Prominent colonists in the plantation South and in cities such as Charleston, New York, and Philadelphia belonged to the
    a. Presbyterian Church.
    b. Anglican Church.
    c. Catholic Church.
    d. Congregational Church.

44. In eighteenth-century New England, the Congregational Church
    a. was popular, but plurality was the norm.
    b. was not as popular as the Anglican Church.
    c. was supported by taxes paid by all residents.
    d. tried to undermine the Puritan Church, which was losing membership.

45. In colonial America, deists
    a. came from the middle class and questioned the existence of God.
    b. were usually educated and followed the ideas of European Enlightenment thinkers.
    c. rejected intellectual thought and sought to find gods in natural phenomena.
    d. believed in predestination and a vengeful god.

46. Topics discussed at the American Philosophical Society, led by Benjamin Franklin, revolved around
    a. ways to improve society.
    b. a new approach to science.
    c. new inventions to improve farming equipment.
    d. the true purpose of life.

47. The Great Awakening can best be described as
    a. a movement to convert Catholics.
    b. a revival movement to convert nonbelievers and revive the piety of believers.
    c. an appeal to the head, not the heart.
    d. an appeal to Protestants to band together as one.

48. In addition to their competition for land, colonial settlers and Indians clashed over
    a. fishing rights.
    b. French protection.
    c. access to British imports.
    d. the fur trade.

49. Colonial governors had difficulty gaining the trust and respect of influential colonists because
    a. their terms of office were often less than five years, and they had no access to patronage positions.
    b. they all lived in England and rarely came to the colonies.
    c. they were poorly paid and accepted bribes.
    d. the colonists believed that they should not be tied to England.

50. During the eighteenth century, colonists in America
    a. thought of themselves as both British subjects and colonists.
    b. were ready to break with England.
    c. became remarkably homogeneous given the number of immigrants.
    d. worked incessantly to make their society thoroughly colonial, rejecting as much of British culture and fashion as possible.

Terminology Matching   Select the word or phrase from the Terms section that best matches the definition or example provided in the Definitions section. Some terms may be used more than once; some may not be used at all.

TERMS

a. Anglican Church

b. Congregational Church

c. creole

d. deists

e. Edwards, Jonathan

f. Enlightenment

g. Franklin, Benjamin

h. gentry

i. Great Awakening

j. Middle Passage

k. natural increase

l. New England

m. partible inheritance

n. Pennsylvania

o. redemptioners

p. slave codes

q. southern colonies

r. task system

s. Walking Purchase

t. yeoman farmers

DEFINITIONS

1. Author of *Poor Richard's Almanack,* a very popular publication begun in Pennsylvania in 1733 that promoted the idea of worldly payoff for hard work. _____

2. Region in colonial America where great numbers of German farmers settled. _____

3. Demographic term that means "growth through reproduction" in referring to a population. _____

4. This region lagged behind the other colonies in population growth, in part because it was relatively inhospitable for religious dissenters and those indifferent to theology. _____

5. A practice of subdividing land equally among male siblings which was carried out by the original New England settlers. _____

6. Farmers in this colonial region grew diversified crops for subsistence agriculture and did not produce huge marketable surpluses. _____

7. Merchants dominated the commercial economy of this colonial region, the most successful of them living in seaports. _____

8. Penniless German and Scots-Irish immigrants who would obtain money from relatives or friends in the colonies to pay for their passage, or would sell themselves as servants. _____

9. Repressive laws passed in South Carolina after the Stono rebellion of 1739 which were designed to guarantee the upper hand to whites. _____

10. Infamous strategy used to settle a dispute with Indians in northern Delaware in 1737 regarding land granted to the Penn family; approximately doubled the size of the Penns' claim. _____

11. The crossing of the Atlantic Ocean in the hold of a slave ship. _____

12. An arrangement in the lower South that gave slaves some control over the pace of their work and some discretion in the use of the rest of their time. _____

13. Term used to describe slaves who were born in the colonies. _____

14. Rice and indigo were major export products of this colonial region. _____

15. This social group dominated the politics and economy of the South in a self-perpetuating oligarchy. _____

16. This was the officially established, tax-supported church in New England. _____

17. This was the officially established, tax-supported church in the South. _____

18. Persons who look for God's plan in nature more than in the Bible. _____

19. Original organizer of the American Philosophical Society in Philadelphia. _____

20. A multifaceted intellectual movement that challenged many eighteenth century conventional ideas. _____

21. This 1730s movement is associated with revival meetings aimed at reviving the piety of the faithful. _____

Chronology   Place the events in chronological order.

SET ONE

A. American Philosophical Society is founded.

B. Slaves rebel at Stono, South Carolina.

C. Benjamin Franklin arrives in Philadelphia.

D. *Poor Richard's Almanack* is published.

E. *New England Courant* begins publication.

First _____

Second _____

Third _____

Fourth _____

Fifth _____

SET TWO

A. Scots-Irish immigration to America begins to increase.

B. Georgia is founded.

C. Colonists move south from Pennsylvania into the southern backcountry.

D. Large numbers of German immigrants come to the American colonies.

First _____

Second _____

Third _____

Fourth _____

Short Answer   Write a paragraph in response to each question.

1. Eighteenth-century colonial America was characterized by a rapidly growing, diverse population. Identify the two major sources of this growth and diversity and the major ethnic and racial groups that contributed to this diversity, and explain the way in which this population shift changed the demographic profile of the American colonies from 1670 to 1770.

2. Provide evidence that supports the following statement: Demographically, communities in New England during the eighteenth century were more homogeneous than communities in the middle and southern colonies.

3. Identify the stipulations of the agreements that enabled "redemptioners" to immigrate to the middle colonies.

4. By what process was a resident of an African village transformed into a southern colonial slave? What mortality rate and possible causes of death did slaves face during the trip to America?

5. Describe the process known as "seasoning" in regard to newly arrived Africans, and explain why this helped colonial planters reap maximum profits from a slave purchase.

6. The slave rebellion at Stono, South Carolina, was not followed by any similar uprisings during the colonial period. Describe the actions of the slaves, explain how the rebellion was suppressed, and identify the long-term consequences of this rebellion.

7. Though the societies of New England, the middle colonies, and the southern colonies grew increasingly differentiated during the eighteenth century, colonists throughout British North America shared certain unifying experiences. Identify three of these experiences and briefly explain how they unified the colonists.

8. During the eighteenth century, American colonists exhibited a distinctively dual identity as loyal British subjects and as American colonists who acted in their own best interests. Cite an example of each side of this dual identity and explain why the colonists were able to resist British interference in some instances.

9. Describe the reciprocal nature of the trading relationship that existed between Indians and colonists during the eighteenth century along the frontier edges of settlements, and identify the dilemma this relationship created for the Indians.

10. Explain the revolutionary effect James Franklin's regularly published newspaper, the *New England Courant,* had on eighteenth-century colonial society.

Essay   Respond to each of the following questions in an essay of three to four paragraphs. Your responses should include specific evidence and your interpretation of the significance of historical events and concepts.

1. The rapid increase in the population of eighteenth-century colonial America resulted in an expanding economy, which sharply contrasted with the results of population booms in Europe. In an essay, discuss the fundamental economic environment that sustained New England's rapidly growing population. Include in your discussion the major causes of New England's significant population growth, and analyze the effects of New England's growing population on land distribution, land usage, and the overall economy.

2. A common saying among Scots-Irish and Germans during the eighteenth century was "Pennsylvania is heaven for farmers [and] paradise for artisans." Write an essay in which you explain the attraction Pennsylvania held for immigrants. Include an analysis of the extent to which immigrants achieved success in this region.

3. The labor system of slavery transformed the South during the eighteenth century. Write an essay in which you discuss the impact of slavery on the economy of the South, as well as its impact on southern society and politics.

4. During the eighteenth century, British North American colonists became accustomed to thinking of themselves as individuals who had the power to make decisions that influenced the quality of their lives. Write an essay in which you explore the connections the Enlightenment and the "Great Awakening" had to the idea of an empowered individual. Include in your discussion the significant features of each of these movements, and explain the influences each had on eighteenth-century colonial America.

Map Questions   Answer the questions below using Map 4.1, Europeans and Africans in the Eighteenth Century (p. 107).

READING THE MAP

1. In the eighteenth century, what group was concentrated to the west of other immigrant groups?

2. Which immigrant group had the greatest geographical distribution in the eighteenth century?

CONNECTIONS

1. Which immigrant group tended to settle in coastal areas in both the North and South? Why was the Atlantic coastline settled predominantly by this group?

2. Why was there a large concentration of slaves along the South Carolina coast? North Carolina seems to have had few slaves — why was that?

THE BRITISH EMPIRE AND THE COLONIAL CRISIS

5

1754–1775

Multiple Choice   Choose the letter of the best answer.

1. The French and Indian War (called the Seven Years' War in Europe) resulted from
   a. dispute between Indians, Virginians, and the French over territory in the Ohio Valley.
   b. dispute between Indians, the French, and the British over territory in the Ohio Valley.
   c. French claims to fur trapping along the Ohio Valley.
   d. navigation of the Ohio River.

2. One important goal of the Albany Congress (June 1754) was to
   a. restructure imperial authority in the colonies.
   b. win support from the Iroquois Nation.
   c. elect a colonial-appointed military liaison with the English.
   d. provide for taxation of the colonies.

3. The Albany Plan of Union, as proposed by Benjamin Franklin and Thomas Hutchinson, was
   a. accepted by all of the colonies.
   b. accepted by the colonies and turned down by England.
   c. helpful in gaining the pledge of the Iroquois to fight the French.
   d. approved by neither the colonies nor England.

4. The representatives of the Iroquois League at the Albany Congress
   a. made no commitment to helping the British fight the French.
   b. refused to accept gifts from the colonists.
   c. agreed to join the fight against the French.
   d. pledged to continue their support of British troops.

5. The turning point of the French and Indian War was probably William Pitt's
   a. negotiations with the Iroquois Nation.
   b. capture of the French fortress city of Quebec.
   c. willingness to commit massive resources to the war.
   d. guerilla tactics and extreme bravery.

6. The terms of the Treaty of Paris included
   a. the English receiving Canada, all land east of the Mississippi, and islands previously held by the French.
   b. England receiving lands east of the Mississippi River, and Spain receiving lands west of the Mississippi River.
   c. England winning rights to all land east of the Mississippi, and the Indians of the Ohio Valley receiving land to the west of the Mississippi.
   d. France retaining possession of Canada, Martinique, and Guadeloupe, with Spain holding onto Cuba.

7. As a result of the French and Indian War,
   a. cracks in the English-American alliance were mended.
   b. colonists had a new respect for British military leaders.
   c. England's royal treasury was filled, due to war booty.
   d. Indians lost their land and had to face colonists moving west.

8. After the French and Indian War, the earl of Bute decided to keep ten thousand British troops in America to
   a. keep the peace between the colonists and the Indians.
   b. punish the colonists for their smuggling activities during the war.
   c. prevent the French from trying to regain lost territory.
   d. protect settlers who moved west of the Appalachian Mountains.

9. Pontiac's rebellion had the success it did because
   a. Indians from several tribes coordinated uprisings.
   b. the British had abandoned their western forts.
   c. the Indians received help from the French.
   d. colonists had recently been hit hard by disease.

10. The Proclamation of 1763 was meant to
    a. establish a permanent boundary line dividing Indian land and colonial claims.
    b. protect the French fur trade.
    c. protect the Iroquois Indians from French settlers encroaching upon their lands.
    d. prevent colonists from settling west of the Appalachian mountains.

11. The Proclamation of 1763 was meant to
    a. permit American colonists to advance west of the Mississippi River.
    b. give the colonial assemblies control over westward movement.
    c. keep the peace between Indians and colonists.
    d. threaten the Indians of the Ohio Valley.

12. The Paxton Boys
    a. were hanged for the murder of some Indians.
    b. sought to retaliate against Indian attacks.
    c. murdered Chief Pontiac.
    d. were Scots-Irish inhabitants of Virginia.

13. Growing colonial resentment of British authority during the 1760s could be attributed to
    a. increased trade possibilities.
    b. increased taxation and intrusion by Britain.
    c. increased exports from other countries.
    d. continuous abuse by the British soldiers.

14. In 1764, in an effort to generate income for England, George Grenville initiated the
    a. Currency Act, popularly called the Stamp Act.
    b. Revenue Act, popularly called the Sugar Act.
    c. Molasses Act, popularly called the Sugar Act.
    d. Sugar Act, popularly called the Sweet Act.

15. George Grenville engineered the Currency Act of 1764 to
    a. pacify London merchants who were losing revenue because of paper money in the colonies.
    b. lubricate the colonies' war-weary economy.
    c. allow the colonies to print more paper money.
    d. slow the flow of gold and silver coins into the colonies.

16. An important difference between the Sugar Act and the Stamp Act was that the latter
    a. was merely a revision of a previously existing tax, so colonists could not object.
    b. instituted a tax that was to be paid mainly by merchants and shippers.
    c. received united support from members of Parliament and therefore could be effectively enforced.
    d. was an internal tax that few colonists could escape.

17. Thomas Hutchinson, lieutenant governor of Massachusetts, lobbied quietly against the Stamp Act because
    a. he felt most colonists could not afford to pay more taxes.
    b. it trampled the colonies' right to tax themselves.
    c. he felt Britain did not need more tax revenue.
    d. he was personally opposed to higher taxation.

18. George Grenville claimed that Americans had "virtual representation" because
    a. the colonists were allowed to send delegates to the House of Commons.
    b. the colonies had their own assemblies.
    c. the members of the House of Commons represented all British subjects, wherever they were.
    d. the colonists were represented in the Continental Congress.

19. The Stamp Act of 1765
    a. affected only New England.
    b. was consistent with past parliamentary efforts to regulate trade.
    c. seemed to set an ominous precedent in the eyes of the colonists.
    d. required the consent of the colonial assemblies before going into effect.

20. The Virginia Resolves, authored by Patrick Henry of Virginia, were a response to the
    a. Revenue Act.
    b. Stamp Act.
    c. Townshend Duties.
    d. Coercive Acts.

21. The Sons of Liberty, protestors against the Stamp Act, organized a large demonstration that showed colonists
    a. that British authority would quell such riots in the future.
    b. that stamp distributors were more popular than they had realized.
    c. the ability of the British police force to subdue protests.
    d. their ability to affect politics.

22. American opposition to the Stamp Act took the form of
    a. burning an effigy of a stamp collector, breaking windows, and ransacking an official's home.
    b. street fighters who maimed or murdered anyone who supported the act.
    c. gangs of seamen who tarred and feathered stamp distributors.
    d. congressional meetings in Philadelphia to protest the legislation to the King.

23. The Stamp Act Congress, held in New York in 1765,
    a. was a failure, as the nine colonies represented could not agree on a unified policy.
    b. protested the "state of slavery" imposed by the Stamp Act and, by extension, the enslavement of slaves in the South.
    c. formulated a set of resolves that threatened rebellion against Britain.
    d. encouraged intercolonial political action and insisted on the linkage of liberty and property.

24. In response to the colonial reaction to the Stamp Act, the British government
    a. revoked the act and slowly began to return colonial lawmaking to the colonies.
    b. reinforced all British garrisons in North America and prepared for a long conflict.
    c. concluded that the colonies were incapable of cooperating and that the next phase of imperial restructuring should begin.
    d. repealed the act but reaffirmed parliamentary power by passing the Declaratory Act.

25. The Declaratory Act was much more damaging to the colonists than the Stamp Act had been, as it
    a. asserted Parliament's right to legislate for the colonies "in all cases whatsoever."
    b. drew many objections from the colonial governors.
    c. gave colonists authority to tax themselves.
    d. left unclear the extent to which Parliament could extend its authority in the colonies.

26. As chancellor of the exchequer in 1767, Charles Townshend
    a. favored imperial reforms that would make the colonists pay for the cost of British troops in America.
    b. set aside his antagonism toward the colonies.
    c. tried to revive the Stamp Act in modified form.
    d. increased the English land tax to cover military expenses.

27. In 1767, Charles Townshend enacted the Revenue Act, which
    a. levied an internal tax.
    b. placed new duties on such imported items as tea, glass, lead, paper, and painters' colors.
    c. was a form of income tax.
    d. taxed building materials, such as brick and wood.

28. The Revenue Act of 1767
    a. reflected Townshend's conciliatory attitude toward the colonies.
    b. reorganized the customs service and directed that some of the revenue gained be used to pay the salaries of royal governors.
    c. replaced the American Board of Customs Commissioners with royal oversight.
    d. was a relief to the colonists after the Stamp Act conflagration.

29. In response to the New York assembly's refusal to enforce the Quartering Act of 1765, Charles Townshend
    a. required New York residents to pay two-thirds more duties.
    b. took no action, allowing the assembly to ignore the act in return for gold.
    c. had the assembly's acts declared null and void until it met its obligations to the army.
    d. quickly revoked the act, fearing that other states would follow.

30. Which of the following statements best characterizes the colonial boycott (nonimportation) efforts of 1768–1769?
    a. The boycott failed because southern merchants refused to support the northern organizers.
    b. Merchants and consumers needed little persuasion to join the boycott.
    c. Consumers in the various colonies disagreed over which imported items to boycott.
    d. By 1769, merchants from New England to Charleston were supporting the boycott.

31. The Daughters of Liberty urged women to participate in public affairs and protest the Townshend duties by
    a. participating in nonconsumption agreements.
    b. growing their own tea plants.
    c. joining the Sons of Liberty in street protests.
    d. marching on the governor's mansion as a group.

32. Mounting tensions between Bostonians and British soldiers in early 1770 led to the Boston Massacre,
    a. a riot that killed two hundred people before it was brought under control.
    b. a confrontation in which a customs official was murdered.
    c. a skirmish in which five people were killed.
    d. a mutiny aboard British ships carrying tea.

33. Which of the following statements best characterizes the Boston Massacre of March 5, 1770?
    a. The Boston Massacre was prompted by a similar episode in New York in January.
    b. The British deliberately planned the incident to flush Boston rebels out into the open.
    c. The incident was aptly named, as the injuries on both sides were unprecedented up to that time.
    d. It was over in minutes, and the British regiments were then moved to an island in the harbor for their protection.

34. John Adams, cousin of Samuel Adams, represented British captain Thomas Preston and his soldiers who were involved in the Boston Massacre to
    a. please his cousin.
    b. prove that the colonists had the upper hand.
    c. punish the British offenders.
    d. show that the Boston leaders were defenders of British liberty and law.

35. In the early 1770s, several incidents brought the colonies' conflict with England into sharp focus; one was the
    a. burning of the *Gaspée.*
    b. proposal by Lord North to pay the salaries of superior court justices out of the Townshend duties.
    c. repeal of the Townshend duties.
    d. smuggling of Dutch tea.

36. The *Gaspée* incident of 1772 caused many towns in Massachusetts and other colonies to set up a communications network of standing committees known as
    a. "assemblies for protest."
    b. "committees of public safety."
    c. "committees of correspondence."
    d. "forums on change."

37. According to the British, the major purpose of the Tea Act of 1773 was to
    a. break the American boycott of tea imported from England.
    b. raise more revenue from the sale of tea to cover military costs in North America.
    c. boost sales for the financially strapped British East India Company.
    d. punish the Americans for importing tea from Holland.

38. Dissenting colonists believed that the real goal of the Tea Act of 1773 was
    a. to start a war.
    b. to put Dutch tea companies out of business.
    c. to show colonists that the British wanted to cooperate on trade.
    d. increased revenue to pay royal governors and judges, a reminder of Parliament's taxation and legislation power.

39. Bostonian reaction to the Tea Act culminated in December of 1773 with the dumping of 342 chests of tea into Boston Harbor, an action eventually known as the
    a. Defiance by Bostonians.
    b. Boston Tea Party.
    c. Boston Port Incident.
    d. East India Protest.

40. The Coercive Acts, passed by Parliament to punish Massachusetts for dumping the tea, included
    a. a law closing the Boston harbor until the destroyed tea was paid for.
    b. an addendum to the Declaratory Act.
    c. a law stipulating that any Massachusetts colonist accused of a capital crime would be tried in Canada or England.
    d. the appointment of Benedict Arnold as the new governor of Massachusetts.

41. The Quebec Act affronted many Americans because it
    a. denied political rights to Roman Catholics.
    b. permitted criminal cases to be settled without the use of juries.
    c. gave French Canadians unrestricted entry into northern New York and New England.
    d. gave Roman Catholic Quebec control of the Ohio River valley.

42. The Coercive Acts (or Intolerable Acts) spread alarm among the colonists, who feared that
    a. their liberties were insecure.
    b. tea prices would continue to rise.
    c. their home industries might not be able to meet the colonies' textile needs.
    d. independence was just around the corner.

43. The First Continental Congress created the Continental Association, whose purpose it was to
    a. abolish individual colonial governments.
    b. enforce a staggered and limited boycott of trade.
    c. provide a forum whereby representatives of all the colonies would be able to share plans for resisting British oppression.
    d. devise a method of collecting all taxes until the former Massachusetts charter was restored.

44. The First Continental Congress
    a. renounced American allegiance to George III.
    b. denied Parliament's right to tax the colonies but acknowledged its authority to legislate for the colonies and regulate their trade.
    c. denied Parliament's right to tax and legislate for the colonies but acknowledged its authority to regulate their trade.
    d. denied that Parliament had any authority in America.

45. Early in 1775, as royal authority collapsed in Massachusetts, General Thomas Gage
    a. realized the seriousness of the situation and endorsed Pitt's plan for reconciliation with the colonies.
    b. believed that he could suppress rebellion by arresting the leaders of the resistance and making a show of force.
    c. realized the seriousness of the situation and requested twenty thousand additional troops from England.
    d. attempted to negotiate with the leaders of the resistance.

46. General Gage planned a surprise attack on an ammunition storage site in Concord
    a. to put down the small group of rabble-rousers he believed was causing all the colonial dissent.
    b. because the site contained all the firepower in the area.
    c. because he knew it would be unguarded.
    d. because he was ordered to quell the dissenters before they became more organized.

47. The first shot at Lexington was fired by
    a. a British soldier.
    b. an American militiaman.
    c. a member of the Continental army.
    d. an unknown person.

48. Following the battles of Lexington and Concord, Lord Dunmore, the royal governor of Virginia, issued a proclamation
    a. promising freedom to defecting, able-bodied slaves who would fight for the British.
    b. saying that he would free his own slaves, along with all female, young, and elderly slaves who would fight for the British.
    c. stating that all Virginians should join him in freeing their slaves so they could fight for the British.
    d. saying that any slave caught fighting for the British would be hanged immediately.

49. Northern slave Phyllis Wheatley used bitter sarcasm in a 1774 newspaper essay exposing the hypocrisy of local slave owners; her accomplishments included
    a. leading Bostonian women in promoting spinning bees.
    b. writing poetry about freedom for slaves.
    c. inciting slaves to rebel against the British in Boston.
    d. starting the underground railroad.

50. Slaves were aware of the colonies' evolving political struggle with England; some slaves tried to promote their bid for freedom by
    a. stashing away ammunition for a planned uprising.
    b. volunteering to serve in the colonial militia.
    c. talking back to their masters.
    d. fleeing to the West.

Terminology Matching   Select the word or phrase from the Terms section that best matches the definition or example provided in the Definitions section. Some terms may be used more than once; some may not be used at all.

TERMS

a. Albany Congress

b. Boston Port Act

c. Declaratory Act

d. Dinwiddie, Robert

e. French and Indian War

f. Grenville, George

g. Henry, Patrick

h. Hutchinson, Thomas

i. North, Frederick, Lord

j. Proclamation of 1763

k. Quartering Act

l. Quebec Act

m. Sons of Liberty

n. Stamp Act

o. Stamp Act Congress

p. Sugar Act

q. Tea Act

r. Townshend duties

s. Treaty of Paris

t. Virginia Resolves

u. virtual representation

DEFINITIONS

1. Nine colonial assemblies sent twenty-seven delegates to this meeting in New York City in the fall of 1765 to discuss taxation and representation. _____

2. Formally ended the French and Indian War in 1763. _____

3. He was the much-hated royal governor of Massachusetts in the 1770s. _____

4. A group of delegates who did not approve an effort to unify the colonies for mutual defense. _____

5. An order issued by the British government that forbade colonists to settle west of an imaginary line drawn from Canada to Georgia along the Appalachian Mountains. _____

6. This 1765 act proposed a tax on various colonial documents — newspapers, pamphlets, contracts, etc. _____

7. A series of resolutions on the Stamp Act that were written by Patrick Henry. _____

8. According to George Grenville, the manner in which colonists were represented in Parliament, due to the fact that the House of Commons represents all British subjects. _____

9. He served as prime minister for King George from 1770–1782 and was responsible for enacting the Tea Act of 1773. _____

10. The fifth of the Intolerable Acts, it gave disputed lands throughout the Ohio River valley to Quebec. _____

11. Governor of Virginia who in 1753 sent George Washington to warn the French that they were trespassing on Virginia land. _____

12. A conflict that ended with the North American continent divided between the Spanish and British. _____

13. This act, also known as the Revenue Act of 1764, lowered the duty on French molasses and raised penalties for smuggling. _____

14. To protest the Stamp Act, this group of men found ways to pressure stamp distributors to resign. _____

15. This act, one of the Coercive Acts, closed Boston harbor to all shipping traffic. _____

16. He was responsible for the passage of the Sugar Act to stop American smuggling and generate income for the British Empire. _____

17. He was the author of the Virginia Resolves. _____

18. This act, passed after the Stamp Act was repealed, gave Parliament the right to legislate for the colonies "in all cases whatsoever." _____

19. This 1765 act directed the colonies to furnish shelter and provisions for the British army. _____

20. External taxes on tea, glass, lead, paper, and painters' colors imported into the colonies. _____

Chronology   Place the events in chronological order.

SET ONE

A. The French and Indian War ends with the Treaty of Paris.

B. The Albany Plan of Union is proposed.

C. The Intolerable Acts are passed.

D. Parliament passes the Currency Act.

E. The first shot is fired at Lexington and Concord.

First _____

Second _____

Third _____

Fourth _____

Fifth _____

SET TWO

A. The colonists agree to nonimportation agreements to protest British duties.

B. A standing army is left in America to enforce the Proclamation Act.

C. The First Continental Congress meets.

D. Parliament passes the Revenue Act.

First _____

Second _____

Third _____

Fourth _____

Short Answer   Write a paragraph in response to each question.

1. What were the conflicting interests in the Ohio valley before the French and Indian War, and what was the outcome of the war for each of the parties?

2. What circumstances caused the British government to issue the Proclamation Act of 1763, and what were the terms of the act?

3. Briefly describe the Sugar Act and the Currency Act, two of George Grenville's attempts to generate income for Britain in 1764. Why did the colonists object to these measures?

4. Why were the colonists opposed to "virtual representation"?

5. Explain why Americans opposed to the Stamp Act adopted the rallying cry of "Liberty and property."

6. Explain how the imposition of the Townshend duties led to the Boston Massacre.

7. What was the purpose of the "committees of correspondence," and how did their role develop in the early 1770s?

8. Why did Bostonians throw tea overboard into Boston Harbor in December 1773?

9. What did the members of the First Continental Congress discuss when they met in September 1774?

10. Why was Thomas Gage, the royal governor of Massachusetts, ordered to attack a suspected ammunition storage site at Concord in April 1775? Did he agree this was the best course of action?

Essay   Respond to each of the following questions in an essay of three to four paragraphs. Your responses should include specific evidence and your interpretation of the significance of historical events and concepts.

1. Following the French and Indian War, England began taxing the colonies and placing restrictions upon settlement beyond the Appalachian Mountains. Using specific examples, explain some of these measures and why the mother country adopted them.

2. Choose any four acts of Parliament, and discuss the terms of the acts and the effect they had on the colonists.

3. Discuss the Sons of Liberty and Daughters of Liberty. Include their goals and accomplishments.

4. Was tarring and feathering a common means of punishment in the colonies? Who were the victims of this unjust act, and what were some of the offenses or supposed crimes committed to warrant tarring and feathering? In general, what part did violence and terrorism such as tarring and feathering play in the colonial struggle for independence from Britain?

Map Questions   Answer the questions below using Map 5.2, North America before and after the French and Indian War (p. 150).

READING THE MAP

1. Before the French and Indian War, France held roughly what percentage of the American continent? And after the war?

2. What part of French land holdings went to England? To Spain?

CONNECTIONS

1. Why was the Proclamation Line of 1763 established by England?

2. What was the major outcome of the French and Indian War? Who lost the most lands?

THE WAR FOR AMERICA

1775–1783

Multiple Choice   Choose the letter of the best answer.

1. About a month after the skirmishes at Lexington and Concord, delegates from all of the colonies except Georgia met to discuss their course of action at the
   a. Continental Association.
   b. First Continental Congress.
   c. Second Continental Congress.
   d. House of Burgesses.

2. The initial goal of the Second Continental Congress was to
   a. declare independence from England immediately.
   b. raise and supply an army and negotiate a reconciliation with England.
   c. send the Continental army to Massachusetts.
   d. elect a president of the group.

3. By the middle of 1775, royal authority in the colonies
   a. was virtually dead due to violent local rebellions.
   b. was virtually dead due to the spread of government by colonial committees and a lack of royal power or loyalty.
   c. was tightened in response to the recent incidents at Lexington and Concord.
   d. tried to work with the colonial committees on compromise rule.

4. Most of the delegates to the Second Continental Congress initially were not prepared to break with England, and total independence was out of the question for delegates from
   a. Maryland and Virginia.
   b. South Carolina and Georgia.
   c. Massachusetts and New Jersey.
   d. New York and Pennsylvania.

5. The delegates to the Second Continental Congress chose George Washington as commander in chief because
   a. he was an excellent general.
   b. he had done such a good job in the French and Indian War.
   c. picking a southerner would show England that there was widespread commitment to war beyond New England.
   d. he was a wealthy plantation owner and had the time to commit to an all-out war.

6. The Battle of Bunker Hill
   a. was a victory for the Patriots.
   b. made the British realize they should quickly move westward to defeat the new Continental army.
   c. showed George Washington's leadership abilities.
   d. was an expensive victory for the British.

7. When George Washington took control of the Continental army he found
   a. excellent facilities but insubordinate troops.
   b. enthusiastic but undisciplined troops.
   c. sober and disciplined troops.
   d. soldiers who came to fight for the duration of the war.

8. The Olive Branch Petition of July 1775
   a. was proposed by Parliament to end the fighting in the colonies.
   b. affirmed loyalty to the monarch, blamed Parliament for all the problems, and asked that American colonial assemblies be recognized as individual parliaments.
   c. proposed that the King repeal all the legislation imposed by Parliament on the colonies.
   d. asked the King to ease up on the colonists and remove all his British troops from America.

9. The author of the radical pamphlet *Common Sense*
   a. called for independence and republicanism.
   b. was actually Benjamin Franklin writing under a pseudonym.
   c. asked the colonists to reconsider their cry for independence to restore harmony in the colonies.
   d. urged the common people to revolt against the wealthy merchants and planters.

10. By May of 1776, most of the colonies supported independence; the four that did not were
    a. Virginia, Maryland, Massachusetts, and Connecticut.
    b. Georgia, New Jersey, Rhode Island, and Maine.
    c. Pennsylvania, Maryland, New York, and South Carolina.
    d. North Carolina, South Carolina, Delaware, and New York.

11. The author of the Declaration of Independence was
    a. Benjamin Franklin.
    b. John Adams.
    c. John Dickinson.
    d. Thomas Jefferson.

12. Revisions to the Declaration of Independence included those made by Georgia and South Carolina, which struck from the document
    a. any mention of the issue of slavery.
    b. any mention of the natural equality of "all men."
    c. the phrase "give me liberty or give me death."
    d. the idea that governments derive their powers from the consent of the governed.

13. When New York delegates endorsed the Declaration of Independence on July 15, 1776, it meant that
    a. only South Carolina and Pennsylvania were left to endorse the resolution.
    b. the resolution for independence had passed unanimously.
    c. the resolution had the required majority to pass, but it was far from unanimous.
    d. war with England was over, and the new nation could get on with its democratic government.

14. One of the main obstacles the British army faced in the Revolutionary War was
    a. that they were highly motivated to destroy and conquer.
    b. that the loyalists were spread too thin among the colonies.
    c. the logistics of supplying an army with food and supplies across three thousand miles of water.
    d. that they had too many generals of little experience.

15. The British goal in fighting the war in America was
    a. to keep the colonists from obtaining help from other foreign nations.
    b. to gain support from Indian tribes and loyalists.
    c. to take control of the southern colonies and then defeat New England and the middle states.
    d. to regain colonial allegiance, not to destroy the colonies.

16. In order to raise the necessary troops for the Continental army, the congress
    a. offered a bonus for enlistment and land grants to those who committed for the war's duration.
    b. relied on the trained local militias.
    c. offered a land grant of five hundred acres to anyone who signed on for one year or more.
    d. required that soldiers sign on for the duration of the war.

17. Individual states raised troops for the war against the British by
    a. drafting all able-bodied men and men of position in the community.
    b. offering free rifles, uniforms, and adequate monthly salaries.
    c. drafting marginal men and those men suspected of being loyalists.
    d. promising the men adequate food and allowing them to bring their wives.

18. As manpower needs in the Continental army increased
    a. the southerners allowed their black slaves to serve.
    b. free blacks were welcomed into service in the northern states.
    c. about twenty thousand black men enlisted in the Revolutionary War.
    d. Indians were promised their land back if they would assist in the cause.

19. One of the many weaknesses of the Continental army was that
    a. it was inexperienced and undermanned.
    b. it was fighting on its own soil.
    c. there were too many pockets of loyalists in the colonies.
    d. it was undermanned because military service was not politically fashionable.

20. The American strategy in the war with Britain was to
    a. maintain and protect all the seaports.
    b. keep a strong force in New York.
    c. turn the British back and defeat their invading armies.
    d. utilize the state militias as much as possible.

21. The British strategy in the war in America was to
    a. destroy the colonies at almost all costs.
    b. recapture the thirteen colonies in a divide-and-conquer approach, with loyalist help.
    c. ravage the American towns and countryside in hopes of wearing the people down.
    d. amass as many men as possible in the North, the nerve center of the colonies.

22. The American goal of capturing Montreal and Quebec early in the war
    a. showed that the Americans were not just reacting to the British invasion of Massachusetts.
    b. was swiftly accomplished in 1775.
    c. was quickly and bloodlessly accomplished only in Quebec.
    d. was foiled when Indians in the area joined British troops.

23. In the fall of 1776, the British hired approximately eight thousand Hessian mercenaries and
    a. brought in ten thousand additional troops from Scotland.
    b. concentrated their military might in New York.
    c. concentrated on protecting their holdings in Canada.
    d. further swelled their ranks by cleaning out the jails in England.

24. In one of the early battles of the war, the Battle of Long Island,
    a. British troops, led by General Howe, forced the Americans to retreat to Manhattan Island.
    b. Washington and the Continental army scored their first major victory over British forces.
    c. General Howe demanded the unconditional surrender of Washington and his troops.
    d. British troops and a loyalist regiment accidentally fired on each other.

25. The Continental army enjoyed its first victory over the British on Christmas night in 1776, when the Americans
    a. attacked and captured Quebec.
    b. became firmly entrenched on Long Island and from there moved on to the middle colonies.
    c. crossed the Delaware River to surprise the Hessians at Trenton.
    d. retook the city of Philadelphia.

26. In the first year of the Revolutionary War, what really saved the American army may have been
    a. Britain's lack of naval support.
    b. the many casualties within British ranks produced by their recklessness.
    c. British reluctance to follow through militarily when they had the advantage.
    d. the inability of the British to hold New York City.

27. At the time of the war with Britain, white women
    a. were forbidden to talk of politics.
    b. participated in political rallies aimed at boosting morale.
    c. were allowed to join the army as male recruits became scarce.
    d. began to participate in politics through talking and fundraising.

28. The most visible and dedicated loyalists (also called Tories by their enemies) were
    a. Maryland Catholics.
    b. local judges, customs officers, wealthy merchants, and urban lawyers.
    c. Quakers and Moravians.
    d. small New England landowners and southern planters.

29. Treasonable acts, as defined by state laws in 1775 and 1776, included
    a. joining the British army or providing it with food or ammunition.
    b. being a Quaker or Mennonite.
    c. being the son or daughter of a traitor.
    d. offering blacks their freedom if they joined the British army.

30. During the Revolution, punishment for a treasonable act might include
    a. being put on public display in stocks.
    b. house arrest, suspension of voting privileges, and confiscation of property.
    c. wearing an embroidered *T* on the back of your coat or shirt.
    d. being sent to the front line of fighting.

31. During the Revolution, the Continental Congress and the various states issued paper money, which resulted in
    a. deflation and low prices.
    b. easy sales of bonds.
    c. inflation and escalating prices.
    d. low-interest foreign credit becoming available.

32. Well into the Revolutionary War, congress was forced to procure supplies and labor and to pay soldiers by
    a. using the black market.
    b. offering land bounties and issuing certificates of debt.
    c. taxing property in all the colonies.
    d. borrowing money from the Spanish.

33. In 1777, the British moved large numbers of men into Quebec in an effort to
    a. isolate New England by controlling the Hudson River.
    b. bring a swift end to the war.
    c. gain the support of the Iroquois Indians.
    d. capture Allentown.

34. Burgoyne's defeat at the second Battle of Saratoga was a decisive moment in the Revolutionary War because
    a. it caused Benedict Arnold to defect to the British.
    b. it brought France into the war on the side of the Patriots.
    c. it discredited Horatio Gates, resulting in his being replaced by Nathaniel Greene.
    d. it vindicated Burgoyne's strategy of mounting an attack from Canada.

35. When the British troops under General Howe captured Philadelphia in September 1777 and Washington suffered a defeat at Brandywine Creek, the British government
    a. proposed a truce and offered independence to the Americans.
    b. proposed to end the war as a tie.
    c. proposed a settlement which did not include American independence.
    d. offered monarchial protection if the patriots surrendered.

36. Continental army morale during the winter of 1777–78 was
    a. high, because the army had won a string of victories.
    b. high, because the British appeared ready to surrender.
    c. increasing, because American support for the troops was at an all-time high.
    d. low, because corruption was undermining the patriots' cause.

37. Relationships between Americans and Indians in the Revolutionary War were increasingly characterized by
    a. hostility and violent anti-Indian campaigns.
    b. cooperation in fighting a common enemy, the British.
    c. antagonism, as most Indians joined the British in fighting the Americans.
    d. cooperation, as the Indians allied with the French in fighting the British.

38. After the American victory at Saratoga, France allied with the Americans because it
    a. saw an opportunity to defeat England, France's archrival.
    b. wanted to gain a foothold in Canada once the Americans beat back the English.
    c. wanted to link the New England colonies with Quebec.
    d. wanted to extract revenge on England for France's defeat in the French and Indian War.

39. What immediate impact did the Americans' alliance with France in 1778 have on the British?
    a. The British were undaunted in their optimism for winning the war.
    b. A British troop commander argued for an immediate negotiated settlement, and the commander of the British navy argued for abandoning the war.
    c. The King was devastated, but his naval commander convinced him that the British would still win.
    d. Parliament called for a truce.

40. In their campaign in the South in 1778, the British
    a. quickly captured Charleston, South Carolina, without encountering any Continental army regiments.
    b. planned to use loyalists to fight back country regulators who had always supported the patriot planters.
    c. targeted Virginia as the first southern colony to capture.
    d. captured Georgia and South Carolina and dealt General Gates a devastating defeat at Camden, South Carolina.

41. In the final phases of the Revolutionary War, the British
    a. decided to mount a naval battle to exploit American weaknesses.
    b. tried to undermine the Revolution by enlisting the support of American loyalists in the South.
    c. enlisted large numbers of Indian tribes to aid in their cause.
    d. put slaves on the front lines to fight the patriots.

42. British gains from their southern campaign partly resulted from information provided to them by an American traitor,
    a. Nathaniel Greene.
    b. General William Howe.
    c. Benedict Arnold.
    d. Major John André.

43. News of Benedict Arnold's treason
    a. ended rebel support in the South for good.
    b. caused the French to withdraw their support of the Americans.
    c. made American morale sink to an all-time low.
    d. inspired renewed patriotism in America.

44. In the course of England's southern campaign late in the Revolutionary War,
    a. small bands of American guerrillas fought a series of fierce battles in the southern backcountry.
    b. British forces were buoyed by increasing loyalist strength in the South.
    c. Cherokee units in the Carolina backcountry switched to the patriots' side.
    d. the French convinced the Indians to fight the British along with French forces.

45. After Cornwallis achieved the upper hand in Virginia, the picture changed dramatically because
    a. Washington now had better information about Cornwallis's position and more troops with which to attack.
    b. the French gave military support to Washington.
    c. British intelligence information was accurate.
    d. Cornwallis had momentum in his favor.

46. The most decisive factor in ending the Revolutionary War at Yorktown was
    a. Lafayette's arrival at Yorktown from the west.
    b. the introduction of more sophisticated cannons.
    c. the French forces taking control of the Chesapeake, thus commanding the bay and the coasts of Virginia and North Carolina.
    d. General Cornwallis's troops being unprepared for attack.

47. By the terms of the Treaty of Paris of 1783,
    a. the king acknowledged that the United States were "free Sovereign and independent States."
    b. the Indians retained the Ohio Valley.
    c. loyalists' land was to be returned to them.
    d. the Americans were given Florida and half of Louisiana.

48. For the Indians, the peace that began in 1783
    a. meant displacement and only a temporary lull in fighting.
    b. was the beginning of the reservation system.
    c. meant their land was returned to them.
    d. led to unification.

49. The British lost the Revolutionary War primarily because
    a. their food supply was cut off by heavy rains every few months.
    b. there were very few loyalists to help them win the war.
    c. of America's alliance with France, which doomed the British to defeat.
    d. royal governors were imprisoned early in the war.

50. The war for independence took five and a half years, and the subsequent peace negotiations and British evacuation took an additional
    a. two years.
    b. five years.
    c. month.
    d. nine months.

Terminology Matching   Select the word or phrase from the Terms section that best matches the definition or example provided in the Definitions section. Some terms may be used more than once; some may not be used at all.

TERMS

a. André, Major John

b. Arnold, Colonel Benedict

c. Battle of Bunker Hill

d. Battle of Long Island

e. Battle of Saratoga

f. Battle of Ticonderoga

g. Battle of Yorktown

h. Burgoyne, General John

i. Chesapeake Bay

j. *Common Sense*

k. Cornwallis, General Charles

l. Declaration of Independence

m. French alliance

n. Gates, General Horatio

o. Hessians

p. loyalists

q. Olive Branch Petition

r. Paine, Thomas

s. Rochambeau, comte de

t. Second Continental Congress

u. Treaty of Paris

DEFINITIONS

1. The author of *Common Sense*. _____

2. An appeal to the king by the Second Continental Congress that was ultimately rejected. _____

3. They began meeting May 10, 1775, and while they had no legal authority, they assumed power on their own. _____

4. The 20 to 30 percent of the colonists who did not favor independence from England. _____

5. The battle that unofficially ended the Revolutionary War. _____

6. This British general surrendered to George Washington in October 1781, unofficially ending the war for independence. _____

7. This battle, fought on October 17, 1777, was the first decisive victory for the Continental army. _____

8. He became a traitor and traded information about the Continental army to the British for money. _____

9. A document drafted by Thomas Jefferson and his committee that was formally adopted on July 4, 1776, and signed on August 2. _____

10. This British general lost at the second Battle of Saratoga. _____

11. German soldiers hired by the British to defeat the colonists. _____

12. This document, which argued for complete independence from England, sold more than 150,000 copies in a matter of weeks. _____

13. In this formal agreement signed in February 1778, the French promised the colonists full military and commercial support in the war with England. _____

14. He and the large French army under his command changed the course of the Revolutionary War when they joined George Washington in Rhode Island. _____

15. After a significant loss of men in this battle, General Washington retreated to Manhattan Island. _____

16. The French command of this location was a decisive factor in ending the Revolutionary War. _____

17. This peace agreement was nearly two years in the making after the Battle of Yorktown. _____

18. He was sent by the British to meet with Benedict Arnold to negotiate payment for Arnold's services and was later arrested for spying and hanged. _____

19. Congress passed a resolution in June 1775 saying these people would be considered traitors. _____

20. One of the tasks of this group was to raise and supply a colonial army. _____

Chronology   Place the events in chronological order.

SET ONE

A. Cornwallis occupies Yorktown, Virginia.

B. Congress offers the Olive Branch Petition.

C. Burgoyne surrenders at Saratoga.

D. France enters the war on the American side.

E. *Common Sense* is published.

First _____

Second _____

Third _____

Fourth _____

Fifth _____

SET TWO

A. The Battle of Bunker Hill.

B. The British lay siege to Charleston, South Carolina.

C. The siege of Yorktown.

D. American armies march on Montreal and Quebec.

First _____

Second _____

Third _____

Fourth _____

Short Answer   Write a paragraph in response to each question.

1. How did Thomas Paine justify his case for complete independence from England in his pamphlet *Common Sense*? How was his pamphlet received in the colonies?

2. List at least two of the grievances in Thomas Jefferson's Declaration of Independence and Congress's response to these grievances.

3. Discuss several of the advantages and disadvantages for the British in fighting a war against the colonists.

4. Discuss some of the advantages and disadvantages for the patriots in rebelling against England.

5. Who were the loyalists during the Revolutionary War? Where were they located within the colonies?

6. What financial problems existed for the colonists during the Revolutionary War? What did the Continental Congress do to finance the war?

7. What impact did the French alliance have on the outcome of the Revolutionary War?

8. Why did the British decide to move their Revolutionary War campaign south in 1778? Was this strategy successful?

9. What events led up to Cornwallis's surrender in October 1781?

10. Discuss the terms of the Treaty of Paris. What issues were left unresolved?

Essay   Respond to each of the following questions in an essay of three to four paragraphs. Your responses should include specific evidence and your interpretation of the significance of historical events and concepts.

1. Discuss the two tasks facing the Second Continental Congress when the delegates met on May 10, 1775. What initial steps did they take to carry out their goals?

2. Discuss the differing attitudes toward colonial independence that are expressed in "Documenting the American Promise: The Issue of Independence."

3. Discuss the role of women and blacks in the Revolutionary War, both at home and on the battlefields.

4. Discuss why the British lost the Revolutionary War. What advantages did they misuse?

Map Questions   Answer the questions below using Map 6.1, The War in the North, 1775–1778 (p. 196).

READING THE MAP

1. Where were Washington's winter quarters in 1776–77 and 1777–78?

2. How many British victories occurred in the North between 1775 and 1778? How many American victories occurred in the North during the same period?

CONNECTIONS

1. Why did the British leave Boston to concentrate on New York in 1776?

2. Burgoyne had much better resources in upper New York than the Continental army, so why did he surrender at Saratoga?

3. With eight American victories and seven British victories early in the war, why did the two sides continue fighting for three more years?

BUILDING A REPUBLIC

1775–1789

Multiple Choice   Choose the letter of the best answer.

1. The weaknesses of Congress under the Articles of Confederation included its
   a. lack of an executive or judicial branch and of the power to levy taxes.
   b. inability to get money to finance the war.
   c. lack of a way to amend the Articles should that be needed.
   d. inability to conduct foreign relations.

2. Under the Articles of Confederation, delegates to Congress
   a. would be appointed by state governors.
   b. would number two to seven delegates from each state, selected annually by the state legislature.
   c. could serve four years at a time.
   d. were selected every six years by popular vote.

3. Under the Articles of Confederation
   a. all thirteen states had to approve routine decisions.
   b. five states had to approve war-making decisions.
   c. three-quarters of the states had to vote to approve or amend the Articles.
   d. each state had a single vote in Congress.

4. The Articles of Confederation were finally approved in 1781 when all the states agreed to surrender their
   a. power to regulate trade.
   b. power to make war.
   c. claims to western lands.
   d. right to levy their own taxes.

5. Early problems that confronted Congress under the Articles of Confederation included
   a. absenteeism and the lack of a quorum needed to conduct business.
   b. a permanent location that was too far away for many delegates to travel on a routine basis.
   c. overcrowding, as state legislatures sent more than their allotted share of delegates.
   d. the lack of a place to meet.

6. A shared feature of all the state constitutions drawn up during the American Revolution was
   a. a governor with strong powers.
   b. the conviction that government rests on the consent of the governed.
   c. a call for a strong centralized government.
   d. two houses, upper and lower.

7. In devising their new constitutions, most states
   a. abolished the lower house.
   b. gave veto power to the governor and kept an appointed upper house.
   c. reduced the powers of the executive branch of government.
   d. gave veto power to the governor, who had a four-year term.

8. Virginia's constitution was the first one to
   a. include longer terms for the governor.
   b. give more power to the governor.
   c. abolish the upper house altogether.
   d. include a bill of rights.

9. Most of the new states spelled out their citizens' rights and liberties in written contracts because
   a. Americans did not trust the federal government to uphold their freedoms.
   b. they wanted to be able to amend their bills of rights on a yearly basis.
   c. they hoped to become separate nations in the future and wanted to be able to attract new settlers.
   d. the unwritten nature of the British political traditions had led to Americans being denied liberties they had assumed they possessed.

10. Property qualifications for voters and candidates in the new states
    a. were replaced by a minimum-age requirement of twenty-two.
    b. disfranchised one-quarter to one-half of all adult white males.
    c. ensured that free blacks in the North would be able to vote.
    d. were so liberal that essentially all adult white males could vote.

11. Writers of the new state constitutions believed that voting requirements
    a. should reflect colonial property qualifications to keep women and very poor people from demanding the vote.
    b. should open up the political process to a wider group.
    c. should be tied to literacy.
    d. should be widely debated so that all citizens could have a voice.

12. The states were reluctant to include "equality language" in their bills of rights and constitutions because
    a. they were afraid that the words could be construed to apply to slaves.
    b. slaves might sue in court to gain their freedom.
    c. women might think they were equal to men and want the vote.
    d. children as young as twelve might think they could vote.

13. In the quarter century after 1775, legislatures provided for the immediate or gradual abolition of slavery
    a. in Maryland, Virginia, and most northern states.
    b. in Maryland and most northern states.
    c. in most northern states.
    d. in all of the original thirteen colonies.

14. In the deep South immediately after the Revolution,
    a. no slaves achieved their freedom.
    b. the largest emancipation of blacks in the country occurred because of their association with the British.
    c. some states legislated gradual emancipation.
    d. the idea that the ideals of the Revolution applied to slaves began to catch on among people of all classes.

15. Factors leading to the postwar depression that began in the mid-1780s included
    a. the lack of governmental power to print money.
    b. the fact that each state had its own currency.
    c. wage fixation that had occurred early in the war.
    d. huge state and federal war debts, private debt, and rapid expenditure.

16. Robert Morris proposed to increase the revenue of the confederation government by
    a. amending the Articles of Confederation to allow the government taxing powers without state approval.
    b. passing a 5 percent import tax.
    c. taxing all goods that flowed between states.
    d. expanding the economic base of the confederation.

17. While Robert Morris's tax proposal didn't take effect and the Bank of North America did not resuscitate the economy in the 1780s, the confederation still had the potential to obtain wealth through
    a. the sale of the huge territory ceded by Virginia, which became the national domain.
    b. the stabilization of the economy with gold and silver.
    c. borrowing from France and Germany.
    d. the retiring of the war debt.

18. In the land ordinances of 1784 and 1785, Congress
    a. set out a rectangular grid system for surveying land and established township perimeters.
    b. prohibited slavery and involuntary servitude in the Northwest Territory.
    c. specified that western lands would be sold first to people with no property.
    d. established the Southwest Territory in the lands south of the Ohio River.

19. The Ordinance of 1785 set guidelines for land sales in the Northwest Territory; land would be sold
    a. only to people who pledged to have no slaves or to free their current slaves.
    b. only to speculators by closed bidding on acreage.
    c. by public auction at a minimum purchase price of a dollar per acre and in minimum parcels of 640 acres each.
    d. only with bank loans, as confederation money was worth so little.

20. The most serious obstacle to settlement in the Northwest Territory was
    a. heavy tree growth that prevented easy farming.
    b. heavy taxation imposed by the government on industrial development.
    c. the lack of government policy on slavery in the area, which hindered farmers and caused the eruption of violent protests.
    d. clashes with the Indian tribes that occupied the land.

21. The Northwest Ordinance of 1787
    a. prohibited slavery in the Northwest Territory.
    b. funded an exploratory party to locate the Northwest Passage.
    c. provided for the eventual creation of eight to ten new states.
    d. required compulsory elementary education in each new township.

22. Shays's Rebellion of 1786 was the result of
    a. debt-strapped farmers in Pennsylvania.
    b. increased taxes and foreclosures on farms in Massachusetts.
    c. commercial and eastern creditors' harsh payment terms.
    d. Samuel Adams inciting farmers in Massachusetts.

23. Massachusetts responded to Shays's Rebellion with a
    a. dispatch of armed militiamen.
    b. moratorium on private debt.
    c. new issue of paper money.
    d. reduction of taxes.

24. The immediate outcome of Shays's Rebellion was
    a. jail for the dissidents after their leaders fled.
    b. tax relief for farmers in the state.
    c. the passage of a Riot Act outlawing illegal assemblies.
    d. the execution of ten dissidents and jail for the rest.

25. The major legacy of Shays's Rebellion was
    a. a series of similar revolts by farmers in other states.
    b. action by state legislatures to curb the powers of Congress.
    c. the realization that the Articles of Confederation were inadequate and thus a reworking of the national government was needed.
    d. the idea that civil disobedience was an American liberty.

26. The two men who were instrumental in calling for the Philadelphia meeting in May 1787 to discuss revising the Articles of Confederation were
    a. Jefferson and Madison.
    b. Madison and Hamilton.
    c. Washington and Franklin.
    d. Washington and Madison.

27. The delegates to the Constitutional Convention generally
    a. wanted a stronger federal government.
    b. defended the Articles of Confederation as they stood.
    c. thought the federal government's powers should be restricted.
    d. were disturbed that Massachusetts had quelled free speech in putting down Shays's Rebellion.

28. The constitutional convention's delegates
    a. were dominated by farmers from the mid-Atlantic and southern states.
    b. tended to be lawyers.
    c. included artisans and day laborers.
    d. were merchants, shippers, and businessmen.

29. The fundamental issue at the constitutional convention was
    a. whether the new national government should be more powerful or less powerful than the confederation government.
    b. whether or not slavery should be abolished.
    c. how to balance the conflicting interests of large and small states.
    d. whether the presidential powers should be increased.

30. At the constitutional convention, the proposal to create a bicameral national legislature, with representation in both houses based proportionally on each state's population, was known as the
    a. New Jersey Plan.
    b. Connecticut Plan.
    c. Three-Fifths Plan.
    d. Virginia Plan.

31. The major objection to the Virginia Plan by the smaller states at the Constitutional Convention was the proposal for
    a. proportional rather than equal representation of the states in Congress.
    b. direct election of the president.
    c. the creation of a national judiciary.
    d. a council of revision to review legislation.

32. The New Jersey Plan proposed at the constitutional convention
    a. called for severely limited powers for the Congress.
    b. reserved control over taxation, revenue, and commerce to the individual states.
    c. featured a bicameral legislature elected by voters.
    d. called for a unicameral legislature in which each state would have one vote.

33. The New Jersey Plan departed from the Articles of Confederation by
    a. changing the legislature to a two-house form.
    b. creating a plural presidency to be shared by three men elected by the congress from among its membership.
    c. giving the states total control over taxation and regulating trade.
    d. endowing the presidency with the power to declare war.

34. The constitutional convention deadlocked over the issue of
    a. representation.
    b. executive power.
    c. the electoral college.
    d. Congress's authority to levy taxes.

35. As a part of the Great Compromise, delegates at the Philadelphia Convention agreed
    a. that voters would elect the members of the upper house, the Senate, directly.
    b. upon the Supreme Court and a system of lower national courts.
    c. upon a lower house whose seats would be apportioned on the basis of population and an upper house, the Senate, that would have two senators per state.
    d. upon a procedure for direct election of a chief executive.

36. At the Philadelphia convention, the following was the compromise reached on the issue of who counted as population for the purpose of deciding representation:
    a. slaves were counted under the three-fifths clause.
    b. slaves were not to be counted as persons in a population count.
    c. Indians were to be counted only if they were assimilated.
    d. no state could reclaim a slave who had taken refuge in a free state.

37. When the Constitution was drafted, slavery
    a. was not named, but its existence was recognized and guaranteed.
    b. was the most hotly debated issue.
    c. was euphemistically outlawed.
    d. was explicitly named as being a landowner's liberty.

38. In a new distinction between democracy and republicanism, the delegates to the constitutional convention
    a. thought America should move closer to pure democracy.
    b. gave a direct voice to the people only in the House.
    c. gave a direct voice to the people in both the House and the Senate.
    d. believed that only the elite should govern.

39. To create a presidency out of the reach of direct democracy, the delegates to the constitutional convention
    a. devised the electoral college.
    b. said that the state legislatures would choose the president.
    c. provided for a popular vote to elect the president.
    d. said that the Senate and House would vote for a president.

40. Before the Constitution could go into effect it had to be ratified
    a. by the state legislatures of twelve states.
    b. by a simple majority of the states.
    c. by all thirteen states.
    d. in ratifying conventions in nine of the thirteen states.

41. The Constitution most clearly shifted the balance of power in favor of
    a. northern over southern states.
    b. large over small states.
    c. mercantile over agrarian interests.
    d. national over state governments.

42. Opposition to the Constitution came from substantial majorities in the three most populous states,
    a. North Carolina, Virginia, and Pennsylvania.
    b. Virginia, Massachusetts, and New York.
    c. Massachusetts, Pennsylvania, and Georgia.
    d. North Carolina, Virginia, and New York.

43. Pro-Constitution forces called themselves
    a. Antifederalists.
    b. Pro-Constitutionalists.
    c. Federalists.
    d. the Constitutional Party.

44. The first state to ratify the Constitution was
    a. Delaware.
    b. New York.
    c. Virginia.
    d. Massachusetts.

45. Antifederalists tended to be
    a. large landowners and slaveholders.
    b. merchants, lawyers, and urban artisans.
    c. rural, western, and noncommercial.
    d. those who favored a strong centralized government.

46. The core of Antifederalists' opposition to the Constitution centered on
    a. the power it gave to the common man.
    b. the creation of a stronger chief executive.
    c. the doctrine of separation of powers.
    d. their fear of a distant power that might infringe on people's liberties.

47. To persuade the powerful state of Virginia to ratify the Constitution, Federalists promised that
    a. George Washington would become the first president.
    b. a bill of rights would be added to the Constitution.
    c. the national capital would be in New York City.
    d. the national capital would be in Virginia.

48. Antifederalism in New York centered on
    a. a feud with Virginia over the new national capital.
    b. the proposed bicameral legislature.
    c. the state's size and power in relation to the new federal government.
    d. the fear that federalism would hurt commercial interests.

49. The authors of *The Federalist* essays originally wrote them
    a. as newspaper articles in favor of ratifying the Constitution.
    b. to provide an authoritative commentary on the Constitution.
    c. as a history of the constitutional convention.
    d. as a pamphlet promoting the Bill of Rights.

50. In essay number 10 of *The Federalist*, James Madison maintained that the constitutional government would
    a. eliminate the need for political parties.
    b. protect the rights of individual states against incursions by the central government.
    c. prevent any one faction from becoming dominant.
    d. bring focus and order to American foreign policy.

Terminology Matching   Select the word or phrase from the Terms section that best matches the definition or example provided in the Definitions section. Some terms may be used more than once; some may not be used at all.

TERMS

a. Antifederalists

b. Articles of Confederation

c. bill of rights

d. Congress

e. Constitution

f. electoral college

g. *Federalist, The*

h. Federalists

i. Great Compromise

j. Jefferson, Thomas

k. Land Ordinance of 1785

l. Madison, James

m. Mason, George

n. New Jersey Plan

o. Northwest Ordinance

p. Shays's Rebellion

q. three-fifths clause

r. Virginia Plan

s. Virginia Statute of Religious Freedom

DEFINITIONS

1. John Dickinson drafted this document during the American Revolution to specify the powers and structure of the national government. _____

2. A list of basic individual liberties that governments cannot abridge. _____

3. This plantation owner authored the Virginia bill of rights. _____

4. A land act dividing up the Northwest Territory into three to five states with boundaries conforming to geographic features. _____

5. This 1787 land act prohibited slavery in the entire region north of the Ohio River and east of the Mississippi. _____

6. A tax revolt by western Massachusetts farmers. _____

7. This Virginian is referred to as the Father of the Constitution. _____

8. This 1787 plan for restructuring the government called for representation in both houses of Congress to be dependent upon population, which would weaken the smaller states. _____

9. This 1787 plan for restructuring the government called for a plural presidency and a very powerful single-house congress in which each state would have one vote. _____

10. This 1787 agreement broke the logjam between two proposed plans to restructure the government and adopted a bicameral legislature. _____

11. A compromise that settled the question of whom to count among a state's population in determining the number of its representatives to Congress. _____

12. The only function of this group is to elect the president and vice president. _____

13. The end result of the Convention that met from May to September of 1787. _____

14. This political group advocated passage of the Constitution. _____

15. This political group opposed ratification of the Constitution. _____

16. The author of the Virginia Statute of Religious Freedom. _____

17. This bill to establish religious liberty was finally passed with the help of James Madison in 1786. _____

18. The most widespread objection to the Constitution was that this was lacking. _____

19. These essays were written by Alexander Hamilton, James Madison, and John Jay in an effort to promote ratification of the Constitution. _____

Chronology   Place the events in chronological order.

SET ONE

A. Constitution is ratified.

B. Northwest Ordinance allows self-government and prohibits slavery in the Northwest Territory.

C. State constitutions are completed.

D. Shays leads rebellion in Massachusetts.

E. Articles of Confederation are ratified.

First _____

Second _____

Third _____

Fourth _____

Fifth _____

SET TWO

A. Virginia adopts state bill of rights.

B. Second Continental Congress begins.

C. Arguments are made and compromises are reached in the constitutional convention.

First _____

Second _____

Third _____

Short Answer   Write a paragraph in response to each question.

1. What were the major components of the final version of the Articles of Confederation, and what were the Articles' shortcomings?

2. In the debate over the Articles of Confederation, how did five small states clash with the eight states with western land claims?

3. Discuss the provisions of the various state constitutions written after May 1776. Did they all retain a two-chamber assembly? If not, what did they choose?

4. Discuss various ways in which the institution of slavery began to be eroded in the North after 1776.

5. Discuss the country's financial predicament following the American Revolution.

6. How did the Northwest Ordinance of 1787 deal with the problem of slavery in the Northwest Territory?

7. Discuss the delegates to the constitutional convention and their commonalties, positions in society, wealth level, and background.

8. Describe the basic structural features of the U.S. Constitution as set forth in the Great Compromise.

9. Compare the Federalist and Antifederalist positions on the ratification of the Constitution.

10. New York's ratification of the Constitution assured the solidity and legitimacy of the new government, but the state was one of the last to approve the Constitution. What measures were taken in that state to promote ratification?

Essay   Respond to each of the following questions in an essay of three to four paragraphs. Your responses should include specific evidence and your interpretation of the significance of historical events and concepts.

1. The Continental Congress gave the job of organizing the Northwest Territory to Thomas Jefferson. Discuss the terms of the three bills that subsequently evolved and passed Congress.

2. Discuss the events that led to Shays's Rebellion, the revolt itself, and the outcome of the revolt.

3. Ratification of the Constitution was not an easy thing to accomplish. Discuss the various states and their reasons for or against ratification.

4. Why did Virginia and New York hold out in ratifying the Constitution? What compromise prompted these states to ratify it?

Map Questions   Answer the questions below using Map 7.3, Ratification of the Constitution, 1788–1790 (p. 244).

READING THE MAP

1. Several of the Atlantic coast states ratified the Constitution early on in the process. Which states were they?

2. Which state was last to ratify the Constitution?

3. Which states were most divided over the issue of ratification?

CONNECTIONS

1. Discuss the demographics of the first five states to ratify the Constitution.

2. Why would the two largest states, with much commerce and trade, be reluctant to ratify the Constitution?

THE NEW NATION TAKES FORM

8

1789–1800

Multiple Choice   Choose the letter of the best answer.

1. As president, George Washington
   a. was a brilliant thinker and strong political strategist.
   b. was congenial and outgoing.
   c. was virtuous, aloof, resolute, and dignified.
   d. did not like pomp and ceremony.

2. The authors of the Constitution did not include or allow for
   a. a voice for the smaller states.
   b. a way to amend the Constitution.
   c. a two-party system.
   d. divisiveness among the congressmen.

3. Among Washington's first duties as president was
   a. selecting cabinet members to serve him.
   b. asking Congress for a judiciary bill.
   c. deciding on the number and names of cabinet offices.
   d. choosing his vice president.

4. Washington chose this man to be his secretary of the treasury.
   a. Henry Knox
   b. Thomas Jefferson
   c. James Madison
   d. Alexander Hamilton

5. As vice president, John Adams was not invited to cabinet meetings; his only official duty was to
   a. sit in on Supreme Court hearings.
   b. preside over the Senate.
   c. tour the country on goodwill missions.
   d. help assemble items for the budget.

6. In response to Antifederalists' complaints and to promises that had been made in order to obtain ratification of the Constitution, James Madison drew up
   a. the first ten amendments to the Constitution, commonly called the Bill of Rights.
   b. the Judiciary Act of 1789.
   c. the Whiskey Bill.
   d. the Fugitive Slave Act.

7. A significant omission in the Bill of Rights was
   a. religious freedom.
   b. the right to vote.
   c. the right to bear arms.
   d. freedom of speech.

8. According to republican ideals of the late eighteenth century, women and mothers were most important in
   a. teaching virtuous sons.
   b. running an orderly household.
   c. volunteering for church activities.
   d. their duty to obey their husband.

9. In the new republic, traditional gender relations
   a. were briefly reversed due to the war sparing more women than men.
   b. remained largely unaltered from the norm.
   c. shifted as women abandoned domestic duties for a new role in the political sphere.
   d. were altered in light of republican ideals that pointed out the equality of men and women.

10. American cotton production underwent a real boom in the late 1790s because of
    a. market conditions and the invention of the horse-drawn plow.
    b. transportation innovations, especially the improved canal system.
    c. market conditions and the invention of the cotton gin.
    d. the increased need for cotton due to the burgeoning population.

11. In the 1790s, road building and commercial stagecoach travel failed to progress south of the Potomac River like it did in New England and the Middle Atlantic states, primarily because
    a. Southerners envisioned the coming of railroads.
    b. passenger demand was low.
    c. Southerners didn't have the money to build roads and to fund stagecoach companies.
    d. elite Southerners were opposed to improvements.

12. During the 1790s, the U.S. economy was stimulated by
    a. an increase in overseas grain and cotton trades and the development of commercial banking.
    b. Hamilton's manufacturing program, which began to create business opportunities.
    c. a decrease in the slave trade.
    d. a decrease in interstate business alliances and an increase in overseas trade.

13. Before the government settled upon Washington, D.C., as its permanent home, the capital had been moved from
    a. Philadelphia to Baltimore.
    b. New York City to Baltimore.
    c. Philadelphia to New York City.
    d. New York City to Philadelphia.

14. To restore faith in the credit of the federal government, Hamilton proposed
    a. the issuance of paper currency backed by gold and silver.
    b. measures to reduce or prevent private speculation in public securities.
    c. that the federal government redeem securities issued by the confederation government with new notes paying 12 percent interest.
    d. that the federal government assume the unpaid war debts of the states.

15. To meet the interest payments on the national debt under his assumption plan, Alexander Hamilton convinced Congress to pass
    a. an excise tax on whiskey of 25 percent.
    b. an increased import duty.
    c. an increased export duty.
    d. legislation making it illegal to smuggle.

16. Which of Hamilton's economic programs was attacked as unconstitutional by Thomas Jefferson?
    a. the creation of a national bank
    b. federal assumption of state debts
    c. the placement of an excise tax on whiskey
    d. the passage of protective tariffs

17. In response to Hamilton's bill to establish the Bank of the United States,
    a. Jefferson championed the bill and argued for its constitutionality.
    b. President Washington agreed with Hamilton's interpretation of the Constitution and signed the bill.
    c. the bill passed, but the sale of its stock went largely unnoticed by the public.
    d. President Washington questioned the morality of a public bank in which private citizens could invest.

18. The main purpose of the moderate tariff that Hamilton proposed in his *Report on Manufactures* was to
    a. raise all the money the federal government needed to operate.
    b. protect and foster domestic manufacturing.
    c. punish the British for their discriminatory tariffs.
    d. raise the price of domestic products so that merchants and manufacturers, Hamilton's main supporters, would prosper.

19. Of the economic programs presented by Hamilton, the only one not to be approved by Congress was the
    a. funding of bondholders.
    b. assumption of state debts.
    c. tariff recommended in the *Report on Manufactures.*
    d. national bank.

20. The Whiskey Rebellion
    a. was led by Federalist merchants who sold imported liquor.
    b. occurred among city workers angered by the high price of whiskey.
    c. was led by tavern keepers on the frontier.
    d. was a protest by grain farmers against the excise tax on whiskey.

21. In response to the Whiskey Rebellion of 1794, President Washington
    a. suggested that Congress repeal the tax.
    b. demanded that the governor of Pennsylvania take action to enforce the national law.
    c. nationalized the Pennsylvania militia and led the effort to put down the revolt.
    d. waited until the rebellion died down before acting.

22. Alexander Hamilton viewed the Whiskey Rebellion as
    a. an indication of an unjust policy needing change.
    b. a serious threat to the stability of the federal government.
    c. a minor protest unworthy of government action.
    d. a serious threat to the public safety.

23. Which of the following best describes the U.S. government's early policy toward Indians in the Northwest Territory?
    a. Displace the Indians and clear the way for permanent American settlement in Ohio.
    b. Obtain their lands with generous treaties providing money, supplies, and resettlement.
    c. Engage the Indians in brutal warfare followed by extermination.
    d. Leave them alone and hope American settlers could get along with them.

24. When the U.S. government's early policy toward the Indians in the Northwest Territory did not reap the anticipated results,
    a. the troops that had been stationed there were withdrawn.
    b. an expansion of military forces led to the total defeat of General St. Clair's army.
    c. expanded military efforts by General St. Clair's army pushed the Indians back and made way for new settlement.
    d. President Washington told all settlers to refrain from crossing the Ohio River to settle.

25. In 1794, General Anthony Wayne's defeat of the Indians at Fallen Timbers resulted in
    a. the Treaty of Fallen Timbers.
    b. escalated fighting in the Northwest Territory.
    c. the Treaty of Greenville.
    d. the Indians ceding all of their tribal lands in the Northwest Territory.

26. Of the treaty goods offered to the Indians in the Treaty of Greenville, the most detrimental to the tribes was
    a. knives and guns.
    b. farming equipment.
    c. liquor.
    d. contaminated food and blankets.

27. What was President Washington's first reaction to the war between England and France that began in 1793?
    a. He pledged American support for the French.
    b. He pledged American support for the English.
    c. He tried to negotiate peace between the two countries.
    d. He issued a Neutrality Proclamation.

28. Which of the following best describes American sentiment regarding the English-French struggle in 1793?
    a. The Federalists favored the English.
    b. The Republicans favored the English.
    c. The country was overwhelmingly in favor of remaining neutral.
    d. Many Americans were angered by an official declaration of neutrality.

29. John Jay's 1795 treaty with England
    a. failed to pass the Senate and House.
    b. was widely seen as benefiting only a small group of merchants in the overseas trade.
    c. was well received by Americans.
    d. ended our relationship with England.

30. How did the Haitian Revolution of 1791–1804 affect white Americans?
    a. They wanted to send American militia to help put down the rebellion.
    b. They paid no attention to the rebellion.
    c. They became fearful that the rebellion might spread to American shores.
    d. They felt sympathy for the slaves.

31. The first signs of rival U.S. political parties appeared
    a. during Washington's second term.
    b. during the election of 1796.
    c. at the constitutional convention in 1787.
    d. after John Adams took office.

32. In his farewell address, President Washington spoke against
    a. America forming alliances with foreign countries and forming political parties.
    b. Federalist policies.
    c. Republican policies.
    d. a president serving more than two terms in office.

33. In the 1796 presidential election, John Adams and Thomas Jefferson
    a. ran on the same ticket.
    b. had very similar political outlooks.
    c. pledged to disband the electoral college.
    d. ended up being president and vice president.

34. In the election of 1796, a procedural flaw resulted in the election of political rivals as president and vice president; this flaw was
    a. redressed by having each elector to the electoral college vote again.
    b. corrected by passage of the Twelfth Amendment in 1804.
    c. left uncorrected, as Congress believed the situation would not occur again.
    d. corrected by dismantling the electoral college.

35. During President Adams's one term in office, Vice President Jefferson
    a. had an amicable relationship with Alexander Hamilton.
    b. refused to cooperate with the president from the very beginning.
    c. was overshadowed by Alexander Hamilton.
    d. agreed with Adams on foreign policy.

36. In the fall of 1797, in order to avert a war with France, President Adams
    a. sent three men to negotiate peace with France.
    b. called for immediate full-scale military preparedness to scare the French.
    c. advised American privateers to cease shipping to England.
    d. called for a boycott of English goods.

37. X, Y, and Z were the code names for
    a. three American diplomats sent to France to avert war.
    b. three unnamed French agents sent by Tallyrand to meet with American representatives.
    c. secret agents sent to France to avert war.
    d. English spies located in France to gather intelligence.

38. Following the XYZ Affair,
    a. President Adams chose to submit to Tallyrand's demands.
    b. Americans seemed mildly disturbed, but they were more interesting in the workings of the new federal government.
    c. Congress repealed all prior treaties with France and launched into an undeclared war called the Quasi War.
    d. Congress called for a boycott on trade with France.

39. In an effort to muffle the heated opposition to President Adams's anti-French foreign policy,
    a. Adams stockpiled guns and ammunition at his house.
    b. Congress passed the Sedition Act of 1798.
    c. the Adams administration began arresting all suspected French sympathizers.
    d. all newly arrived French were deported.

40. The basic intent of the two Alien Acts passed by Congress was
    a. to jail newly arrived French residents and confiscate their property.
    b. deport any French person who had been in the U.S. for less than a year.
    c. to harass French immigrants to the United States and discourage others from coming.
    d. to discourage all immigration to the United States.

41. The Sedition Act mainly targeted
    a. Republican newspaper editors who freely published criticism of the Adams administration.
    b. any private citizen who spoke out in public against the Federalist Party.
    c. any gathering of people questioning Adams or his foreign policy.
    d. postal employees delivering Republican pamphlets.

42. The Virginia and Kentucky Resolutions
    a. called for the impeachment of President Adams.
    b. were a condemnation of the Alien and Sedition Acts.
    c. were written to protect those indicted of seditious acts.
    d. were an attempt to protect the institution of slavery in the South.

43. The Virginia and Kentucky Resolutions put forth the novel idea that
    a. states have the right to judge the constitutionality of federal laws and can nullify laws that infringe on liberties as defined in the Bill of Rights.
    b. the federal government had overstepped its powers.
    c. Adams and the Federalists were promoting an undeclared war with France.
    d. slavery should be a right protected by the federal constitution.

44. The Virginia and Kentucky Resolutions were authored by
    a. Alexander Hamilton.
    b. Thomas Jefferson and James Madison.
    c. proponents of the Alien and Sedition Acts.
    d. Matthew Lyon and James Bayard.

45. When President Adams arranged a negotiated end to the Quasi War in 1799,
    a. he ensured his bid for reelection.
    b. the French revolted.
    c. it was still years before the fighting actually ended.
    d. he lost his party's support.

46. In the election of 1800
    a. Adams's chief opponent was Alexander Hamilton.
    b. party lines were drawn between Republicans and Federalists.
    c. Adams gained momentum because of his work in resolving the crisis with France.
    d. Republicans began switching to the Federalist Party.

47. Jefferson's inaugural address suggested
    a. that government should be all powerful.
    b. that party politics had no influence in America.
    c. that political parties were instrumental to democracy.
    d. that the Republicans would begin undoing everything the Federalists had accomplished.

48. Which of the following statements characterized the Federalists in 1800?
    a. They were pro-French.
    b. They opposed commercial advancements.
    c. They were made up of farmers and artisans.
    d. They advocated a strong centralized government.

49. Issues that in the 1790s divided the country while under Federalist presidencies included
    a. Indian policy.
    b. the election of Adams in 1796.
    c. the Jay Treaty and the Quasi War.
    d. Adams's dismissal of Hamilton as secretary of the treasury.

50. In 1800, Republicans could be described as
    a. promoting a strong federal government.
    b. sympathetic to French republican ideals.
    c. pro-British.
    d. alarmed about the excesses of democracy.

Terminology Matching   Select the word or phrase from the Terms section that best matches the definition or example provided in the Definitions section. Some terms may be used more than once; some may not be used at all.

TERMS

a. Adams, John

b. Alien Acts

c. *Federalist, The*

d. Hamilton, Alexander

e. "His High Mightiness"

f. Jay, John

g. Jay Treaty

h. Jefferson, Thomas

i. Knox, Henry

j. L'Ouverture, Toussaint

k. Madison, James

l. Neutrality Proclamation

m. public debt

n. Quasi War

o. Randolph, Edmund

p. *Report on Public Credit*

q. Sedition Act

r. Twelfth Amendment

s. Virginia Resolution

t. Wayne, General Anthony

u. Whiskey Rebellion

v. X, Y, and Z

DEFINITIONS

1. This act was aimed at quieting Republican newspaper editors critical of the Adams administration. _____

2. America's first secretary of state. _____

3. He was the first chief justice of the Supreme Court, and he negotiated a controversial treaty with Britain. _____

4. Name given a series of protests and demonstrations by a group of western Pennsylvania farmers hostile to an excise tax proposed by Alexander Hamilton. _____

5. In 1794 his forces defeated the Indians at Fallen Timbers in Ohio. _____

6. He was a staunch Federalist in charge of the first administration's financial affairs. _____

7. He led slaves in a revolt in Haiti. _____

8. Amount of money owed by the federal government when it began in 1789. _____

9. Anonymous Frenchmen sent to solicit bribes from U.S. peace treaty negotiators. _____

10. This pronouncement said the United States would stay out of the conflict between England and France and remain friendly to both countries. _____

11. Washington chose this man to be the first U.S. attorney general. _____

12. The first U.S. war department secretary. _____

13. He drew up the Bill of Rights, the first ten amendments to the Constitution. _____

14. This agreement with England was not well received in the United States because of its concessions to the British. _____

15. This legislation was aimed at stopping French immigration to the United States. _____

16. This was added to the Constitution in 1804 to correct a procedural flaw that appeared in the election of 1796. _____

17. This argued that states should be able to nullify a federal law that infringes on the liberties of the people. _____

Chronology   Place the events in chronological order.

SET ONE

A. Whiskey Rebellion.

B. Treaty of Greenville.

C. Election of 1800.

D. XYZ Affair.

E. Hamilton's *Report on Manufactures.*

First _____

Second _____

Third _____

Fourth _____

Fifth _____

SET TWO

A. President Washington issues the Neutrality Proclamation.

B. XYZ affair.

C. Jay Treaty passes through Congress.

D. United States launches its Quasi War with France.

First _____

Second _____

Third _____

Fourth _____

Short Answer   Write a paragraph in response to each question.

1. How was the issue of a federal bill of rights resolved in 1789, and what was the resulting amendments' most salient omission?

2. Briefly describe the economic changes taking place in America in the 1790s due to developments in agriculture and transportation.

3. Why was Washington, D.C., an area not controlled by any state, chosen as the location of the permanent federal capital?

4. What problems confronted Alexander Hamilton when he first took the office of secretary of treasury?

5. In what way can the Whiskey Rebellion be seen as more than just a revolt by farmers unhappy with paying a tax?

6. What were the terms of the Treaty of Greenville, and what were its long-term effects on the Indians?

7. What was the Jay Treaty, and why were Americans generally opposed to it?

8. How was news of the Haitian Revolution received by most white Americans?

9. What problems plagued John Adams in his one term as president?

10. What were the differences between the Federalists and the Republicans in 1800?

Essay   Respond to each of the following questions in an essay of three to four paragraphs. Your responses should include specific evidence and your interpretation of the significance of historical events and concepts.

1. Discuss Hamilton's three-part economic program for the new federal government and the success of each of the three components.

2. Describe in detail the Indian policy of the Washington administration. Include conflicts and their outcomes and solutions for both the U.S. government and the Indians.

3. In the 1790s, America had conflicts with both England and France. Include specific examples to explain how both Washington and Adams handled these situations as they arose.

4. In your opinion, were the Alien and Sedition Acts constitutional? If you believe they were not, justify your answer using evidence from the Bill of Rights.

Map Questions   Answer the questions below using Map 8.2, Western Expansion and Indian Land Cessions to 1810 (p. 270).

READING THE MAP

1. Where were the battles of the 1790s concentrated? Was this area in the early or later land cessions?

2. When did the U.S. government acquire land west of the Mississippi River?

CONNECTIONS

1. What events led to the loss of Indian lands north of the Ohio River?

2. What country ceded land west of the Appalachian Mountains to the U.S. government, and why?

REPUBLICAN ASCENDANCY

1800–1824

Multiple Choice   Choose the letter of the best answer.

1. When Thomas Jefferson referred to his successful bid for the presidency in 1800 as the "revolution of 1800," he meant that
   a. the political strife and turmoil in the United States in 1800 might well have degenerated into bloody opposition to Jefferson's presidency rather than the peaceful transfer of power the nation witnessed.
   b. since he was the chief author of the Declaration of Independence, his rise to the presidency was reminiscent of the American Revolution.
   c. he thought it truly revolutionary that a man espousing the political views he held could actually be elected president.
   d. he was astonished that Aaron Burr did not win the contest.

2. As the presidential election of 1800 played out in the House of Representatives, Federalist Alexander Hamilton supported Thomas Jefferson over Aaron Burr because
   a. Hamilton had been pulling for Jefferson to win the election all along.
   b. Hamilton and Jefferson had made a deal which required Jefferson to support certain of Hamilton's programs in return for Hamilton's support of Jefferson in the presidential contest.
   c. while Hamilton was no fan of Jefferson, he believed that the corrupt Burr would prove much more dangerous to the Republic should he be elected president.
   d. Burr had angered Hamilton by challenging him to a duel, and Hamilton wanted to get even.

3. The slave insurrection planned in 1800 by the Virginia slave Gabriel is a powerful testament to the fact that
   a. slave revolts always failed because many of those involved simply could not keep the plans a secret.
   b. enslaved African Americans sometimes waited too long to consider their options before taking matters into their own hands.
   c. many slaves in the South were aware of successful slave uprisings elsewhere as well as the rhetoric of revolution, freedom, and equality sweeping the Atlantic world.
   d. the South's slaveholding ruling class always knew precisely what their servants were up to.

4. The slave Gabriel's aborted rebellion of 1800 unnerved Virginia's white leaders, who ultimately reacted by
   a. hanging every black Virginian thought to be part of the plot.
   b. manumitting a large portion of the state's slave population.
   c. deporting all of Virginia's troublesome blacks.
   d. proposing, and then abandoning, a scheme to deport rebellious slaves.

5. A guest visiting President Thomas Jefferson in 1804 found him attired in a red waistcoat, green velveteen breeches with pearl buttons, and "slippers down at the heels," all calculated, in Jefferson's mind, to
   a. make Americans believe he was an able and focused president because he paid no attention to his personal appearance.
   b. make an important point about republican simplicity and manners.
   c. hide his true identity in order to solicit visitors' candid views about his administration.
   d. enable him to play practical jokes on diplomatic visitors, a pastime Jefferson relished.

6. One of the major criticisms Thomas Jefferson leveled against Alexander Hamilton's vision of government was that
   a. it would lead to another major war with European powers.
   b. it was unconstitutional to promote financial schemes that would allow rich men to become richer without enhancing the natural productivity of America.
   c. it would undercut the appropriations necessary for a strong U.S. military.
   d. it had already rendered the United States a virtual monarchy.

7. According to Thomas Jefferson, the source of true freedom in America was
   a. the virtuous, independent farmer who owned and worked his land both for himself and for the market.
   b. the rising class of mechanics in American cities, single-minded men who allowed no one to push them around.
   c. the political party system that had come about in the late eighteenth century.
   d. the continuation of property qualifications for voting.

8. President Jefferson believed that a properly limited federal government
   a. raised money only through federal internal taxes, not customs duties.
   b. would maximize the number of government jobs so more citizens could have input.
   c. ran the postal system, collected customs duties, conducted a periodic census, and had no federal internal taxes.
   d. had a strong executive branch to balance the power of the legislature against.

9. In his last weeks as president in 1801, John Adams appointed his famous "midnight judges" as a way to
   a. help Thomas Jefferson assume the nation's highest office by making sure he did not have to spend his valuable time filling minor federal posts.
   b. leave as many Federalists as possible in government positions as political counterweights to the incoming Republican administration.
   c. make sure that experienced candidates were installed in these sensitive positions.
   d. make sure that Jefferson's inauguration ceremonies went smoothly by having on hand plenty of people who knew their way around Washington, D.C.

10. The most lasting effect of *Marbury v. Madison* (1803) was
    a. that the Supreme Court awarded William Marbury the largest monetary settlement in such cases until the Civil War.
    b. that the Supreme Court awarded William Marbury the government post he had been denied, at twice the original salary.
    c. that the Supreme Court ruled, for the first time, that a case should logically be heard in a federal district court.
    d. the Supreme Court's claim to the right of judicial review.

11. Events in the Louisiana Territory in 1802 alerted the United States to a potential national security problem, as
    a. England was negotiating to buy the territory from France.
    b. Spain had turned over the territory to France, which was then under the rule of powerful expansionist Napoleon Bonaparte.
    c. a large confederation of native Americans had hatched a plan to cross the Mississippi River and attack the United States.
    d. a large contingent of slaves from Saint Domingue had taken refuge there and were planning to capture New Orleans.

12. Representatives from New England voted almost unanimously against the Louisiana Purchase because
    a. they felt that allowing the Indians to settle in that area would be a good solution to land disputes in the West.
    b. the dominant Republicans there felt the government would not remain democratic if the country gained that much more land.
    c. they felt the purchase was unconstitutional.
    d. they were concerned about upsetting the geographic balance of power in the United States.

13. The exploration of the Spanish and Indian territory west of the Mississippi River by Meriwether Lewis and William Clark was successful in
    a. finding a waterway between the East and West Coasts of the United States.
    b. negotiating treaties to ensure peace with all of the Indian tribes from the Mississippi River to the Columbia River.
    c. establishing good relations with many Indian tribes and collecting scientific and anthropologic information.
    d. preparing later American explorers and settlers so their western journeys were completely free of hardship.

14. Aaron Burr challenged Alexander Hamilton to a duel in 1804 because
    a. Hamilton owed Burr money and refused to pay.
    b. Burr was still smarting from Hamilton's support of Thomas Jefferson in the presidential contest of 1800.
    c. disparaging remarks made by Hamilton about Burr had found their way into the press, remarks that Burr believed had cost him the governorship of New York.
    d. he sought to challenge the fact that dueling was illegal by staging a duel with his political nemesis.

15. Impressment, one of the key issues that led the United States into war with England in 1812, was
    a. the practice of American naval vessels stopping English ships to search for prohibited goods.
    b. the practice of the British navy removing American citizens from U.S. ships as supposed deserters and impressing them into royal naval service.
    c. the practice of the British navy confiscating U.S. ships on the high seas because His Majesty's navy was experiencing a shortage of vessels.
    d. the practice of the U.S. merchant fleet taking, or "impressing," goods from ports in the West Indies when American ship captains were short on funds.

16. The Embargo Act of 1807 was passed by Congress to
    a. forbid American ships from engaging in trade with England only, thus depriving the English of American goods while Americans were free to trade with any other country.
    b. forbid American ships from engaging in trade in any foreign port and thus make England suffer while preventing illegal trade through secondary ports.
    c. use economic coercion to force England into war.
    d. forbid the U.S. navy from using force against French ships but not against English vessels.

17. The Embargo Act of 1807 affected the U.S. by
    a. raising the nation's stature with European powers.
    b. causing the British to stop impressment when its agricultural supplies dwindled.
    c. idling New England ships, closing off foreign outlets for U.S. agricultural produce, and contributing to a marked rise in unemployment.
    d. causing most citizens to rally in support of President Jefferson.

18. The Non-Intercourse Act of 1809 directly helped
    a. English farmers.
    b. South American ports trading with England.
    c. French shippers.
    d. New England shippers and southern planters.

19. In 1810, while war with Europe was brewing, the northernmost Indian tribes in America
    a. had alliances with one another and with British Indian agents and Canadian fur traders as well.
    b. coalesced under Tecumseh to fight with the French against the Americans.
    c. were resisting attempts by Tecumseh and his brother Tenskwatawa (the Prophet) to unite them.
    d. united under Tecumseh in the belief that each tribe held its own land and could exchange it freely as long as no money was exchanged.

20. In negotiating the Treaty of Fort Wayne in 1809, William Henry Harrison angered the Shawnee chief Tecumseh by
    a. negotiating with several native American chiefs who had no legitimate claims to the land they ceded to the U.S. government.
    b. promising to exchange the Indiana land for land west of the Mississippi.
    c. offering him gold and silver in exchange for land, which Tecumseh claimed was "owned" only by the Great Spirit.
    d. all of the above

21. The battle at Tippecanoe Creek in 1811 pitted native Americans under Tenskwatawa against a force of a thousand men commanded by William Henry Harrison and was
    a. an unqualified disaster for the troops under Harrison.
    b. heralded as a glorious victory for the American forces and was the moment that turned Harrison into a military hero.
    c. fought to a standstill.
    d. the confrontation that completely broke the Shawnee nation in the old Northwest Territory.

22. War Hawks were young congressmen who
    a. were enthusiastic for western expansion, ready to subdue native Americans standing in the way of white settlement, and eager to declare war on England for the humiliation it had heaped on the United States.
    b. believed the United States should declare war on France for the abuse to which it had subjected the nation on the high seas.
    c. as New Englanders went against the political tide in their home states by advocating that America declare war on England.
    d. believed that Spain was responsible for America's international woes and supported plans to take significant portions of Spain's crumbling New World empire.

23. The war with Great Britain declared by Congress in 1812
    a. was certain to end with an American victory from the beginning, due to the country's military preparedness.
    b. was as much about insult and honor as about the search and seizure of American ships.
    c. was averted when the British agreed to end impressment.
    d. was predicted to end in an easy victory and, indeed, was much shorter than expected.

24. When British soldiers entered Washington, D.C., in 1814 they
    a. met with President Madison and attempted to negotiate a preliminary peace settlement.
    b. paraded up and down the city's major thoroughfares in an effort to persuade those in the capital to surrender.
    c. set fire to much of the city.
    d. stole all the government's vital documents and then left the city.

25. "The Star-Spangled Banner" was originally a
    a. song composed about the 1814 British attack on Washington, D.C.
    b. poem composed about the 1814 British attack on Baltimore.
    c. short story about the 1814 British attack on Baltimore.
    d. political essay about the need for the United States to defend its honor against British impressment.

26. While Andrew Jackson's defeat of the British at New Orleans cemented his status as a military hero, what he did not know at the time was that
    a. a huge contingent of British reinforcements was right behind those he had just defeated, but these troops had orders not to attack.
    b. the War of 1812 had been over for two weeks.
    c. he was extremely lucky, as his men had just run out of ammunition.
    d. win or lose, his men had decided to return home after this battle.

27. The Treaty of Ghent ending the War of 1812
    a. paved the way for an important exchange of territory between the United States and England.
    b. settled the ongoing dispute over shipping rights.
    c. set up a commission to determine the exact boundary between the United States and Florida.
    d. actually settled few of the issues that had led to war.

28. As a result of the War of 1812, the Federalist Party
    a. gained new strength because of New Englanders' support for the conflict.
    b. basically died as a political force, having opposed a war that most Americans chose to view as a nationalistic and patriotic victory over England.
    c. put forth a constitutional amendment that the nation's capital be moved farther west to accommodate the country's shifting population.
    d. proposed that the Constitution be amended to allow for concurrent presidents, one representing the North and one representing the South.

29. The group that suffered the greatest losses in the War of 1812 was
    a. the Indians.
    b. the British.
    c. the United States.
    d. the War Hawks in Congress.

30. In the early nineteenth century, the Anglo-American view of women was embodied in the legal concept of *feme covert,* which held that
    a. single women were the legal responsibility of all adult males over twenty-one years of age in a household.
    b. legally, the need for men to control their wives was an antiquated notion.
    c. a wife's civic or legal existence was completely subsumed by that of her husband.
    d. single women were not legally responsible for their own actions until the age of twenty-five.

31. *The Law of Baron and Feme,* a standard treatise on family law published in 1816 in Connecticut, made it clear that
    a. lawyers believed it was high time that women be accorded more rights within the confines of marriage.
    b. lawyers believed the unequal power relations between men and women in marriage were the heart of the institution and never considered challenging that inequality.
    c. lawyers were on the cutting edge of arguing for a more liberal education for all married women.
    d. many lawyers had begun to doubt the validity of marriage as constituted in America at the time.

32. By 1820, divorce in the United States
    a. remained illegal in all states.
    b. was possible only in southern states.
    c. was the one aspect of family law that had changed since the eighteenth century, and, while difficult, was possible in most states.
    d. was possible in every state, but only by petition to the state's legislature.

33. A woman in the early Republic who owned and conveyed property, made contracts, and initiated lawsuits was probably
    a. friends with influential men in her neighborhood.
    b. single.
    c. married.
    d. a lawyer.

34. Slave marriages were not governed by the unequal power relations characteristic of white marriages because
    a. as property themselves, slaves could not enter into contractual obligations, including marriage.
    b. slave owners ultimately controlled slaves and enforced equality in slave unions.
    c. African custom ensured equality between husbands and wives.
    d. married slaves wanted to make sure they did not follow any customs of white society.

35. Jemima Wilkinson was an exhorting woman; specifically, she
    a. was a Quaker who took her message to the deep South.
    b. dressed in men's clothes and preached openly in Rhode Island and Philadelphia.
    c. was the first woman to be ordained as an Anglican minister, a practice sanctioned in New York between 1790 and 1820.
    d. was the most successful female clothier in Philadelphia between 1815 and 1825.

36. The biblical injunction "Let your women learn to keep silence in the churches" appeared from time to time in a Baptist periodical published in Massachusetts in the early 1800s and indicated that
    a. women had taken over the leadership of numerous Baptist churches in New England.
    b. men believed it was the duty of church women to ensure that children were quiet during worship services.
    c. more than a few religious men were frustrated about what they considered the unseemly practice of women preaching.
    d. men were frustrated with the large number of women who insisted on singing in church choirs.

37. A contemporary newspaper dubbed the two terms of President James Monroe the "Era of Good Feelings," a designation indicating that
    a. Americans enjoyed amazingly good health on a personal level during these years.
    b. Americans were feeling an intense nationalistic pride in the aftermath of the U.S. "victory" over Great Britain in the War of 1812.
    c. party politics and wrangling completely disappeared from the American scene.
    d. Republicans of the Jeffersonian stripe had no serious political challengers able to win national elections.

38. James Tallmadge Jr.'s amendments to the Missouri statehood bill of 1819 were controversial because their ultimate effect would have been to
    a. reduce Missouri's representation in the House of Representatives.
    b. make Missouri a free state.
    c. make Missouri a slave state.
    d. make Missouri a separate republic.

39. The Missouri Compromise of 1820 was successful in Congress chiefly because
    a. Henry Clay cast the deciding vote that pushed it through.
    b. twenty southern congressmen tipped the balance in favor of the bill.
    c. seventeen northern congressmen voted with their southern colleagues in the interest of sectional political harmony.
    d. John C. Calhoun had secured enough votes in the state legislature of South Carolina to support secession should Missouri not be allowed to enter the Union as an unrestricted slave state.

40. In 1823, President James Monroe issued what became known as the Monroe Doctrine, a statement that the Americas
    a. "will ultimately come under the rule of one republic, the United States."
    b. "are henceforth not to be considered as subjects for future colonization by any European power."
    c. "have no interests in Europe that supercede the Western Hemisphere's domestic tranquility."
    d. "are destined to become one economic unit with laws and procedures by which Europe must abide."

41. Henry Clay's American System was
    a. a national economic program that included protective tariffs and federally funded internal improvements.
    b. a program that revised the steps by which aliens might become naturalized U.S. citizens.
    c. a system of trade agreements with European nations stipulating that imports and exports must be made available in equal amounts.
    d. a bill in Congress stipulating that only native-born Americans could occupy important government and military posts.

42. The presidential election of 1824 was notable because it was the last
    a. that was contested.
    b. in which a candidate with fewer popular votes than his nearest challenger became president.
    c. to be decided in the House of Representatives.
    d. in which a candidate from Massachusetts was elected president.

43. If Andrew Jackson had any doubts that John Quincy Adams became president in 1824 as a result of a "corrupt bargain" with Henry Clay, he became confident that he was right when
    a. Clay's letters to Adams were leaked to the press.
    b. it was discovered that money had been exchanged between the two men.
    c. Adams made Clay his secretary of war.
    d. Adams made Clay his secretary of state.

44. John Quincy Adams was a one-term president primarily because
    a. he proved to lack a sense of diplomacy.
    b. he had not developed the political savvy necessary to survive in America's rough and tumble world of electoral politics.
    c. of repeated scandals in his administration.
    d. so many congressmen opposed his programs that he wisely chose not to run again.

45. By proposing federally funded internal improvements, scientific research, and a national university located in Washington, D.C., President John Quincy Adams believed
    a. he was picking up where Jefferson and Madison had left off, using the power of the government to advance knowledge.
    b. he was actually forwarding a program that would save Americans millions of dollars in other areas of government.
    c. he was picking up where his own father had left off as president in his efforts to employ the government as an engine of reform.
    d. he was forging the basis of a new political party able to counter the upsurge of popular voting.

46. In 1807, Connecticut clockmaker Eli Terry contracted to produce four thousand clocks in three years, a goal he was able to reach because of his successful utilization of
    a. complete pre-pressed brass clock movements.
    b. a warehouse full of experienced clockmakers who worked very quickly.
    c. a system of interchangeable parts.
    d. steam-powered machinery.

47. Eli Terry's shelf clock revolutionized timekeeping by
    a. being so accurate that numerous localities ordered them to keep official municipal time.
    b. producing a fairly accurate clock cheap enough to be affordable to practically anyone desiring a clock in his or her home.
    c. being so small that one could carry it instead of a pocket watch.
    d. making it unnecessary ever to rely on the sun to set time pieces.

48. Eli Terry's pillar and scroll clocks of the 1820s were decorated with pictures of farmyards and country landscapes, rather curious when we consider that
    a. scenes such as these were not very popular in other areas of American decorative arts.
    b. there are few documented cases of farmers owning any of Terry's clocks.
    c. although Terry was not known as an artist, he decorated many of his clocks himself.
    d. his clocks paved the way for America's future of rapid transit, factory discipline, and industrial capitalism.

49. The nineteenth century opened with President Thomas Jefferson attempting to create a more limited government than that erected by his Federalist predecessors, an effort that
    a. was remarkably successful, considering the political complexities of the era.
    b. proved impossible because of continued westward expansion and the nation's continuing interaction with foreign powers.
    c. splintered old political alliances and made Jefferson's first administration basically unsuccessful.
    d. many Federalists, seeing the error of their ways, enthusiastically supported.

50. U.S. involvement in the War of 1812 encouraged economic growth
    a. in the Western Hemisphere, as Americans opened up new markets in Latin America.
    b. in the South, as farmers there sold more agricultural produce to other sections of the nation.
    c. in the manufacturing sector, as the embargo and trade stoppages meant that American factories received a temporary respite from competition with the English.
    d. in the North, as shippers there were forced to switch over to other industries due to the embargo and trade stoppages.

Terminology Matching   Select the word or phrase from the Terms section that best matches the definition or example provided in the Definitions section. Some terms may be used more than once; some may not be used at all.

TERMS

a. Adams-Onis Treaty

b. Big Knives

c. Crawford, William

d. election of 1820

e. election of 1824

f. Gabriel

g. Great Pacifier, the

h. Jackson, Andrew

i. Key, Francis Scott

j. Livingston, Robert R.

k. Louisiana Territory

l. *Marbury v. Madison*

m. Monroe, James

n. Northwest Territory

o. Pierce, Deborah

p. Prophet, the

q. Tecumseh

r. Tippecanoe

DEFINITIONS

1. Authored the "Star-Spangled Banner" after the British attack on Baltimore in 1814. _____

2. America's minister in France who negotiated the Louisiana Purchase. _____

3. Authored *A Scriptural Vindication of Female Preaching, Prophesying, and Exhortation* to support the practice of women exhorters. _____

4. Shawnee Indian who created a pan-Indian confederacy in the Great Lakes area. _____

5. His two presidential administrations spanned the period known as the "Era of Good Feelings." _____

6. This was used by Supreme Court Chief Justice John Marshall to implement the principle of judicial review. _____

7. Henry Clay's skill at congressional compromise earned him this sobriquet. _____

8. Shawnee name for whites in the Ohio country. _____

9. The first presidential election in which the popular vote could be fairly accurately measured. _____

10. Nickname for the Shawnee who urged other Indians to give up their borrowings from white society. _____

11. This American general commanded troops in impressive victories at Horseshoe Bend and New Orleans. _____

12. Presidential candidate of choice in 1824 among powerful Republicans in New York and Virginia. _____

13. The creek where William Henry Harrison had an important victory, and Harrison's nickname in 1840. _____

14. The geographical name for the region made up of Illinois, Ohio, Indiana, Wisconsin, and Michigan. _____

15. This agreement secured Florida from Spain. _____

Chronology   Place the events in chronological order.

SET ONE

A. Thomas Jefferson and Aaron Burr tie in electoral college.

B. *Marbury v. Madison* declares part of Judiciary Act of 1789 unconstitutional.

C. Missouri Compromise admits Missouri as a slave state and Maine as a free state.

D. Burr-Hamilton duel ends in Alexander Hamilton's death.

E. U.S. declares war on Great Britain.

First _____

Second _____

Third _____

Fourth _____

Fifth _____

SET TWO

A. Monroe Doctrine asserts independence of Western Hemisphere from European intervention.

B. Battle of New Orleans won by forces under Andrew Jackson.

C. "Corrupt bargain" election of John Quincy Adams.

D. Non-Intercourse Act forbids trade with England, France, and their colonies.

E. Death of Tecumseh at the Battle of the Thames.

F. Battle of Tippecanoe won by troops under William Henry Harrison.

First _____

Second _____

Third _____

Fourth _____

Fifth _____

Sixth _____

Short Answer   Write a paragraph in response to each question.

1. Describe how Tecumseh's formative years influenced his later attitude toward white settlers in the Ohio country.

2. Explain how President Thomas Jefferson sought to apply the principle of republican simplicity in his first administration.

3. Explain the importance of the Mississippi River to Americans around 1800.

4. What specific effects did the Embargo Act of 1807 have on the U.S. economy?

5. Explain how battles such as the one at Tippecanoe Creek in the Indiana Territory in 1811 were viewed and manipulated by victorious whites.

6. Who were the War Hawks, and why were they so interested in taking on England in another war?

7. How did the legal doctrine of *feme covert* apply to enslaved African American women?

8. What circumstances and events led to the issuance of the Monroe Doctrine?

9. How did Henry Clay come to find himself in such an influential position regarding the outcome of the presidential election of 1824, and why did he support John Quincy Adams?

10. Why was John Quincy Adams a one-term president?

Essay   Respond to each of the following questions in an essay of three to four paragraphs. Your responses should include specific evidence and your interpretation of the significance of historical events and concepts.

1. Although Gabriel's planned slave insurrection in Virginia in 1800 failed to materialize, knowledge of it caused white leaders to sit up and take notice. Compose an essay in which you identify the main ideas that inspired Gabriel and his followers and the sources of those ideas. Also discuss how the actions of men such as Thomas Jefferson and James Monroe made it clear that they understood how these ideas were problematic in a slave society.

2. How did the reaction of New England Federalists to the War of 1812 demonstrate the volatility of American politics, the divergence of sectional interests, and the fragile nature of the Union?

3. In a sense, the outcome of the War of 1812 can be interpreted as a feeble "nationalistic awakening" for the United States. Examine the validity of this interpretation by considering the foreign and domestic concerns that contributed to the war, the military situation during the war, the actual settlement of the war, and America's place in the international world in 1815.

4. Compose an essay in which you analyze the national political implications of the Missouri Compromise of 1820. Why did American leaders place so much importance on keeping the issue of slavery out of national politics? Why had maintaining a sectional political balance become so important? What does this settlement suggest to you about the way American leaders were able to divorce the institution of slavery from the people it enslaved?

Map Questions   Answer the questions below using Map 9.2, The Louisiana Purchase and the Lewis and Clark Expedition (p. 295).

READING THE MAP

1. Which countries laid claim to the areas explored by Lewis and Clark?

2. Did Lewis and Clark remain together throughout the expedition? If not, how did their routes differ?

CONNECTIONS

1. What was the logic behind beginning the Lewis and Clark expedition at St. Louis?

2. What were the most obvious political hazards faced by Lewis and Clark as they traversed the Oregon Country?

THE EXPANDING REPUBLIC 10

1815–1840

Multiple Choice   Choose the letter of the best answer.

1. A hallmark of the Jacksonian era was
   a. a country finally united under a single political party.
   b. a faith that people and societies can shape their own destinies.
   c. the belief that equality for all, as set forth in the Declaration of Independence, would finally be realized.
   d. the desire for the federal government to solve all of the nation's problems.

2. The market revolution experienced by Americans after the War of 1812
   a. brought increasing numbers of people out of old patterns of rural self-sufficiency into the wider realm of national market relations.
   b. gave rise to a huge factory system that pulled millions from the cities to labor in the country-side.
   c. was seen to have limited impact on most Americans, who were relatively poor and not much affected by the economic growth.
   d. was hardly revolutionary, as many Northerners refused to do business with southern slave masters, whom they regarded as immoral.

3. Funding for transportation improvements in America between 1815 and 1840 came mostly from
   a. the federal government.
   b. private investment.
   c. state governments.
   d. private and state funding.

4. The transportation innovation that most dramatically reduced travel time in the early nineteenth century was the
   a. growth of the stagecoach system.
   b. development of the canal system.
   c. development of steamboat travel.
   d. invention of the diesel engine.

5. The most horrifying hazard faced by people traveling on steamboats in the early nineteenth century was
   a. running aground in shallow, poorly charted rivers.
   b. long delays because of inefficient routing and scheduling.
   c. being injured or killed by the frequent boiler explosions.
   d. the constant threat of Indian attacks from the shore.

6. The 1824 Supreme Court decision in *Gibbon v. Ogden*
   a. upheld the practice of states granting monopolies to steam transportation companies.
   b. opened the avenues of economic expansion by declaring that navigation on rivers traversing more than one state came under the jurisdiction of the federal government and that state-granted transportation monopolies on such rivers were invalid.
   c. set a limit on the number of steamboat companies that could operate on U.S. rivers.
   d. instituted strict licensing requirements for all steamboat companies operating on U.S. waterways and thus improved the safety of steamboat travel.

7. Canals were an important innovation in the early nineteenth century because
   a. they provided speedier transport of merchandise than had been previously possible.
   b. they allowed cheaper transport by virtue of greatly increased loads.
   c. they were primarily privately funded and thus were not dependent on government support.
   d. by using animal power, they reduced the pollution that was generated by steamboats and railroads.

8. The first railroad lines in the United States
   a. were the death knoll for canal transport of freight.
   b. were a nationwide system that provided an efficient distribution system for goods.
   c. were funded completely by the government.
   d. were generally short and inefficient for the transport of goods.

9. The Waltham system that developed in New England after 1814
   a. was designed to employ a permanent class of wage laborers.
   b. was designed to provide cheap, transitional labor for early textile factories, unlike the permanent class of poor industrial workers found in Western Europe.
   c. failed to fill the labor requirements of early New England factories.
   d. was linked initially to producing shoes.

10. Employees of early textile mills in New England were
    a. mainly young women seeking long careers in America's expanding economy.
    b. mainly young men seeking careers in America's expanding economy.
    c. mainly young women seeking a new degree of autonomy in their lives that was difficult to achieve by remaining on the family farm.
    d. mostly immigrant families trying to escape the factory system in Europe.

11. In the 1820s and 1830s, shoebinding, an important component of shoe manufacturing,
    a. was highly skilled work performed by men.
    b. was comparatively low-paying women's work that was performed at home.
    c. was usually undertaken by boys who lived and worked on the site of the shoe factory.
    d. was the most highly unionized segment of the early-nineteenth-century factory system.

12. State-chartered banks served ordinary consumers in Jacksonian America by
    a. issuing a uniform U.S. currency.
    b. issuing a uniform state-level currency.
    c. issuing banknotes that were used just like money.
    d. making sure that the circulating media passing as money were evenly distributed throughout the economy.

13. In the economy of Jacksonian America, bankers
    a. stimulated the economy by making loans to entrepreneurs.
    b. had great power in deciding who would get loans and what the discount rates would be.
    c. issued banknotes, which effectively became the currency of the country.
    d. all of the above

14. Shifts in legal attitudes and the law aided the market revolution that began in 1815 were refleccted by
    a. courts increasingly supporting contracts based on their fairness to all parties, especially by ensuring that contracting parties were not cheated.
    b. courts increasingly supporting legally binding contractual agreements regardless of the fairness of the outcome.
    c. Congress staunchly defending the rights of workers.
    d. the diminishing importance of lawyers in many economic transactions.

15. In the evolving legal environment of Jacksonian America, lawyers worked through legislatures and courts to
    a. help workers gain unprecedented workplace protection.
    b. ensure that the practice of granting government privileges did not continue.
    c. create the legal foundation for an economy that favored the maximization of wealth by ambitious individuals.
    d. give aggrieved workers the right to strike in protest of unfair treatment or dangerous conditions.

16. In large measure, the panic of 1819 occurred as a result of
    a. exceedingly inept management of all facets of the U.S. economy.
    b. the optimism and exuberance on the part of U.S. banks in circulating ever larger issues of banknotes, a pattern that fueled the more speculative aspects of the economy.
    c. basic pessimism concerning U.S. economic prospects.
    d. the slackening of consumer demand for numerous goods.

17. Between 1828 and 1836, the second American party system took shape; it
    a. featured a revival of the Federalists to challenge Jeffersonian Republicans.
    b. offered little more than new political labels pasted over old political organizations with the same philosophies and beliefs.
    c. was chiefly sectional in nature: Whigs tended to be Northerners, and Democrats tended to be Southerners.
    d. was, by 1836, a fully functioning, national, two-party political system with the appearance of the Whig and Democratic parties.

18. One of the key elements in the political landscape of Jacksonian America was the upsurge of universal white male suffrage,
    a. in spite of increased property qualifications for voters in most states.
    b. as most states abolished property qualifications for voting.
    c. though voting became more difficult because many states levied poll taxes.
    d. as poll taxes were often paid by members of political parties in return for votes.

19. Newspapers became crucial to party politics in Jacksonian America because
    a. they remained the only source of information about matters of political concern.
    b. the press during this period was known for its unbiased coverage of political issues.
    c. they published numerous political cartoons that helped illiterate Americans decide on which candidate they wanted to vote for.
    d. many newspapers were under the control of a particular political party and actively pushed that party's agenda.

20. The presidential election of 1828 seems quite modern in that
    a. it was the first national election in which scandal and character questions were as important as, or more important than, policy issues.
    b. analysts offered early state-level projections regarding which candidate had won the election.
    c. several states contested the electoral vote tally.
    d. voters tended to vote against a particular candidate rather than for one.

21. The "personality contest" in the presidential election of 1828 taught American leaders that
    a. they had been right all along: political parties were extremely subversive.
    b. political parties were necessary to mobilize and deliver voters in order to win elections.
    c. political parties were of marginal utility and that what was really required to win elections was a sober, dispassionate discussion of substantive issues.
    d. voters were incredibly gullible.

22. As president, Andrew Jackson favored
    a. an unprecedented reach of the government into the lives of ordinary citizens and the economic development of America.
    b. a bipartisan cabinet that could advise him without regard to political interests.
    c. a limited federal government and the establishment of a federal Indian policy.
    d. big government and expanded opportunities for Americans regardless of race, creed, or sex.

23. In *Advice to American Women*, Mrs. A. J. Graves represented the new ideas about gender relations in Jacksonian America in her support for the concept of
    a. limiting the size of American families.
    b. separate spheres for men and women, based on the middle-class notion that women have a unique contribution to make in the home as more men venture into the competitive world of market relations.
    c. women courting men in a more aggressive fashion so as to secure the most desirable husbands.
    d. raising the legal age of marriage for men and women.

24. After 1815, the idea of separate spheres and separate duties for men and women was strengthened by the fact that
    a. most women went to work in the newly established mills and factories.
    b. an experiment in which males and females had attended the same colleges and gone on to similar jobs proved unsuccessful.
    c. most men worked at home, either in farming and cottage industries, and separation of men from women was necessary to avoid discord and distraction.
    d. men's work was newly disconnected from the home and increasingly brought cash to the household.

25. The advent of "common schools" in the 1820s and 1830s made education more accessible to students and affected teaching by
    a. initiating a shift toward hiring women as cheap, temporary instructors.
    b. elevating the status of teachers as professionals.
    c. raising the pay of most teachers.
    d. requiring that all teachers have college degrees.

26. The Troy Seminary in New York and the Hartford Seminary in Connecticut were schools for women founded in the 1820s on the belief that
    a. men and women should never attend school together.
    b. all-female schools with male teachers offered the best opportunity for young women to get an education.
    c. women made better teachers than men.
    d. women educating women would weaken the middle-class idea of separate spheres for men and women in society.

27. A typical pattern for boys not remaining on the farm in the 1820s and 1830s was to
    a. leave school at the age of fourteen and become either an apprentice in a trade or an entry-level clerk.
    b. attend college in preparation for a career in a profession.
    c. enter the military.
    d. enter the ministry.

28. Penny press newspapers became popular with American readers in the 1830s by featuring
    a. sophisticated analysis of political issues.
    b. highbrow literature in serialized form.
    c. sensationalized crime reporting and irreverent editorials on current events.
    d. all of the above

29. The most common form of shared entertainment for Americans in the 1830s was
    a. attending political rallies.
    b. going to the theater.
    c. participating in outdoor religious rallies.
    d. going to the circus.

30. To become a successful lawyer, politician, or minister in the 1830s, one had to master the art of
    a. sprinkling one's public utterances with catchy slogans and phrases.
    b. speed-reading.
    c. exaggerating the truth just enough to hold an audience's attention.
    d. formal elocution.

31. The Second Great Awakening
    a. was a philosophical offshoot of the market revolution emphasizing the pitfalls of a society run by bankers and lawyers.
    b. brought forth an outpouring of evangelical religious fervor that offered salvation to anyone willing to eradicate individual sin and accept faith in God's grace.
    c. constituted a second wave in a temperance movement that had failed in its first attempt.
    d. was the spiritual component accompanying the second party system.

32. The leading exemplar of the Second Great Awakening, Charles Grandison Finney, insisted that
    a. "The world is divided into two great political parties" — the party of Satan and the party of Jehovah.
    b. women had too much influence in the church already, and any more would rock its very foundations.
    c. "Alcohol is the devil's work."
    d. the legal system taking hold in the United States was the work of Satan and that only the business class was benefiting from societal changes.

33. Alcohol consumption in America in the decades up to 1830 was
    a. characterized by moderate drinking.
    b. widespread, rising, and often tended toward abusive amounts.
    c. very low due to the increased safety of urban drinking water sources.
    d. confined to persons over eighteen years of age.

34. By 1845, the American Temperance Union and other temperance advocates
    a. had convinced twelve states to ban entirely the sale or manufacture of alcoholic beverages.
    b. were demanding that their adherents consume only sacrificial wine.
    c. had backed down and were demanding that their adherents abstain from alcohol only on Sunday.
    d. had succeeded in decreasing alcohol consumption in the United States.

35. The nationally circulated *Advocate of Moral Reform* was
    a. a newsletter published by a consortium of powerful evangelical ministers.
    b. a magazine published by women that condemned prostitutes for possessing low moral character.
    c. a newspaper published by women that took men to task for the sexual sin of frequenting prostitutes and perpetuating prostitution.
    d. a best-selling novel satirizing Americans' preoccupation with fixing their broken society.

36. The most radical reform movement of the 1830s proved to be
    a. the temperance movement.
    b. the effort to abolish slavery.
    c. the effort to reform prisons and insane asylums.
    d. the southern version of the Second Great Awakening.

37. In 1831, William Lloyd Garrison launched
    a. *An Appeal to the Colored Citizens of the World*, a periodical advocating that the U.S. government pay each black American $100,000 and arrange for passage to Liberia.
    b. the *Liberator*, an abolitionist newspaper advocating an immediate end to slavery.
    c. the *Boston Emancipator*, an abolitionist newspaper that advocated negotiating with slaveholders to arrange a gradual, compensated end to slavery.
    d. the *Atlantic Monthly*, a magazine dedicated to freeing slaves and relocating them in the North.

38. Relatively few white Northerners got involved in the campaign to eradicate slavery because
    a. they simply could not spare the time.
    b. they had no idea how bad the institution of slavery really was.
    c. abolition societies charged exorbitant membership fees.
    d. even though they may have viewed slavery as counterproductive or immoral, they tended to be racists.

39. Angelina Grimké, Sarah Grimké, and Maria Stewart, women lecturers who conveyed a powerful antislavery message, encountered hostility in the North because
    a. few were receptive to the substance of their antislavery orations.
    b. while enthusiastic, they were poor speakers.
    c. they affronted a rigid cultural norm by speaking in public and presuming to instruct men.
    d. they insisted on being paid the same as men speaking on the same circuit.

40. The following could be said about the U.S. government's policy of encouraging assimilation of the Indians:
    a. The general failure of assimilation as promoted by previous administrations was a factor in President Jackson's relocation policy in regard to the Indians.
    b. The Removal Act of 1830 was a continuation of the assimilation policy begun by President Jefferson.
    c. The Cherokees were the least assimilated Indian tribe, a factor that led to the Trail of Tears in 1838.
    d. Assimilation as practiced by the Jackson administration grew out of the president's belief that the Indians should be considered foreigners who deserved large hunting grounds.

41. In Jacksonian America, the federal government viewed Native Americans as
    a. potential U.S. citizens.
    b. people who should move out of the path of white settlement whenever and wherever whites desired the land they occupied.
    c. people who should assimilate into white society.
    d. too expensive to relocate and thus better exterminated.

42. In *Worcester v. Georgia* (1832), the Supreme Court ruled that
    a. the Cherokees could not utilize the U.S. court system to sue anyone.
    b. the Removal Act of 1830 was unconstitutional.
    c. the Cherokees in Georgia existed as "a distinct community, occupying its own territory, in which the laws of Georgia can have no force."
    d. the Cherokees in Georgia existed as "a distinct ethnic minority over which only local government has jurisdiction."

43. The doctrine of nullification outlined by John C. Calhoun in response to the Tariff of Abominations argued that
    a. if a state believed it had been harmed by an action of Congress, the Supreme Court had the authority to settle the dispute.
    b. states had the constitutional right to declare null and void any tariff passed by the federal government that raised duties above 35 percent.
    c. the federal government was supreme in the land and, if need be, could invalidate inappropriate statutes enacted by state legislatures.
    d. the Union was a voluntary confederation of states that had yielded only some of their power to the federal government, and when Congress overstepped its powers, states had the right to nullify Congress's acts.

44. A compelling reason underlying South Carolina's argument for nullification in 1828 was
    a. the growing fear among some South Carolinians that Congress was attracting ever larger numbers of northern representatives who were hostile to the institution of slavery.
    b. that South Carolinians wanted to keep the income from higher tariffs for themselves.
    c. that Congress authorized a special tax on slaves, which South Carolinians viewed as discriminatory.
    d. that Congress was debating a peacetime conscription law that would have drafted slaves into the military to fight in foreign wars.

45. Henry Clay wanted to force the issue of the renewal of the charter of the Bank of the United States before the presidential election of 1832, because he hoped to
    a. get the bank rechartered as quickly as possible to continue its stabilizing benefits to the nation.
    b. force Andrew Jackson into an unpopular veto on the issue in order to secure support for Clay as president.
    c. help President Jackson defeat the bank bill.
    d. oust Nicholas Biddle from the presidency of the bank.

46. Andrew Jackson interpreted his reelection in 1832 as a mandate to
    a. deposit even more federal receipts into the Bank of the United States.
    b. destroy the Bank of the United States by obtaining a special congressional authorization to close its doors immediately.
    c. destroy the Bank of the United States before its charter expired, a process he began by removing federal deposits from the bank and depositing them in Democratic-leaning banks throughout the country.
    d. remove Nicholas Biddle as president of the Bank of the United States once and for all.

47. A positive effect of the economic turmoil of Jackson's second administration was that from 1835 to 1837, for the first and only time in U.S. history,
    a. much of the money to finance railroads and canals came from private investors.
    b. the government had a surplus of money.
    c. unemployment was only 5 percent.
    d. the number of women in the workforce equaled the number of men.

48. The Specie Circular, one precipitating cause of the panic of 1837,
    a. stipulated that government land could be purchased only with hard money.
    b. stipulated that government land could be purchased only with banknotes.
    c. initially encouraged bankers to increase loans.
    d. was suggested by Henry Clay to make Andrew Jackson lose public favor.

49. In the presidential election of 1836, three Whig candidates ran against Democrat Martin Van Buren
    a. to show Van Buren he needed to be a more lenient president than Andrew Jackson had been.
    b. to get Van Buren to step down and allow a more suitable candidate to run in his place.
    c. because each candidate had a solid popular regional base but none had the support of all regions.
    d. in an attempt to get a New Englander in the presidency.

50. High rates of voter participation continued into the 1840s and 1850s because
    a. literacy rates continued to rise at a rapid rate.
    b. politics remained the arena where different choices about economic development and social change were contested.
    c. numerous states allowed some women to vote.
    d. so many elections were contested that recounts became a foregone conclusion in some political contests.

Terminology Matching   Select the word or phrase from the Terms section that best matches the definition or example provided in the Definitions section. Some terms may be used more than once; some may not be used at all.

TERMS

a. Berea College

b. Black Hawk

c. canals

d. Finney, Charles

e. Garrison, William Lloyd

f. independent treasury system

g. "Little Magician"

h. Lovejoy, Elijah

i. Lowell, Francis Cabot

j. New England Anti-Slavery Society

k. normal schools

l. nullification

m. Oberlin College

n. "Old Hickory"

o. penny press papers

p. Second Great Awakening

q. separate spheres

r. specie payment

s. steamboats

t. Walker, David

u. Waltham system

DEFINITIONS

1. His *Appeal to the Colored Citizens of the World* struck fear into the hearts of more than a few white Southerners. _____

2. Female labor force begun in 1814 that soon appeared in many towns in New England. _____

3. This Illinois abolitionist editor paid for his antislavery convictions with his life. _____

4. This name was applied to institutions established in the 1840s to train teachers. _____

5. Innovation that allowed for cheaper transportation of goods because of increased loads. _____

6. Transaction in which a banknote was traded in at a bank for its equivalent in gold or silver. _____

7. The first college in the U.S. to admit women and blacks. _____

8. A religious movement that peaked in the 1830s and which held that salvation was available to anyone willing to accept God's grace. _____

9. Martin Van Buren worked to create this to serve as a moderating influence on inflation and the credit market. _____

10. One of the first factory owners to consolidate the production of cloth in one location. _____

11. In the 1830s, this was the best and cheapest place to read about the latest scandal, murder, or general goings-on in the local police court. _____

12. This middle-class doctrine, popular in Jacksonian America, posited that men and women have different contributions to make to society and should make them in two decidedly different places. _____

13. In the 1830s, his refusal to be relocated by the government spawned a brief conflict in which he was captured and more than nine hundred of his people were massacred. _____

14. The first affectionate nickname given to a presidential candidate. _____

15. This doctrine argued that states did not need to accept an act of Congress if Congress had overstepped its powers. _____

Chronology   Place the events in chronological order.

SET ONE

A. Second Bank of the United States is chartered for twenty years.

B. Robert Fulton develops first commercially successful steamboat.

C. American Colonization Society is founded to promote gradual emancipation and relocation of African Americans to Liberia.

D. Andrew Jackson issues Specie Circular, which ordered that public land could be purchased only with hard money.

E. Indian Removal Act appropriates money to relocate Indian tribes west of the Mississippi River.

First _____

Second _____

Third _____

Fourth _____

Fifth _____

SET TWO

A. David Walker's *An Appeal to the Colored Citizens of the World* is published in Boston.

B. William Henry Harrison is elected president.

C. Nullification crisis: South Carolina declares federal tariffs void in the state.

D. William Lloyd Garrison begins publishing abolitionist newspaper the *Liberator*.

First _____

Second _____

Third _____

Fourth _____

Short Answer   Write a paragraph in response to each question.

1. When Andrew Jackson was a presidential candidate, how did his background and personal qualities work both in his favor and against him?

2. How did the nature of steamboating capture the essence of American society between 1815 and 1840?

3. Describe the basic conditions of factory life for women and girls who worked in textile manufacturing in the 1820s and 1830s.

4. Why was the Second Bank of the United States referred to as the Second Bank of the United States, and what was its purpose?

5. Name the two parties that formed America's second party system, and outline the most important differences in their philosophies.

6. Allowing for obvious differences over time, compare the efforts of the Whigs and the Democrats to "sell" their candidates in the election of 1828 with what takes place in modern political campaigns.

7. Describe the ways in which a shared American culture spread through Jacksonian America.

8. How did Charles Grandison Finney employ popular political concepts to get his religious message across?

9. Andrew Jackson referred to the Second Bank of the United States as a "monster" — what did he find so monstrous about it?

10. Explain why Martin Van Buren was a one-term president.

Essay   Respond to each of the following questions in an essay of three to four paragraphs. Your responses should include specific evidence and your interpretation of the significance of historical events and concepts.

1. Discuss the character and impact of the legal revolution on the American economy between 1815 and 1840. Did this revolution have to be so antagonistic toward laborers? Explain your answer.

2. Discuss the ways in which Andrew Jackson's personality and political philosophy trickled down through the Democratic party. Was there actually anything common or ordinary about Jackson? Why was he so popular with so many people?

3. How did the Second Great Awakening mesh with America's market revolution? What did the religious message of this revival offer Americans who were not faring well in the modernizing economy?

4. What qualities of northern society and the abolition movement there made it clear that the commitment to eradicating slavery was anything but universal and was often dangerously divisive?

Map Questions   Answer the questions below using Map 10.1, Routes of Transportation in 1840 (p. 325).

READING THE MAP

1. In 1840, where were most canals located in the United States?

2. A central river system became even more important with the advent of the steamboat. Which three major rivers made up this system?

CONNECTIONS

1. What does the regional positioning of roads seem to indicate about the basic geographical flow of the U.S. economy by 1840?

2. Describe some of the cultural implications of improved transportation, for people and for the exchange of information by 1840.

THE FREE NORTH AND WEST 11

1840–1860

Multiple Choice   Choose the letter of the best answer.

1. One of the factors that fueled economic growth in the United States during the mid-1800s was
   a. the movement of Americans from farms to cities, where they found jobs working in factories.
   b. a decline in family size.
   c. a decline in agricultural productivity that forced industrial growth.
   d. better tariff rates with England.

2. During the 1840s and 1850s, U.S. factories were able to become more productive because
   a. water wheel technology improved.
   b. steam engines began to be used as an energy source.
   c. water and animal power had been phased out.
   d. the use of electricity became widespread.

3. The most important factor behind the phenomenal American economic growth that occurred between 1840 and 1860 was
   a. an adequate supply of laborers.
   b. a constant influx of immigrants.
   c. manufacturing advancements.
   d. an increase in agricultural productivity.

4. The population increased greatly in Indiana, Michigan, Wisconsin, Iowa, and Illinois between 1830 and 1860 because
   a. the Indians of the Midwest were quick to cooperate with the settlers.
   b. land was much less expensive than in other parts of the unsettled country.
   c. the climate there was favorable to settlement.
   d. the relatively treeless setting and rich soil made conditions favorable to farming.

5. Agricultural productivity in the North and West increased in the late 1830s partly because of
   a. water wheels.
   b. John Deere's steel plow.
   c. the invention of thrashers.
   d. the numbers of freed slaves eager for wage-earning work.

6. The increase in U.S. agricultural productivity in the 1840s and 1850s was fundamentally dependent upon the
   a. federal government's generous land policy.
   b. increased yields per acre of cultivated land.
   c. migration of eastern farmers.
   d. development of interchangeable parts.

7. Unlike European manufacturers in the first half of the nineteenth century, American manufacturers were spurred to invent laborsaving methods and devices because
   a. the government offered tax incentives to new innovations and inventions.
   b. workers were unreliable and lacked the work ethic needed for optimal production.
   c. American colleges had superior engineering schools that encouraged innovation.
   d. workers were in limited supply and thus more expensive.

8. The growth of railroads in the 1850s
   a. brought to an end older forms of transportation such as stagecoach and horseback travel.
   b. caused enough pollution to seriously hamper agricultural productivity in the Midwest.
   c. fostered iron production, coal production, and the telegraph industry.
   d. was due almost entirely to federal rather than private funding.

9. The invention of the telegraph
   a. was a unifying force for the young United States.
   b. caused a splintering in the United States as news could spread more rapidly.
   c. caused the postal service to flounder.
   d. caused an immediate rise in school attendance as people wanted to know how to read.

10. The telegraph had the following effect on the railroad industry:
    a. The telegraph provided more jobs in the railroad industry.
    b. Use of the telegraph made it possible to synchronize clocks, which allowed railroads to run safely according to schedules.
    c. The telegraph made the train station the hub of the community.
    d. The telegraph hurt railroads by providing a cheaper method of sending information.

11. The "free labor" system touted in the North and West in the 1840s and 1850s affirmed an egalitarian vision of human potential, and proponents claimed that the system
    a. opened up doors to even the least-hard-working segments of the population.
    b. made it possible for hired laborers to become independent land owners.
    c. gave slaves compensation for their labor.
    d. enforced the puritan ideal of working hard and saving one's money.

12. The free-labor ideal of the 1840s and 1850s
    a. closely mirrored the economic situation of the times.
    b. did not mesh with the economic inequalities of the times and led to a restless and mobile society.
    c. caused a rise in crime, because paying jobs were becoming more and more scarce.
    d. strengthened the abolition movement as the idea of freeing laborers caught on.

13. A large influx of immigrants arrived in America between the years 1840 and 1860; three-fourths of them came from either
    a. Sweden or Norway.
    b. Italy or Germany.
    c. Germany or Ireland.
    d. England or Ireland.

14. Among the reasons why immigrants left their homelands for the United States in the 1840s and 1850s
    a. were famine and deteriorating economic conditions in their mother countries, along with the opportunities in America for skilled artisans.
    b. was a lack of available land for them to buy in their homelands.
    c. was a well-organized immigrant aid society in New England, which actively solicited immigrants in Europe to come work in the growing manufacturing sector.
    d. was religious persecution.

15. Irish immigrants in the 1840s and 1850s often
    a. worked as skilled artisans in the northeastern U.S. cities.
    b. lived up to the ideal of wage laborers who became independent, self-sufficient property holders.
    c. entered at the bottom rung of the free-labor ladder as wage laborers or domestic servants.
    d. were the most sought-after immigrant group because they got along well with the predominantly Protestant population in the Northeast.

16. Transcendentalists believed that
    a. women should get the vote.
    b. nature was the essence of contentment.
    c. competition was good for the economy.
    d. individuals should not conform to the materialistic world.

17. In the 1840s, members of utopian communities sought
    a. truth and guidance by looking within themselves rather than to the materialistic world.
    b. to share their wealth and maximize it by developing the most efficient means of production possible.
    c. perfection through communal living.
    d. equality in all things, including gender and race.

18. The convention at Seneca Falls in 1848 advocated
    a. women's rights and suffrage.
    b. better sanitary conditions to curb the rising infant mortality rate.
    c. the right of property ownership for women.
    d. the abolition of slavery.

19. Why did politicians and editorialists oppose women's groups calling for the vote?
    a. They were afraid that if they gave women the vote, slaves would be next in line.
    b. They thought women should stay home to raise their children and civilize their husbands.
    c. They saw women as a possible voting bloc if women were given the vote.
    d. They felt that women would not be informed voters.

20. Abolitionists in the 1840s and 1850s made their issue more attractive to white Northerners by promoting
    a. a complete and immediate end to slavery in the United States.
    b. slave insurrections to convince plantation owners to end slavery.
    c. limitations on the geographic expansion of slavery.
    d. gradual emancipation for all slaves in the United States.

21. In 1843, Henry Highland Garnet advocated
    a. the immediate freeing of slaves in all states.
    b. slaves' rising in insurrection against their masters.
    c. gradual emancipation.
    d. passive resistance.

22. In 1855, African American leaders saw their most notable success to date when
    a. public schools were integrated in Massachusetts.
    b. blacks received voting rights in Massachusetts.
    c. slavery was abolished in Massachusetts.
    d. gradual emancipation was approved in Massachusetts.

23. Behind the scenes, Harriet Tubman and other free blacks helped fugitive slaves escape from the South
    a. by providing them with clothes and horses.
    b. via the "underground railroad."
    c. via a complex system of tunnels.
    d. by procuring ships for their passage north.

24. In 1845, New York journalist and armchair expansionist John L. O'Sullivan coined the term *manifest destiny*, by which he meant that
    a. America should expand into Canada and Mexico.
    b. Americans were destined by a higher power to create a worldwide empire.
    c. the United States should take advantage of economic turmoil in Europe to gain new markets.
    d. Americans had the God-given right to expand their superior civilization across the continent.

25. The increasing number of white settlers traveling west in wagon trains during the mid-1800s brought devastation to the Plains Indians because whites
    a. began killing off the buffalo for their own use.
    b. were intent on annihilating all Indians they came in contact with.
    c. brought alcohol and diseases like smallpox, measles, cholera, and scarlet fever.
    d. were determined to rid the West of all Indians.

26. When westbound settlers asked the government for protection from the Plains Indians, the government responded by
    a. sending soldiers with each wagon train of settlers headed west.
    b. building forts along the trail and adopting the policy of "concentration" in dealing with Indians.
    c. calling tribal meetings and chastising the Indians for attacking wagon trains.
    d. sending army troops to round up all renegade Indians.

27. Prior to emigrating west to the Great Salt Lake, Mormons
    a. were well received by each community they settled in.
    b. were persecuted by non-Mormons because of their religious practices and were forced to move on.
    c. attracted members who shared their beliefs in the value of materialism and slavery.
    d. settled in Arkansas, only to be burned out by locals.

28. Within ten years of arriving at the territory around the Great Salt Lake, the Mormon community
    a. abolished polygamy.
    b. was dislodged by an invasion of U.S. troops.
    c. developed an efficient irrigation system and made the desert bloom through cooperative labor.
    d. almost perished when faced with hunger and Indian attacks.

29. The migrants who settled on the Texas land granted to Stephen F. Austin by Mexico in the 1820s were
    a. New Englanders who wanted a warmer climate.
    b. Irish Catholics who wanted land of their own.
    c. Southerners, who brought cotton and slaves with them.
    d. *Tejanos.*

30. In 1829, Mexico issued an emancipation proclamation in Texas because
    a. it hoped to discourage any more American settlers from coming to the area.
    b. the Texans were asking for independence.
    c. the Mexicans were opposed to slavery on their land.
    d. Santa Anna had a change of heart and decided that the area was better off undeveloped.

31. Texans gained their independence from Mexico in 1836
    a. when Santa Anna surrendered after a bloodless coup.
    b. when two-thirds of the inhabitants voted to establish the Lone Star Republic.
    c. only after fierce fighting and much bloodshed.
    d. after U.S. government troops defeated Santa Anna's troops at the Alamo.

32. In the 1820s, Americans were beginning to trickle into a thinly populated California; in an effort to increase Mexican migration to the area, the Mexican government
    a. posted guards along the California border.
    b. paid local Indians to discourage American settlers.
    c. built forts to stop further American squatting.
    d. granted *ranchos* — huge estates devoted to cattle raising — to new Mexican settlers.

33. When John Tyler became president in 1841,
    a. it was because President William Henry Harrison had been impeached.
    b. he was immediately more popular than the previous president, William Henry Harrison, had been.
    c. it was not clear whether he could legally exercise the full powers of an elected president.
    d. it was because President William Henry Harrison had suffered a heart attack.

34. Since President Tyler was not really a Whig, he generally opposed all the measures of the Whig party, vetoing most of their bills; in response,
    a. the Whigs formally expelled Tyler from the party, and most of the cabinet resigned.
    b. Henry Clay attempted to take over the leadership of the Whig party.
    c. the president's popularity increased.
    d. Tyler resolved to run for election in 1844 as a Republican.

35. Why was the admission of Texas to the U.S. so attractive to John Tyler?
    a. He was an ardent expansionist and feared the British might add Texas to their empire.
    b. It would tip the scales of Congress in favor of free states over slave states.
    c. It would tip the scales of Congress in favor of slave states over free states.
    d. It would mean that he had truly earned the respect due the office of the presidency.

36. The dominant issue in the 1844 presidential election campaigns was
    a. the annexation of Texas.
    b. the annexation of Oregon.
    c. Henry Clay's American System.
    d. the expansion of slavery into the territories.

37. In the 1844 election, the Democratic Convention nominated James K. Polk over Martin Van Buren for president because
    a. Van Buren had not been successful as president from 1836 to 1840.
    b. Polk was strongly in favor of Texas annexation, and Van Buren was not.
    c. the Democrats knew they could count on Polk to oppose manifest destiny.
    d. Polk favored the acquisition of California from Mexico.

38. Just prior to James K. Polk's taking office in 1845, President Tyler was successful in obtaining the annexation of Texas
    a. through a joint resolution of Congress offering Texas admission to the United States.
    b. through Senate approval of a treaty to annex Texas.
    c. by secretly negotiating with Mexican officials.
    d. by sending John Slidell to Mexico to buy Texas its freedom from the Mexicans.

39. How was President Polk able to add Oregon to U.S. holdings?
    a. He annexed it without the approval of the British.
    b. He authorized military action.
    c. He recommended a continued joint occupation of the territory with Britain.
    d. He renewed an old offer to divide Oregon along the forty-ninth parallel, and the British accepted.

40. What caused a break in diplomatic relations between the United States and Mexico in 1845?
    a. The U.S. annexed Texas.
    b. The U.S. recognized the independence of Texas from Mexico.
    c. The United States annexed Oregon, and Mexico was afraid that Texas would be next.
    d. General Winfield Scott attacked a Mexican regiment.

41. When President Polk sent John Slidell to Mexico to buy Mexico's northern provinces, the Mexican government reacted by
    a. participating in negotiations that ended up in a stalemate.
    b. refusing to sell and sending Slidell back home.
    c. declaring war on the United States.
    d. agreeing to sell part of the territory while keeping the rest.

42. In 1846, the American reaction to the country's first foreign war was
    a. widespread dissent and refusal to fight in a foreign land.
    b. support in the North and dissent in the South.
    c. unanimous support.
    d. nationwide support for the military but division over the principles behind the war itself.

43. The Mexican War was called "Mr. Polk's War" by those who believed that
    a. Polk had been deceitful in saying that Mexico caused the war.
    b. Mexico didn't like Polk and was determined to keep Texas.
    c. Polk's aggression was an attempt to extend slavery.
    d. Mexico was mistaken in claiming the boundary of Texas as the Nueces River.

44. The group most outspoken in its opposition to war with Mexico was the
    a. Democrats.
    b. Southerners.
    c. Northern Whigs.
    d. Republicans.

45. President Polk personally directed the war with Mexico; his strategy to win the war was
    a. called the "anaconda plan."
    b. to divide and conquer Mexico, beginning with the northern provinces.
    c. to quickly defeat the Mexicans in the southern provinces and then take Mexico City.
    d. to occupy Mexico's northern provinces and win a couple of major battles, after which Mexico would sue for peace.

46. By January 1847, Americans had successfully taken what land from Mexico?
    a. Colorado and Utah
    b. New Mexico and California
    c. Arizona and southern Mexico
    d. Arizona and New Mexico

47. After Santa Anna evacuated Mexico City on September 14, 1847,
    a. the troops marched on to Veracruz.
    b. the Americans felt the war was far from over.
    c. President Polk sent a representative to Mexico to negotiate peace.
    d. Nicholas Trist was unable to convince Mexico to end the war.

48. The Mexican War ended with the 1848 Treaty of Guadalupe Hidalgo, under the terms of which
    a. Mexico agreed that the Nueces River was the Texas boundary.
    b. Mexico agreed to pay $15 million to American citizens for claims against Mexico.
    c. Mexico agreed to give up Arizona, New Mexico, and southern Utah.
    d. Mexico gave up all claims to Texas above the Rio Grande and ceded the provinces of New Mexico and California to the United States.

49. A flood of Americans, Chinese, Germans, Mexicans, Irish, and others descended on California between 1849 and 1852 because
    a. the U.S. government had offered land at $1 per acre.
    b. gold had been discovered.
    c. they were rushing to stake their claim to free land.
    d. they recognized an opportunity to get rich with vegetable and fruit farms.

50. The legacy of the war between the United States and Mexico included
    a. the rise of nationalism in Mexico and an increased sense of superiority among Americans.
    b. a lessening of the stereotypes Mexicans and Americans had held of each other before the war.
    c. a realization in America that manifest destiny was a flawed and dangerous concept.
    d. the peaceful and respectful mingling of cultures in the previously Mexican territory.

Terminology Matching   Select the word or phrase from the Terms section that best matches the definition or example provided in the Definitions section. Some terms may be used more than once; some may not be used at all.

TERMS

a. Austin, Stephen F.

b. Bear Flag Revolt

c. Brook Farm

d. Clay, Henry

e. Deere, John

f. Deseret

g. Douglas, Stephen A.

h. Emerson, Ralph Waldo

i. free-labor system

j. manifest destiny

k. McCormick, Cyrus

l. Morse, Samuel F. B.

m. Oneida

n. Oregon

o. O'Sullivan, John L.

p. *ranchos*

q. Seneca Falls

r. Smith, Joseph

s. Stanton, Elizabeth Cady

t. transcendentalists

u. Treaty of Guadalupe Hidalgo

v. Truth, Sojourner

w. Tubman, Harriet

x. Young, Brigham

DEFINITIONS

1. This innovative inventor was the leading plow manufacturer in the Midwest. _____

2. His reaper allowed easier and faster harvesting of wheat beginning in the late 1840s. _____

3. His telegraph revolutionized communication in the United States. _____

4. This was supposed to make it possible for hired workers to become independent property owners. _____

5. He was the most prominent transcendentalist. _____

6. This utopian community functioned mainly as a retreat and did not want to sever ties with the larger society. _____

7. This community of reformers believed that the root of the evil of private property lay in traditional marriage and consequently practiced "complex marriage." _____

8. Site where female reformers held the first women's rights convention in 1848. _____

9. She was instrumental in organizing the women's rights convention in 1848. _____

10. This black abolitionist lectured to reform audiences throughout the North. _____

11. The "underground railroad" was masterminded by this former slave. _____

12. This New York journalist coined the term *manifest destiny* as the justification for white settlers to take the land they desired. _____

13. In 1818, the United States and Great Britain agreed to jointly occupy this territory. _____

14. The name given by the Mormons to the area they settled in the West. _____

15. He led a group of Mormons from Illinois to their new home beside the Great Salt Lake. _____

16. Mexico granted this person a large tract of land, and his settlement attracted many Southern slaveholders. _____

17. Huge estates devoted to cattle ranching that the Mexican government granted to new settlers in California. _____

18. This Whig Senator expected President Tyler to follow his "American System" program. _____

19. This gave the United States the area of Texas above the Rio Grande, as well as New Mexico and California. _____

Chronology   Place the events in chronological order.

SET ONE

A. James K. Polk is elected president on a platform calling for the annexation of Texas and Oregon.

B. Texas declares independence from Mexico.

C. California Gold Rush begins.

D. The term *manifest destiny* is first used as justification for Anglo-American settlers to take land in the West.

E. Congress declares war on Mexico.

First _____

Second _____

Third _____

Fourth _____

Fifth _____

SET TWO

A. Samuel F. B. Morse invents the telegraph.

B. John Deere patents his steel plow.

C. First women's rights convention convenes at Seneca Falls.

D. First U.S. railroad breaks ground.

First _____

Second _____

Third _____

Fourth _____

Short Answer   Write a paragraph in response to each question.

1. What changes in American society led to the phenomenal economic growth that occurred between 1840 and 1860?

2. Why did the Midwest experience a huge growth in population between 1830 and 1860?

3. Railroads had a big impact on America in many ways. Discuss some of the changes brought about by the advent of railroads.

4. Why did Germans and Irish immigrate to the U.S. between 1840 and 1860? What skills did they bring with them, and which trades or jobs did they enter upon arrival?

5. Summarize the beliefs of transcendentalists and utopians in the 1840s and 1850s.

6. When women began to break out of their traditional roles in the 1840s, what were some of the causes they embraced, and how did women promote them?

7. In what ways did individual African Americans contribute to the abolitionist movement?

8. The 1840s were a time of great change in America. Describe the impact of the philosophy of manifest destiny on society and on government policy.

9. Discuss the history of the Mormons before they went to Utah, including the discrimination they faced.

10. What problems and issues did John Tyler face upon taking the office of the presidency after William Henry Harrison died?

Essay   Respond to each of the following questions in an essay of three to four paragraphs. Your responses should include specific evidence and your interpretation of the significance of historical events and concepts.

1. Discuss three or four of the many changes that took place in America between 1840 and 1860 (the antebellum years). Include technology, population, and politics in your discussion.

2. Mexico opened itself up to a future loss of land beginning with the land grant to Stephen F. Austin. Describe how Mexico lost Texas, including the events leading up to the Mexican War of 1846–1848.

3. Why is the Mexican War called "Mr. Polk's War"? Was this a war of greed and expansionism? Include examples to explain your answer.

4. Between 1840 and 1850, the United States gained one-third more land than it had previously, achieving its goal of stretching from the Atlantic to the Pacific. Discuss briefly three major land acquisitions made during that decade. Include important events and their final outcomes and explain what land was added to America.

Map Questions   Answer the questions below using Map 11.3, Texas and Mexico in the 1830s (p. 390).

READING THE MAP

1. How did the southern border of the United States change in 1845?

2. What parts of the border between Mexico and the United States remained unchanged in 1845?

3. Where were some of the major battles fought between Mexico and the United States in the 1820s, and which side won in each battle?

CONNECTIONS Why did Texans push for independence from Mexico? Does the map offer any clues about how geography might have influenced these motives?

THE SLAVE SOUTH
1820–1860

12

Multiple Choice   Choose the letter of the best answer.

1. The biggest fear of whites in the antebellum South was
   a. passive resistance by slaves in the field, which would greatly curtail the work that needed to be done.
   b. the passage of legislation freeing slaves.
   c. slave revolts.
   d. the loss of their field hands.

2. The passage of laws strengthening the institution of slavery and restricting free blacks by the Virginia legislature in 1831 was prompted by
   a. Gabriel Prosser's rebellion.
   b. Denmark Vesey's escape and subsequent organization of free blacks.
   c. the publication of the *Liberator.*
   d. Nat Turner's insurrection.

3. Between 1820 and 1860, the most important factor dividing the North and the South was
   a. the existence of an ever increasing number of slaves in the South.
   b. the industrialization of the North.
   c. railroad expansion in the North.
   d. the agricultural dominance of the South.

4. After 1820, what caused slavery to become more vigorous and profitable, which in turn increased the South's political power?
   a. Tobacco production increased exponentially.
   b. Cotton production expanded to the west.
   c. The natural birth rate increased.
   d. The invention of the plow led to greater agricultural productivity.

5. In 1831, a French visitor to the United States astutely observed that the major differences between the North and South revolved around
   a. the vast amounts of free land available to Southerners.
   b. the fact that the northern states were crowded, which fostered an ill-tempered society.
   c. Southerners wanting states' rights and a weak centralized government.
   d. the southern institution of slavery.

6. The cultivation of cotton was well suited to the South because
   a. the South had so many slaves.
   b. of the South's climate and geography.
   c. the South did not have very many towns or cities.
   d. rainfall in the South was above average.

7. By 1860, how much of the world's supply of cotton was produced in the southern United States?
   a. 10 percent
   b. 25 percent
   c. 50 percent
   d. 75 percent

8. In 1790, there were fewer than 700,000 slaves in the South; by 1860, that number had increased to
   a. 800,000.
   b. 1 million.
   c. 4 million.
   d. 12 million.

9. The growth in the southern slave population between 1790 and 1869 occurred primarily because of
   a. the importation of slaves from Africa.
   b. natural reproduction.
   c. miscegenation.
   d. Southerners buying slaves from the North, where the practice was waning.

10. In the Lower South in 1860,
    a. blacks outnumbered whites in all states.
    b. whites outnumbered blacks in all states.
    c. the numbers of whites and blacks were about equal.
    d. there were about as many blacks as there were in the North; the only difference was that in the South most blacks were slaves, whereas in the North most were free.

11. Antebellum southern whites of all classes were unanimous in their commitment to
    a. the teachings of Christianity.
    b. white supremacy.
    c. keeping cotton their primary source of income.
    d. keeping industrial growth to a minimum in the South.

12. Initially, the white South defended slavery as a "necessary evil"; eventually, however, intellectuals began to argue that slavery was
    a. a positive good, as it civilized blacks and brought them Christianity.
    b. a long-standing institution and for that reason alone should be continued.
    c. essential to the cotton industry.
    d. a segment of southern society that could not be dismissed.

13. The effect of the institution of slavery on southern society was that
    a. poor whites identified more with free blacks than with planters and agitated for laws to protect them.
    b. people who owned no slaves generally disapproved of the planters' practices.
    c. planters treated whites who owned no slaves as far inferior to themselves.
    d. whites were unified around race rather than divided by social class.

14. Most white Southerners in the antebellum South
    a. worked small farms with the help of only a few slaves.
    b. had about twenty slaves, including domestic servants.
    c. did not own slaves.
    d. considered themselves planters.

15. According to historians, a planter in the antebellum South may be distinguished from a farmer by virtue of his
    a. owning at least twenty slaves.
    b. owning at least one hundred slaves.
    c. owning at least one hundred acres of land.
    d. earning all of his income from cotton.

16. The staple crop in the tidewater area from the Carolinas into northern Georgia, which required canals, dikes, and huge numbers of slaves, was
    a. tobacco.
    b. cotton.
    c. sugarcane.
    d. rice.

17. During the antebellum years, the southern economy was based on agriculture; the North developed an economy based on
    a. a healthy banking system.
    b. growing only one crop in an area, which ended up depleting the soil.
    c. mining as well as agriculture.
    d. agriculture, commerce, and manufacturing.

18. Why did the antebellum South remain agriculturally based instead of diversifying its economy?
    a. Southerners were afraid that factories would bring a lot of foreigners to the South, and the politically powerful planters were opposed to that concept.
    b. Planters made good profits from cotton, and they feared that economic change would threaten the plantation system.
    c. There were too few cities in the South to support industry.
    d. The South's earlier experiment with textile manufacture had failed, and investors were wary of further attempts at industrialization.

19. Because the antebellum South lacked economic diversity,
    a. newly arrived European immigrants tended to settle in the North.
    b. it was dependent upon the North for food products.
    c. the government dragged its feet in creating an effective banking system there.
    d. railroads were reluctant to build in the South.

20. As late as 1850, there were no statewide public school systems in the South because
    a. the South had no money for schools.
    b. state legislatures failed to provide many essential services, and planters saw no need to educate their workforce.
    c. Southerners sent their sons and daughters to the North for schooling.
    d. Southerners were too involved in making money for themselves.

21. Plantation owners often described the master-slave relationship in terms of "paternalism,"
    a. which meant that masters had no direct contact with their slaves.
    b. a concept whereby a slave's labor and obedience was exchanged for the master's care and guidance.
    c. which meant that the master's relationship with his slave mirrored his relationship with God.
    d. which is to say that the master was the father and slaves were the children.

22. After 1808, masters began to treat their slaves marginally better because
    a. the United States stopped importing slaves, and so it was in the master's best interest to treat his slaves well enough that they could have children.
    b. legislatures passed laws mandating a certain minimum level of physical welfare for slaves.
    c. masters became more afraid of slave uprisings with the passage of time.
    d. masters realized that healthy slaves were a matter of honor.

23. The most common punishment meted out to slaves was
    a. neck and wrist chains.
    b. to withhold their food for three days.
    c. whippings.
    d. miscegenation.

24. Miscegenation existed in the antebellum South primarily because
    a. slavery gave white men extraordinary power over black women.
    b. there were no laws to forbid it.
    c. the plantation mistresses encouraged it.
    d. it gave the slaves power.

25. Plantation values strongly influenced southern life before the Civil War; these values included
    a. slavery, godliness, and cleanliness.
    b. chastity, honor, and virtue.
    c. respect for whites, hatred of blacks, and love of God.
    d. slavery, honor, and male domination.

26. In the antebellum South, plantation mistresses were like slaves in that their husbands
    a. treated them unkindly.
    b. demanded that they be subordinate.
    c. admired their physical strength.
    d. did not allow them to carry out their duties without supervision.

27. The antebellum southern lady has been idealized in history; in reality
    a. she was waited on by servants and had few responsibilities.
    b. she managed up to a dozen servants, nursed sick slaves, and tended the henhouse and dairy.
    c. she was often idle, because her only responsibility was to bear children.
    d. she was responsible for entertaining and for the education of her children.

28. The typical plantation mistress
    a. rode into town occasionally to purchase manufactured goods.
    b. went to church every Sunday, often separately from her husband.
    c. volunteered for community betterment associations.
    d. did not live a life of leisure and spent most of her time on the plantation.

29. Most plantation mistresses kept their opinions on issues to themselves, but the diarist Mary Boykin Chesnut echoed most women in railing against
    a. miscegenation.
    b. her endless responsibilities.
    c. slavery itself.
    d. women's subordination to men.

30. As a system, slavery was
    a. found almost exclusively on plantations.
    b. found in almost every occupation in the antebellum South.
    c. found to be successful only on farms.
    d. frowned on by many southern whites who did not own slaves themselves.

31. When slaves reached their elder years, they
    a. were honored by the chance to retire from the plantation.
    b. swept the big house floors and shooed flies.
    c. carried water to the fields for field hands.
    d. cared for small children, spun yarn, fed livestock, or cleaned stables.

32. There were several advantages to being a house servant in the antebellum South; for instance, house servants
    a. had more time for themselves.
    b. were treated better by the mistress and master.
    c. enjoyed less physically demanding work, better food, and more comfortable living quarters.
    d. did not have to answer to the master or mistress as much as field workers did.

33. The rarest job on the plantation for slaves was that of driver, the person who
    a. transported the slaves to the fields from their quarters and then back again at the end of the day.
    b. worked alongside the carpenter, driving in nails.
    c. sat in the farm equipment and managed the animals that pulled it.
    d. made sure all slaves worked hard.

34. Central to slave life was the importance slaves placed on
    a. family, religion, and community.
    b. being able to keep small gardens to give their families a variety of food.
    c. being good workers so the master wouldn't sell them or their families.
    d. keeping their African culture alive.

35. Planters in the nineteenth century promoted Christianity in the slave quarters because
    a. they didn't want infidels playing with their children.
    b. they knew the preachers would bring joy and thus make the slaves happier and live longer.
    c. they believed that the slaves' salvation was part of their obligation and that religion would make slaves more obedient.
    d. evangelicals were advocating Christianizing the slaves.

36. African American Christianity, created by slaves themselves,
    a. was an interpretation of the Christian message that emphasized justice and salvation for all.
    b. delivered the same message taught by white preachers.
    c. was a combination of witchcraft and African traditions.
    d. emphasized obedience and passive resistance.

37. Slaves most commonly reacted to their bondage by
    a. suffering quietly and passively.
    b. fighting with one another because of their frustration with their situation.
    c. engaging in daily forms of resistance such as feigning illness, breaking farm equipment, or playing dumb.
    d. periodically organizing rebellions.

38. Probably the most active and widespread form of slave protest was
    a. killing chickens and pigs by poisoning them.
    b. running away.
    c. scorching the family's clothes on ironing day.
    d. burying the family's silver.

39. Open slave revolts were uncommon in the South because
    a. whites outnumbered blacks two to one by 1860 and were heavily armed, so there was no chance for blacks to succeed at rebelling.
    b. slaves were not allowed to have firearms or machetes.
    c. vicious hunting dogs were used by planters to keep blacks in tow.
    d. slaves lacked the organizational skills needed to stage a revolt.

40. Free blacks numbered 260,000 by 1860; what restrictions were placed on this segment of southern society?
    a. Curfews said that all blacks must be off the streets in urban areas by 8 P.M.
    b. Free blacks were denied interstate travel, schooling, and participation in politics and were forced to carry "freedom papers."
    c. Free blacks could not attend white churches, legally marry, or own property.
    d. Free blacks could not borrow money from lending institutions or own slaves.

41. The free black population in the antebellum South was
    a. not allowed to own slaves.
    b. concentrated in the lower South.
    c. gradually assimilated into the rural white society.
    d. typically rural, uneducated, and made up of unskilled laborers.

42. In 1860, the largest number of white Southerners
    a. were planters.
    b. owned no land at all.
    c. were nonslaveholding yeoman farmers.
    d. owned a small number of slaves.

43. Yeomen in the plantation belt of the antebellum South
    a. got along well with their planter neighbors, who sometimes shipped and sold their cotton for them.
    b. were looked down upon and mistreated by their wealthier neighbors.
    c. tried to avoid their richer neighbors and carve out their own market niche.
    d. were opposed to slavery.

44. The typical plantation belt yeoman in the antebellum South aspired to
    a. the destruction of his neighbor's crops because of his envy and resentment.
    b. moving up to the planter class.
    c. leaving the farm and opening a shop in town.
    d. higher education for his children so they could compete against the planter's children for jobs.

45. In the antebellum South, upcountry yeomen, who lived in the hills and mountains,
    a. concentrated on raising tobacco rather than cotton, with the help of one or two slaves.
    b. raised hogs, cattle, and sheep and were independent and self-sufficient.
    c. were commonly opposed to the slavery system of their plantation neighbors.
    d. were as well educated as the average Northerner.

46. Southern plain folk, whether they lived upcountry or in the flatlands,
    a. valued education.
    b. were not very religious.
    c. were more likely to attend a religious revival than a classroom lecture.
    d. attended traditional church services each week without fail.

47. At the bottom of the social scale in the antebellum South were poor whites, who
    a. owned only ten to twenty acres of farmland.
    b. worked ambitiously and hoped to move up and away from their miserable living conditions.
    c. had no chance or hope of upward mobility.
    d. made and sold moonshine to get by.

48. By the 1850s, the political system of the white South
    a. had extended suffrage for all white males who were at least twenty-one years of age.
    b. had implemented strict voting requirements to keep yeomen from holding office.
    c. was characterized by poor voter turnout.
    d. was largely free from partisan voting.

49. In the nineteenth century, southern politics were democratized, which meant that
    a. the legislatures reflected a representative mix of planters, yeomen, and tradesmen.
    b. a town meeting system like that in New England began to emerge to encourage the political participation of ordinary citizens.
    c. planters were losing their status as leaders.
    d. a greater number of ordinary citizens voted, but yeomen and artisans were still only infrequently elected to the legislatures.

50. The antebellum South's elite class protected slavery by
    a. making sure slaveholders paid more in taxes than other whites relative to their wealth, to ensure the continued support of the poorer people.
    b. trying to keep yeoman farmers and other nonslaveholders from voting.
    c. criticizing people who did not own slaves and by trying to convince them to join the slaveholding class.
    d. stifling its harsher critics.

Terminology Matching   Select the word or phrase from the Terms section that best matches the definition or example provided in the Definitions section. Some terms may be used more than once; some may not be used at all.

TERMS

a. Barrow, Bennet H.

b. Chandler, Thomas

c. Chesnut, Mary Boykin

d. chivalry

e. cotton curtain

f. driver

g. European immigrants

h. field hands

i. Garrison, William Lloyd

j. Georgia

k. house servants

l. Louisiana

m. Lower South

n. Mason-Dixon line

o. miscegenation

p. paternalism

q. rice

r. sugarcane

s. tenants

t. tobacco

u. Tocqueville, Alexis de

v. Turner, Nat

w. Whitney, Eli

x. yeomen

DEFINITIONS

1. He led an 1831 slave insurrection in which he and his followers slaughtered fifty-seven whites in Virginia. _____

2. This Massachusetts abolitionist published a fiery newspaper entitled the *Liberator.* _____

3. Surveyor's mark that divided the free North and the slave South. _____

4. This French political observer believed that the main differences between the North and the South in the first part of the nineteenth century originated with slavery. _____

5. Tier of states from South Carolina west to Texas. _____

6. The original plantation crop in North America, which had shifted westward from the Chesapeake to Tennessee and Kentucky by the nineteenth century. _____

7. The most physically demanding staple crop in the antebellum South. _____

8. State with most of the sugar plantations in the early nineteenth century. _____

9. Probably the most expensive staple crop to grow in the antebellum South. _____

10. Working this crop was both dangerous and extremely uncomfortable to the slaves. _____

11. Former tutor and inventor who created the cotton gin, which revolutionized the cotton industry. _____

12. There were fewer of these people in the South than the North because the South had few cities and industrial jobs. _____

13. Name used by historians to describe the master-slave relationship in the nineteenth century. _____

14. Sexual mixing of the races. _____

15. The South's romantic ideal of male-female relationships, glorifying the lady even while subordinating her. _____

16. This South Carolina plantation mistress wrote negatively of slavery, yet she endured it because it was the foundation of her world. _____

17. Role carried out by a majority of slaves in 1860. _____

18. Slave whose role it was to force other slaves to work harder in the fields. _____

19. Small southern farmers who owned their own land. _____

20. Nickname given to restrictions on free speech on the slavery question in the 1830s. _____

Chronology   Place the events in chronological order.

A. Nat Turner leads a slave revolt.

B. The external slave trade is outlawed in the United States.

C. Denmark Vesey is executed for planning a slave rebellion in South Carolina.

D. The southern slave population reaches nearly 4 million.

First _____

Second _____

Third _____

Fourth _____

Short Answer   Write a paragraph in response to each question.

1. Why did Southerners move westward in 1815? Where did they tend to settle?

2. Discuss why the South was so well suited for cotton growth in the nineteenth century.

3. The large numbers of blacks in the antebellum South had profound effects on the region. Give several examples of how blacks influenced southern culture.

4. After 1820, the South began passing strict slave codes and put a great deal of effort into justifying the institution of slavery. What were some of the defenses southerners used to justify slavery?

5. The four major staple crops grown in the antebellum South were tobacco, sugar, rice, and cotton. Briefly discuss the methods used in producing these crops and the impact these methods had on the need for slave labor.

6. Why did the South remain agricultural when the economy of the North was diversifying?

7. List and describe the various kinds of jobs slaves held both on a plantation and elsewhere in the South.

8. How did southern whites view free blacks in the antebellum period, and what kinds of legislation did they pass in regard to their rights?

9. Explain how plain folk in both the plantation belt and the upcountry viewed the idea of white supremacy, and what led them to adopt these views.

10. Explain the "cotton curtain" that descended on the South in the 1830s. What effect did it have on small farmers in the South?

Essay   Respond to each of the following questions in an essay of three to four paragraphs. Your responses should include specific evidence and your interpretation of the significance of historical events and concepts.

1. Describe in detail the family, religious, and community life of slaves. Were slaves able to retain any of their African culture?

2. There were some free blacks in the South during the antebellum years. Describe this group of people, including how they were treated by whites, what their status was in society, what kinds of labor they performed, and whether they owned any slaves.

3. Besides planters and their slaves, the population of the antebellum South included plantation belt yeomen, upcountry yeomen, and poor whites. Characterize each group, describing their relationship to the planter class, their aspirations, and their viewpoints on slavery.

4. Slaveholders wielded most of the political power in the antebellum South. What methods did they use to ensure the continuation of the institution of slavery?

Map Questions   Answer the questions below using Map 12.2, The Agricultural Economy of the South, 1860 (p. 416).

READING THE MAP

1. Which states grew cotton as their staple crop?

2. In which states was corn grown?

3. Where was sugar harvested?

4. In which states was tobacco grown?

CONNECTIONS

1. In 1860, which staple crop dominated in the southern states? Why was this the dominant crop?

2. Which states grew rice in 1860, and why was that crop confined to such a small geographic area?

THE HOUSE DIVIDED 13
1846–1861

Multiple Choice   Choose the letter of the best answer.

1. The precise objectives of John Brown's assault on Harpers Ferry, Virginia, in 1859 remain hazy, but most believe he wanted to
   a. steal arms from the arsenal to take back to New England.
   b. set up a training camp for militant abolitionists.
   c. initiate a slave insurrection.
   d. shut down the federal arsenal so it could no longer manufacture weapons.

2. The Mexican War was the event that
   a. awakened the South to the realization that slavery could never survive in the Southwest.
   b. forced the issue of slavery and its prospective expansion back onto the national political stage.
   c. gave rise to the Peace Democrats.
   d. convinced Americans that continuing to support military heroes as presidential candidates was unwise.

3. The Wilmot Proviso of 1846 proposed that
   a. slavery be allowed to expand only into the area below the southern boundary of Missouri ceded by Mexico.
   b. any slaves taken in the area ceded by Mexico be freed at age twenty-eight.
   c. slavery be prohibited in California but allowed in the remainder of the area ceded by Mexico.
   d. slavery be prohibited throughout the entire area ceded by Mexico.

4. Support for the Wilmot Proviso of 1846 came primarily from
   a. Northerners desiring to solidify the Democratic Party in their region, reserve new lands for white settlers, and check the power of the South in Congress.
   b. Southerners who had concluded that it was futile to press for slavery expansion in an area where it could not flourish.
   c. Northerners and Southerners who were morally opposed to slavery.
   d. Southerners who could not afford to relocate their agricultural operations to the West.

5. As the battle over the expansion of slavery intensified in the 1840s, Senator Lewis Cass of Michigan proposed the doctrine of "popular sovereignty," a measure that would allow
   a. a vote by Supreme Court justices to decide whether territories might sanction slavery.
   b. a national referendum on the issue of slavery expansion.
   c. the people who settled the territories to decide whether they wanted slavery.
   d. a special congressional commission to decide slavery's fate in the territories.

6. To reunite their party, the Whig strategy in the presidential campaign of 1848 was to
    a. nominate a slaveholder and denounce abolitionists.
    b. nominate a military hero and remain silent on the issue of slavery.
    c. nominate a wealthy Southerner who opposed slavery.
    d. nominate a Southerner who advocated the admission of California as a slave state.

7. When Zachary Taylor became president in 1849, he enraged Southerners by
    a. proposing a ten-year program to phase out slavery in the nation.
    b. introducing a new tariff bill that would affect cotton plantation owners.
    c. unveiling a new railroad-building plan that favored the North over the South.
    d. urging Congress to admit California and New Mexico as free states.

8. In the "Great Debate" of 1849–1850, the major issue was
    a. the balance of power between the North and the South in Congress.
    b. whether the nation should engage in a civil war.
    c. tariffs and interstate commerce regulations.
    d. whether the North, which had more manufacturing than the South, should be more heavily
        taxed for road construction.

9. In the high-stakes debates surrounding the Compromise of 1850, Senator William Seward of
    New York stunned Congress and disagreed with Daniel Webster and Henry Clay when he
    a. announced that it was no longer possible to work with Southerners in Congress in any
        fruitful way.
    b. stated that there was "a higher law than the Constitution" — the law of God.
    c. advocated that the North marshal all its resources to stop slavery expansion in the territories
        and to roll back the institution of slavery where it already existed.
    d. suggested that the North ought to secede from the Union if a proslavery president should
        happen to be elected in 1852.

10. The Compromise of 1850
    a. received wide national support and solved for the foreseeable future all the problems it
        addressed.
    b. passed Congress easily because of the sense of urgency attached to it.
    c. was neither a true compromise nor a final settlement of all the issues it addressed.
    d. saw Millard Fillmore awarded the honorary title of "Great Pacificator" upon the death of
        Henry Clay in 1852.

11. The Fugitive Slave Act, part of the Compromise of 1850,
    a. was designed to operate in conjunction with personal liberty laws.
    b. pleased Northerners weary of the increasing numbers of runaway slaves in their communities.
    c. was the least controversial component of the agreement.
    d. placed the force of the federal government behind Southerners seeking the return of runaway
        slaves.

12. Harriet Beecher Stowe's *Uncle Tom's Cabin* (1852) influenced Northerners' attitudes toward
    slavery
    a. by including some of the earliest research to yield scientific evidence of the effects of slavery
        on those enslaved.
    b. because it was a compelling novel and a vehicle for a stirring moral indictment of slavery.
    c. by arguing that the North was in no way responsible for the institution of slavery.
    d. by suggesting that the federal government should pay the fair market value for all slaves and
        then relocate them west of the Mississippi River.

13. The Whigs lost the election of 1852 because they
    a. included "doughfaces," who were unpopular in the South.
    b. insisted on going with the unpopular incumbent, Millard Fillmore, for president.
    c. were less successful than the Democrats in compromising differences between the northern and southern views.
    d. tried to avoid controversy by having no real platform, a strategy that backfired.

14. In 1853, the United States negotiated the Gadsden Purchase in order to
    a. secure mining rights in the Southwest.
    b. remove troublesome Native Americans from the area ceded by Mexico.
    c. provide a southern route for the transcontinental railroad.
    d. set up James Gadsden as territorial governor and possible presidential candidate.

15. In 1854, Stephen A. Douglas sponsored the Kansas-Nebraska Act and included a section repealing the Missouri Compromise because
    a. he had never supported the Missouri Compromise in the first place.
    b. he needed southern support to pass his legislation, and opening up an area previously closed to slavery seemed the only way to get it.
    c. unbeknownst to his colleagues and constituents, Douglas pocketed large sums of money from southern legislators in return for supporting their causes.
    d. he agreed with the arguments of proslavery theorists about the best way to organize southern society.

16. As a result of the 1854 Kansas-Nebraska Act,
    a. the nation once again had only one functioning political party.
    b. the Whigs gained new strength and vitality.
    c. the nation witnessed the demise of the Whig Party and the eventual rise of a system in which the Democrats dominated the South and the Republican Party was limited to the North.
    d. the Democrats came to dominate northern politics.

17. The American Party, or Know-Nothings, appeared in the mid-1850s as
    a. a reaction to large numbers of Roman Catholics coming to the United States from Germany and Ireland.
    b. a political organization designed to include all Americans.
    c. part of the movement to bind together Americans who had grown apart because of the continuing controversy over slavery.
    d. an organization advocating equal rights for all immigrants.

18. The common thread that wove together northern men into the Republican Party in 1854 was their
    a. conviction that the federal government should do much more to implement social reform in the nation.
    b. belief that Congress should move quickly to abolish slavery where it existed.
    c. belief that citizenship was too easily achieved by ill-prepared foreigners.
    d. opposition to the extension of slavery into any territory of the United States.

19. The Republicans' "glorious defeat" in the presidential contest of 1856
    a. reassured Southerners about the party's intentions regarding the issue of slavery.
    b. alarmed Southerners because the party's favorable showing suggested to slaveholders that this sectional political organization might actually win the election in 1860.
    c. disheartened so many Republicans that they joined the Democratic Party.
    d. was blamed on John C. Frémont's wife, Jessie.

20. When, in 1854, William Seward said, "Come on then, Gentlemen of the Slave States . . . We will engage in competition for the virgin soil of Kansas," his challenge was based on
    a. the idea that many believed the soil of Kansas to be unsuitable for agriculture.
    b. the fact that few people were interested in settling Kansas under any circumstances.
    c. the fact that Kansas had been thrown open for settlement under the concept of popular sovereignty.
    d. the well-kept secret that the Supreme Court was about to declare slavery in the territories unconstitutional.

21. Early in the struggle to win Kansas, proslavery supporters
    a. took control by vote fraud, intimidation, and violence.
    b. provided an excellent example of how the legal and orderly implementation of popular sovereignty might take place.
    c. saw that the cause was lost and retreated from the contest.
    d. got no support from the presidential administration of Millard Fillmore.

22. When the first territorial legislature in Kansas met, it
    a. voted to settle the slavery issue peacefully.
    b. voted to secede from the union.
    c. enacted tough proslavery laws and prompted the organization of a rival government.
    d. voted to repeal the Fugitive Slave Law within the territorial boundaries.

23. John Brown's leadership of a massacre at Pottawatomie Creek, Kansas, led to
    a. the realization of the need for a revote on the popular sovereignty issue.
    b. an increase in the number of proslavery demonstrations nationwide.
    c. government troops declaring martial law in the territory.
    d. guerilla war engulfing the territory.

24. Preston Brooks's caning of Massachusetts senator Charles Sumner in 1856
    a. settled a long-standing personal grievance between the two men.
    b. further inflamed sectional passions over the institution of slavery and its future in the Republic.
    c. was seen in the North as having an appropriately tempering effect upon Sumner for his irresponsible speech entitled "The Crime against Kansas."
    d. resulted in Brooks becoming an outcast in his home state of South Carolina.

25. In the 1857 *Dred Scott* decision, the U.S. Supreme Court ruled that
    a. Dred Scott could not legally claim violation of his constitutional rights because he was not a citizen of the United States.
    b. the Missouri Compromise was constitutional.
    c. black people in the United States could be declared citizens under certain circumstances.
    d. Congress had the power to prohibit slavery in the territories.

26. In his dissenting opinion in the 1857 *Dred Scott* case, Justice Benjamin Curtis argued that
    a. Dred Scott was free, he was a citizen only of the state of Missouri, and the Missouri Compromise was unconstitutional.
    b. Dred Scott was free, he was a citizen of the United States, and the Missouri Compromise was constitutional.
    c. Dred Scott was free, the Missouri Compromise was constitutional, and northern blacks were nominal citizens who must pass a revised examination to become full citizens under the Constitution.
    d. while the Missouri Compromise was unconstitutional, every person born in America had the right to bring suit in any court in the land.

27. The *Dred Scott* decision increased sectional tension by
    a. giving credence to the belief in the North that a Slave Power conspiracy existed and was laboring to subvert northern liberties.
    b. seeming to indicate clearly that the issue of slavery could be determined in any territory long before the moment of statehood.
    c. strengthening the Democratic Party by unifying its northern and southern wings.
    d. none of the above

28. Abraham Lincoln's political hero, with whom he agreed about the Union, slavery, and race issues, was
    a. Stephen A. Douglas.
    b. Frederick Douglass.
    c. Henry Clay.
    d. Daniel Webster.

29. In the mid-1850s, Abraham Lincoln's search for a political home was based on his
    a. commitment to the abolition of slavery everywhere in the United States.
    b. belief that nothing short of an armed confrontation would settle the slavery issue in the country.
    c. desire to fight the *Dred Scott* decision.
    d. opposition to the extension of slavery in the United States.

30. While Abraham Lincoln espoused a typical racial attitude for a white man of his day, he personally believed that slavery
    a. would be acceptable with a few humane modifications.
    b. should be allowed to expand into the territories but be abolished where it already existed.
    c. was morally wrong.
    d. was a dangerously misunderstood institution by most Northerners.

31. Abraham Lincoln understood that humanitarian concern for black people would not motivate Northerners to fight to keep slavery out of the territories, so he promoted the "free soil" concept by asserting that the territories were
    a. places where whites could settle to escape blacks.
    b. excellent destinations for poor people seeking to improve their conditions.
    c. places where blacks could be sent as a way of opening up parts of the East for whites.
    d. excellent places for settlement by all Americans and that the government should give away the land.

32. In the mid-1850s, Abraham Lincoln typified
    a. the white northern male belief that although slavery was not morally wrong, it would eventually destroy national unity and thus should be eliminated.
    b. Republican ideology in asserting that only individual slave owners, and not Congress, could stop the spread of slavery.
    c. Republican ideology in believing that Congress must stop the spread of slavery and put it on the course to extinction.
    d. the legal profession, of which he was a part, in believing that the Supreme Court should end slavery.

33. When proslavery forces in Lecompton, Kansas, drafted a proslavery constitution in 1857 that many felt was fraudulent, Stephen A. Douglas
    a. stood solidly behind southern Democrats and President James Buchanan in supporting the document.
    b. demanded that the votes be recounted before he would take a stand on this issue.
    c. broke with the Buchanan administration and the southern members of his party by coming out against the proslavery constitution.
    d. refrained from making any public statements concerning the framework of the Kansas government.

34. In what became known as the "Freeport Doctrine," Stephen A. Douglas argued that
    a. Northerners need not worry about the effect of the *Dred Scott* decision on the future of slavery in the territories, as the decision would very likely be reversed in the near future.
    b. even though settlers could not at that time pass legislation barring slavery in the territories, they could ban slavery just as effectively by not passing the police laws necessary to protect slave property.
    c. the democratic foundations of the United States made it impossible for a Supreme Court decision to supercede the implementation of a concept such as popular sovereignty.
    d. halting the spread of an institution as economically valuable as slavery would cause dire financial consequences for the United States.

35. Seeking to demagogue the central issues of his debates, slavery and freedom, Stephen A. Douglas tried to depict Abraham Lincoln as
    a. an abolitionist and color-blind egalitarian who loved blacks.
    b. uninformed on some of the key issues pertinent to their debates.
    c. an avid supporter of the Fugitive Slave Act.
    d. pandering to public sentiment by insisting that slavery was wrong, something that Douglas claimed Lincoln did not really believe.

36. As a result of the Lincoln-Douglas debates,
    a. the Democrats shunned Stephen A. Douglas.
    b. Stephen A. Douglas scored a landslide victory against Abraham Lincoln and became a U.S. senator.
    c. Stephen A. Douglas won a senate seat, but Abraham Lincoln became well known.
    d. Abraham Lincoln scored a landslide victory against Stephen A. Douglas and became a U.S. senator.

37. When reflecting on John Brown's raid on the arsenal at Harpers Ferry, Virginia, most Northerners
    a. clearly thought him insane.
    b. applauded the actions of this intrepid foe of slavery.
    c. stated that they were sorry they had not contributed money to his cause.
    d. believed that Brown had acted lawlessly and with unwarranted violence.

38. Ultimately, John Brown's raid on Harpers Ferry, Virginia,
    a. influenced dozens of slave uprisings.
    b. left an increasing number of southern whites unable to distinguish between Northerners who merely opposed slavery and those who advocated violence to eradicate it.
    c. motivated the federal government to remove the arsenal from the community.
    d. caused southern congressmen to propose tighter restrictions on all Northerners wishing to enter the South.

39. "The only persons who do not have a revolver and a knife are those who have two revolvers" is a quote describing
    a. the environment in one of Stephen A. Douglas's favorite taverns.
    b. the state of affairs at a typical nineteenth-century track where horse racing took place.
    c. the environment of the U.S. Congress early in 1860 as congressmen struggled to elect a Speaker of the House.
    d. a popular local contest for woodsmen in Anderson, South Carolina, in the mid-nineteenth century.

40. Democrats meeting in Charleston, South Carolina, in 1860 to choose a presidential candidate wound up
    a. agreeing unanimously on Stephen A. Douglas.
    b. splitting the party into southern and northern wings over the issues of popular sovereignty and a federal code protecting slavery in the territories.
    c. selecting Jefferson Davis as their candidate.
    d. deadlocked over their choice for seventy-two ballots.

41. In the national crisis surrounding the presidential election of 1860, southern moderates refused to support the more radical members of the Democratic Party clamoring for a federal slave code. Instead, they
    a. joined Republicans in an effort to preserve the Union.
    b. attempted to revive the Whig Party.
    c. organized the Constitutional Union Party and put forth an extensive platform much different from anything offered by the Republicans and Democrats.
    d. organized the Constitutional Union Party, a political party that had no platform.

42. Abraham Lincoln became the Republican candidate for president in the election of 1860 because
    a. he supported high tariffs and a Pacific railroad and had begun denouncing the South for the sin of slavery.
    b. he was a moderate on the volatile issue of slavery, demonstrated solid Republican credentials, and represented the crucial state of Illinois.
    c. he threatened to lead his own party-splitting exodus if the party did not nominate him.
    d. fellow Republicans Edward Bates and Salmon Chase lobbied the nominating committee to select Lincoln.

43. Southerners felt such hostility toward the Republican Party during the presidential election of 1860 that they
    a. burned Lincoln in effigy in most major areas of the South.
    b. boycotted the polls in numerous states.
    c. refused to allow Lincoln's name to appear on the ballot in ten of the fifteen slave states.
    d. passed temporary laws allowing women to vote in the hope of defeating the Republicans.

44. Seeking to reduce the fear of many Southerners that the newly elected Abraham Lincoln and the Republican Party meant to tamper with slavery,
    a. Robert Tooms wrote, "The Republicans have pledged to respect our slave property and I know them as honorable men."
    b. Howell Cobb wrote, "Abraham Lincoln has given me his personal assurance that our most cherished institution is safe in the arms of a Republican administration."
    c. James Henry Hammond wrote, "Abraham Lincoln is no abolitionist, that I am certain of."
    d. Alexander Stephens wrote, "Revolutions are much easier started than controlled. I consider slavery much more secure in the Union than out of it."

45. After Lincoln won the presidential election of 1860, southern whites disagreed about
    a. whether the election of a Republican president made secession necessary.
    b. whether they should continue to defend and uphold the institution of slavery.
    c. the exact boundaries of the Mason-Dixon Line.
    d. whether they had a legitimate right to secede from the Union.

46. After Lincoln's election, the vote to secede from the Union was overwhelming only in
    a. Georgia and South Carolina.
    b. Florida and Mississippi.
    c. South Carolina.
    d. Texas.

47. The slave states of the Upper South were not as quick to secede from the Union after Lincoln's election because
    a. they generally believed that secession was an ill-considered idea.
    b. they had great difficulty in getting together a quorum of legislators to debate the issue.
    c. the U.S. army had already assembled on the north bank of the Potomac River as a persuasive deterrent to secession.
    d. they simply did not have as great a stake in slavery as the states in the Lower South had.

48. As the secession crisis loomed over the final weeks of the presidential administration of James Buchanan, his response was to
    a. call several special sessions of Congress to deal with the circumstances.
    b. deny the constitutionality of secession and then proceed to do nothing.
    c. spur the Supreme Court into action to get a ruling on secession before Lincoln took office.
    d. prod Congress to beef up the military in case there was a war.

49. Northerners were apprehensive about Abraham Lincoln as president mostly because
    a. he came into office as a minority president.
    b. he had almost no national political experience and the nation seemed ready to come unglued.
    c. he did not look very presidential.
    d. a huge faction of Congress had already met and threatened not to support Lincoln if he asked that troops be sent against the South.

50. In his first inaugural address, Abraham Lincoln was
    a. reassuring and conciliatory toward the South on the issue of slavery but firm and inflexible concerning the perpetuity of the Union.
    b. rather belligerent toward Southerners, threatening to unleash the army on them if any more states seceded from the Union.
    c. clearly uncomfortable with the principles he espoused regarding the Union.
    d. waiting until the last minute for word about the latest conditions in the South before he delivered his speech.

Terminology Matching   Select the word or phrase from the Terms section that best matches the definition or example provided in the Definitions section. Some terms may be used more than once; some may not be used at all.

TERMS

a. Bleeding Kansas

b. Constitutional Union Party

c. daguerreotype

d. fire-eaters

e. free soil

f. higher law

g. Know-Nothings

h. Lecompton constitution

i. Liberty Party

j. Mexican cession

k. popular sovereignty

l. Scott, Dred

m. secession winter

n. Shadrach

o. Taney, Roger B.

p. Whigs

q. Wilmot, David

r. Wilmot Proviso

DEFINITIONS

1. This fraudulently obtained proslavery document threatened to turn Kansas into a slave state in 1857. _____

2. He proposed legislation that would have prohibited the introduction of slavery into all territory gained from America's war with Mexico. _____

3. These secession-minded Southerners favored turning up the national political heat in order to secure their rights as slaveholders. _____

4. Spawned by anti-immigrant sentiment in the mid-1850s, the members of this new political party considered themselves the real Americans. _____

5. This likeness emanated from what some referred to as the "sunbeam art" and brought photography within the reach of almost all Americans by the 1840s and 1850s. _____

6. Apprehensive about whether the nation would come unhinged, Americans waited and watched during this period stretching from late 1860 into early 1861. _____

7. The brainchild of Lewis Cass of Michigan, this political concept held out every hope of being the all-purpose solution to the dilemma of slavery expansion in the United States. _____

8. In his opinion, the Missouri Compromise was unconstitutional, and so was citizenship for African Americans. _____

9. This notion, introduced by William Seward of New York, took the battle over slavery beyond the confines of constitutional interpretation by introducing a moral component. _____

10. Political party that was badly weakened by a fissure over slavery in the election of 1848. _____

11. The nickname of a territory where civil war broke out in 1856 between proslavery and antislavery forces. _____

12. What most Northerners desired in the territories so that they might continue to take advantage of the promise of America. _____

13. This 1848 territorial addition to the United States opened the controversy over slavery expansion in a new way. _____

14. Organized in the heat of the presidential election of 1860, this political party basically offered a non-platform advising Americans to calm down and obey the law. _____

15. The Supreme Court decision ruling on his plight proved to be one of the darkest moments in American history for African Americans. _____

Chronology   Place the events in chronological order.

SET ONE

A. Gadsden Purchase adds 30,000 square miles of territory in present-day Arizona and New Mexico.

B. *Uncle Tom's Cabin* is published in book form.

C. President Zachary Taylor dies.

D. Opponents of slavery found Free-Soil Party; Zachary Taylor elected president.

E. Wilmot Proviso proposes banning slavery from all land gained in Mexican War.

First _____

Second _____

Third _____

Fourth _____

Fifth _____

SET TWO

A. Armed conflict between proslavery and antislavery forces erupts in Kansas; Republicans run their first presidential candidate, John C. Frémont.

B. Representatives of seven slave states meet in Montgomery, Alabama, to form the Confederate States of America.

C. *Dred Scott* decision declares that African Americans are not citizens and that the Missouri Compromise is unconstitutional.

D. John Brown fails in his attempt to capture the federal arsenal at Harpers Ferry, Virginia.

E. Stephen A. Douglas debates Abraham Lincoln and wins Senate seat.

First _____

Second _____

Third _____

Fourth _____

Fifth _____

Short Answer   Write a paragraph in response to each question.

1. Why was John Brown's raid on Harpers Ferry, Virginia, so frightening to both Northerners and Southerners in America?

2. Explain the basic northern arguments for and southern arguments against the Wilmot Proviso.

3. Why were Southerners so angry with President Zachary Taylor concerning his position on the admission of California to the Union?

4. Explain the process by which Stephen A. Douglas engineered the passage of the Compromise of 1850 and what was contained in this collection of bills.

5. Explain the provisions of the 1850 Fugitive Slave Act and the reaction to it in both the North and the South.

6. Cite the key economic and political factors that motivated Stephen A. Douglas to propose the Kansas-Nebraska Act in the way he did.

7. Cite three reasons why Republican John C. Frémont's showing in the presidential election of 1856 worried Southerners.

8. Identify the chief factors that prompted Republicans to select Abraham Lincoln as their candidate for Illinois senator in 1860.

9. Explain why southern Democrats walked out of the Democratic nominating convention in Charleston in 1860. What did this example of the Lower South Democrats "voting with their feet" say about the nation's sectional party configuration?

10. In his first inaugural address, how did President Abraham Lincoln seek to assure Southerners that they had nothing to fear from a Republican administration?

Essay   Respond to each of the following questions in an essay of three to four paragraphs. Your responses should include specific evidence and your interpretation of the significance of historical events and concepts.

1. The Fugitive Slave Act of 1850 potentially affected all African Americans. Compare and contrast its potential effects on both fugitive slaves and northern African Americans who had always been free. Also compare and contrast the reactions to the act in the North and the South.

2. How did the development of the daguerreotype allow an exciting new technology to reach the masses? How did this photographic process become politicized in the hands of Matthew Brady?

3. Explain how America's political parties realigned between the late 1840s and mid-1850s. What were the most important issues behind this realignment?

4. Although morally opposed to slavery, Abraham Lincoln held the same opinion of African Americans as most white Americans did in the 1850s. Discuss how Lincoln was able to separate his personal feelings about African Americans from his convictions about slavery. Was he disingenuous, politically astute, or something else?

Map Questions   Answer the questions below using Map 13.2, The Compromise of 1850 (p. 457).

READING THE MAP

1. Where was the slave trade ended as a result of the Compromise of 1850?

2. What area did the Compromise of 1850 leave open to slavery based on the principle of popular sovereignty?

CONNECTIONS   Which section of the country, the North or the South, fared better by way of the Compromise of 1850? Why?

THE CRUCIBLE OF WAR
1861–1865

14

Multiple Choice   Choose the letter of the best answer.

1. The title of chapter 14, "The Crucible of War, 1861–1865," is meant to suggest that the American Civil War was a
   a. contest in which the outcome was preordained.
   b. severe test for Americans and the Union.
   c. conflagration that represented the "melting pot" that was the United States.
   d. conflict in which both sides felt intense heat.

2. On March 4, 1861, President Abraham Lincoln delivered an inaugural address in which he revealed his strategy to avoid disunion; that strategy was to
   a. send the Union army to South Carolina because it was the first state to secede.
   b. dispatch special emissaries to the slave states believed most likely to secede to threaten harsh government action should those states proceed.
   c. take measures to stop the contagion of secession and buy time in order for emotions to cool.
   d. send to all slave states specially annotated copies of the Constitution clearly pointing out why secession was illegal.

3. In 1861, armed hostilities between the North and South began officially with
   a. Confederates firing on the frigate *Star of the West* as it attempted to reprovision Fort Moultrie in Charleston harbor in January 1861.
   b. an assault on Washington, D.C., in February 1861 by a ragtag group of Confederate sympathizers from Maryland.
   c. the assault on federal troops passing through Baltimore, Maryland, early in 1861.
   d. Confederates firing on Fort Sumter in Charleston harbor in April 1861.

4. States in the Upper South that were undecided about secession but then decided to exit the Union did so after
   a. President Lincoln called for 75,000 troops to put down the rebellion that began when the Confederates took Fort Sumter.
   b. a special delegation from the deep South toured the upper tier of slave states and convinced the leaders of those states to secede.
   c. minor slave revolts began breaking out, clearly threatening the region's institution of slavery.
   d. the new Confederate government offered those states special tax advantages if they would join the other slave states seeking independence from the government in Washington, D.C.

5. The border states of Missouri, Kentucky, Maryland, and Delaware did not secede from the Union; in these areas
   a. they called the war a "brother's war," because family members were always united in fighting on the same side.
   b. popular sentiment was not unanimously pro-Union.
   c. the decision to go with the Union was unanimous because slaves were such a small part of the population.
   d. the citizens threatened to split off and create their own separate nation.

6. While southern leaders issued somewhat duplicitous statements concerning why they thought it necessary to battle the United States, white Southerners from all classes enlisted to fight Yankees
   a. because they believed the federal government and northern manufacturers were conspiring to raise their taxes and dump cheap manufactured goods on them.
   b. for the sense of adventure they found in proving that a southern farm boy could whip an untold number of Abe Lincoln's hirelings.
   c. to preserve a southern civilization based on slavery and to ensure that African Americans remained subordinate to whites in the region.
   d. all of the above

7. Typically, Northerners viewed secession as
   a. an attack on the best government on earth and a severe challenge to the rule of law.
   b. constitutionally viable but impractical.
   c. too expensive and therefore illegal.
   d. a concept they wished they had thought of first.

8. Southerners believed they had a real chance of winning the Civil War based on
   a. the righteousness of their cause and the character of the southern people.
   b. their belief that southern men were physically tougher than northern men.
   c. their belief that withholding cotton would wreck the northern economy and force England or France to enter the war on the side of the Confederacy.
   d. all of the above

9. When considering the wartime leadership offered by Abraham Lincoln and Jefferson Davis, a central irony emerges in that
   a. neither man was very committed to the efforts he embarked on.
   b. Jefferson Davis made grandiose public statements about what the Confederate States of America might be able to accomplish but privately believed that the South never had a chance.
   c. Abraham Lincoln brought little political experience to his presidency yet rose to the occasion to become a masterful leader, while Jefferson Davis, a seasoned politician, proved to be a relatively ineffectual chief executive.
   d. Lincoln successfully shepherded the nation through an awful war and yet struggled with his own misgivings about America's form of republicanism.

10. The first battle at Manassas (or Bull Run) in July 1861 is significant because it
    a. disheartened Northerners to the extent that men stopped volunteering for the Union army.
    b. demonstrated that Americans were in for a real war, one that would be neither quick nor easy.
    c. was a bloodbath in which thousands of men died.
    d. had an instantly sobering effect on Southerners, who realized they would have to beef up their troops to have a chance at winning the war.

11. When President Lincoln remarked early in the Civil War, "If General McClellan does not want to use the army I would like to *borrow* it," he was expressing
    a. his frustration that McClellan had amassed and trained a huge military force but refused to use it to attack the Confederates.
    b. his confusion regarding McClellan's frequent requests to be reassigned.
    c. his frustration at McClellan's refusal to drill the troops before ten o'clock in the morning.
    d. his desire to have a military command of his own.

12. At the end of 1862, the eastern theater of the Civil War
    a. made it obvious that the rebellion was nearly over.
    b. had been a great success for the Union because the same northern generals stayed on for the duration, getting wiser with each battle.
    c. had seen one Union victory after another.
    d. had reached a stalemate.

13. In the Civil War, military success in the West centered on controlling
    a. the Ozark mountain region.
    b. the region's railroad network.
    c. the Mississippi, Tennessee, and Cumberland rivers.
    d. the region's farmlands and food production.

14. After the battle at Shiloh Church, Tennessee, in April 1862, General Ulysses S. Grant
    a. "believed the war would ruin the nation forever."
    b. "gave up all idea of saving the Union except by complete conquest."
    c. "seriously questioned the war aims of the Lincoln administration."
    d. "believed that God had made it clear which side He supported in the conflict."

15. Initially the Confederacy banked heavily on King Cotton diplomacy, a strategy based on the belief that
    a. cotton-starved western European powers would be forced to enter the conflict by offering diplomatic recognition to the Confederacy and breaking the Union blockade to secure cotton.
    b. raising the price of cotton in the North would give the South more economic leverage to negotiate a peaceful settlement of the dispute.
    c. reducing the price of the cotton the Confederacy sold to England and France would allow those nations to loan the South more money to fight the war.
    d. the North would look more favorably upon the South's bid for independence if cotton planters grew less cotton and released their surplus slaves.

16. When the Civil War broke out, President Lincoln chose not to make the conflict a struggle over slavery because
    a. he believed slavery to be a relatively insignificant issue.
    b. he doubted his right under the Constitution to tamper with the "domestic institutions" of any state, even those in rebellion.
    c. he was not completely confident that destroying slavery was the best thing for African Americans.
    d. he thought that eradicating slavery would unleash millions of angry, violent freedmen on the white South.

17. In March 1862, Congress edged closer to emancipating slaves when it
    a. forbade the practice of returning fugitive slaves to their masters.
    b. labeled all slaves coming within Union military lines as contraband of war.
    c. presented emancipation legislation only to see it defeated by Democrats.
    d. declared all children born of slave parents free.

18. As President Lincoln wavered in his policy of noninterference with slavery, he considered the biggest obstacle to the acceptance of emancipation in the Union to be
    a. the difficulty of finding a suitable place to send the freed slaves.
    b. public concern about the constitutionality of emancipation.
    c. the fears of Northerners that freed slaves would cause overcrowding in schools.
    d. the fears of Northerners that freed slaves, whom they considered "semi-savages," would flood the North, compete for jobs, and try to mix socially with them.

19. On July 17, 1862, Congress adopted a second Confiscation Act, legislation that
    a. declared all slaves everywhere "forever free of their servitude."
    b. made it legal to use slaves as Union army laborers only as long the federal troops were stationed in the slaves' immediate neighborhood.
    c. declared all slaves of rebel masters "forever free of their servitude."
    d. authorized federal soldiers to take any property belonging to any person who openly rebelled against the United States.

20. Abraham Lincoln wrote the Emancipation Proclamation
    a. because he considered emancipation to be "essential to the preservation of the Union."
    b. as a personal moral statement regarding why slaves should be free.
    c. as a response to the constant lobbying of abolitionists pressing him to free the slaves.
    d. as a way to appease the entire Northern population and their cries for freedom for all slaves.

21. To most African Americans, the Civil War was
    a. a struggle for political power between whites in the North and the South.
    b. a military struggle that they wanted to avoid being a part of.
    c. an attempt to save the Union.
    d. a struggle to overthrow slavery and gain racial equality for blacks.

22. From the beginning, the Confederacy faced formidable odds in pursuing its bid for independence; one of the first problems it overcame was
    a. building a powerful army from scratch.
    b. devising a way to finance the war.
    c. creating adequate manufacturing resources to supply war materiel.
    d. overcoming resistance in the disputed border states.

23. The Confederacy's efforts to centralize its government and production facilities encountered resistance because of
    a. the general unwillingness of white Southerners to support the war effort after 1863.
    b. the South's traditional values of states' rights and unrestrained individualism.
    c. the conviction on the part of numerous slaveholders that the Davis government meant to confiscate some of their slaves and sell them to Latin American nations for money to continue the war.
    d. frequent riots by soldiers, who were paid inadequately or not at all.

24. During the Civil War, the "twenty-Negro law" enraged many white Southerners because it
    a. exempted from military service one white man on every plantation with twenty or more slaves.
    b. paid slaveholders scarce government funds for every twenty slaves they owned or supervised.
    c. meant that every slaveholder with at least forty slaves had to turn over twenty of them for use by the Confederate government.
    d. targeted for military service every slaveholder with at least twenty slaves.

25. Throughout the Civil War the Richmond government tried to promote southern unity and nationalism; politicians were aided in this attempt by
    a. yeomen, who understood that they needed to continue to ally themselves with the planters to move up in society.
    b. slaves, who believed that once the war was over they would have a place as free people in the Confederacy.
    c. clergymen, who stated that God had blessed slavery and the new nation.
    d. the lack of Unionists in the entire South.

26. Aside from leading to the legal destruction of slavery, the Civil War itself helped destroy slavery in practice
    a. because thousands of weary and disgusted slaveholders freed their slaves.
    b. by disrupting the routine, organization, and discipline necessary to keep slavery intact.
    c. because most male slaves joined the Union army.
    d. as slave owners increasingly realized the advantages of free labor and began paying their slaves for their labor, though without actually freeing them.

27. White Southerners' greatest fear regarding their slaves during the Civil War was that they would
    a. refuse to work.
    b. run away.
    c. steal even more property than they had stolen before the conflict broke out.
    d. engage in violent revolt.

28. Slaves increasingly used the chaos and turmoil of the Civil War to whittle away at their bondage by
    a. overtly attacking their masters when they had the chance.
    b. banding together to sabotage the efforts of the Confederate army.
    c. indiscriminately poisoning white Southerners.
    d. employing various means to undermine white mastery and expand control over their own lives.

29. Before the federal government could marshal the men, money, and materials necessary to wage an effective war against the Confederacy, it first had to
    a. expand its role in American life, which meant moving beyond the Democratic policies that had for two decades restricted government direction of the economy.
    b. roll back its influence in American life in order to entice more Americans to support its policies.
    c. hold the line on inflation, as voluntary contributions of money were initially an important source of revenue to finance the war.
    d. rid itself of numerous conservative Republicans holding back important measures in Congress.

30. In the early 1860s, the Republicans generated the economic power they needed to fight a successful war
    a. by creating a special class of government bonds which paid investors an attractive rate of interest.
    b. by revolutionizing U.S. banking, monetary, and tax structures.
    c. by creating a new class of banknotes in an effort to get as much money in circulation as possible.
    d. only because they were able to get the cooperation of the Democrats.

31. While the North's industrial production boomed during the Civil War, the working class there found that
    a. they, too, enjoyed unprecedented prosperity.
    b. because their labor was sorely needed, they were able to control the workplace as never before.
    c. inflation and taxes cut so deeply into their wages that their standard of living actually fell.
    d. they could expect quick promotions as well as fatter pay envelopes.

32. Strikes by workers in northern industries calculated to improve wages during the Civil War
    a. often proved remarkably successful.
    b. drastically undermined the patriotism of most workers.
    c. were more effective for women than for men.
    d. rarely succeeded.

33. Thousands of northern and southern women offered their services as nurses during the Civil War; however,
    a. nursing required a high level of medical training, and few women were able to achieve the necessary education.
    b. they bucked tradition in doing so, as women were thought too delicate to deal with sickness and disease on an institutional scale.
    c. the relatively high rate of pay caused males to dominate the field and women were generally refused the chance to participate.
    d. teaching paid much better, so most women in the cash economy stuck with instructing students.

34. Dorothea Dix and Clara Barton are known for their Civil War efforts as
    a. prison camp reformers.
    b. strike leaders in northern industries.
    c. nurses on the battlefield and behind the lines.
    d. surgeons specializing in battlefield amputations.

35. One of the more acute political problems faced by the Confederate States of America was
    a. the lack of well-defined political parties as vehicles for political dialogue and problem solving.
    b. Jefferson Davis's insistence that the Confederate Congress close down because it was not enacting very worthwhile legislation.
    c. the continuing occurrence of vote fraud in most elections.
    d. that Jefferson Davis had so many men resign cabinet positions, which made the formulation of cohesive policies in many areas practically impossible.

36. President Lincoln clashed with northern Democrats over the thorny issue of civil liberties basically because Lincoln believed that
    a. what the government needed to do to ensure the loyalty of northern civilians was resurrect the Alien and Sedition Acts.
    b. the Constitution should be completely suspended until the South was defeated.
    c. free speech tended to be subversive even during peacetime.
    d. the war required a loose interpretation of the Constitution.

37. The former Democratic congressman Clement L. Vallandigham was arrested for treason in 1863 because he
    a. frequently appeared in Richmond to urge Jefferson Davis to change his war strategy.
    b. fomented factory workers engaged in the war effort to strike for higher and more equitable wages and better working conditions since they were aiding their country.
    c. had vigorously criticized the war and President Lincoln's conduct of the war.
    d. had attempted to assassinate President Lincoln.

38. What poor northern men found especially galling about the new draft law of 1863 was that
    a. it allowed a draftee to hire a substitute or pay a $300 fee to avoid conscription.
    b. enlistments for those drafted into the army were twice as long as those for men who volunteered their services.
    c. they had to provide much of their own equipment.
    d. they fell under a special "hostility" clause and were paid less than so-called patriotic men who volunteered.

39. In New York City in the summer of 1863, an Irish-led riot that took the lives of at least 105 people erupted in protest of
    a. the prejudices the immigrant workers faced as they tried to move up the ladder in the booming industrial sector.
    b. the newly enacted draft law, which was inequitable and would force draftees to fight to free black slaves.
    c. inadequate living conditions and high rents, as well as their landlords' failure to restrict their rentals to white tenants.
    d. the plight of the poor and the dangerous working conditions faced by immigrants.

40. The Battle of Vicksburg in July 1863
    a. was an astounding Confederate victory that gave Union commanders pause concerning whether they could actually win the war.
    b. produced a stalemate after horrendous casualties.
    c. was an important Union victory that opened up a large portion of the Mississippi River.
    d. was a Confederate victory that not only upset Union commanders but also rid the lower Mississippi Valley of the federal army.

41. In strict military terms, the Battle of Gettysburg in the summer of 1863
    a. was a crucial turning point for Confederate armies, as it proved to be the last time Confederates launched a major offensive above the Mason-Dixon line.
    b. proved to be a catastrophe for the South in that so much of Robert E. Lee's Army of Northern Virginia was destroyed that it no longer functioned as an effective fighting force.
    c. stimulated an important council of war among major Union generals, who concluded that the North would be better off suing for peace to save the lives of their soldiers.
    d. became an important experiment in which the South got to field-test several new secret weapons.

42. After his victory at Chattanooga, Tennessee, in 1864, General Ulysses S. Grant
    a. asked President Lincoln for a ninety-day furlough to allow for his severe depression and alcoholism to heal.
    b. launched a massive military campaign that would take his troops on a sweep through Virginia toward Richmond and get thousands of them killed in the process.
    c. went back to the western theater of the war to conquer a new rebel threat that had sprung up there.
    d. attempted to end his military service, but President Lincoln talked him out of resigning.

43. In 1864, when General William T. Sherman stated that he intended to "make Georgia howl," he was gearing up for
    a. a military campaign in which his sole purpose was to recruit black men for the Union army.
    b. a military campaign in which he planned to have the men under his command take Georgians' cotton and sell it to England to help finance the northern war effort.
    c. the nation's first military campaign in which biological warfare would be used.
    d. a scorched-earth military campaign aimed at destroying the will of the southern people.

44. Of the 633,000 soldiers who died during the Civil War, most succumbed to
    a. wounds sustained in battle.
    b. diseases such as dysentery, typhoid, pneumonia, and malaria.
    c. infections resulting from amputations.
    d. an amazing number of accidents.

45. President Lincoln's determination to hold elections in 1864 is particularly noteworthy because
    a. with the Union war effort stalled and many Northerners basically weary of much of what the war had heaped on them, the Democrats had an excellent chance of ousting the Lincoln administration.
    b. much of the North's electoral process had shut down and would have to be revived in order to hold elections.
    c. most Union soldiers were so angry that Lincoln had allowed the war to drag on for so long that they were threatening to support the Democratic ticket.
    d. most members of the Republican Party had vowed to oppose his nomination in 1864.

46. In choosing Tennesseean Andrew Johnson as his running mate in the presidential election of 1864, Abraham Lincoln
    a. was demonstrating his desperation at the end of the war: he could find no one else interested in sharing the ticket with him.
    b. picked a Southerner loyal to the Union to demonstrate that Lincoln's party was broad enough to include any uncompromising Unionist.
    c. was taking a huge chance, as Johnson was a political novice with no experience in elected office.
    d. was removing from the battlefield one of the North's most successful generals.

47. Truly desperate to forestall defeat, the Confederacy enacted legislation in March 1865 that
    a. conscripted boys as young as twelve.
    b. authorized suicidal military missions directed at Washington, D.C.
    c. authorized the government to forge an alliance with Mexico in order to defeat the Yankees.
    d. authorized the arming of slaves as Confederate soldiers.

48. General Robert E. Lee's surrender to General Ulysses S. Grant near Appomattox Court House in Virginia on April 9, 1865,
    a. ended the Confederate war effort, as there were no more rebel troops left to fight.
    b. ended the Confederate war effort not because the South was out of troops, but because Lee's surrender demoralized the armies remaining in the field.
    c. was actually a ploy to distract Grant so that other Confederate armies could continue the struggle.
    d. was the signal for southern civilians to launch a guerrilla war.

49. When the Civil War ended, President Lincoln was confident that
    a. the transition to a peaceful nation would be simple compared with the many problems encountered because of the war.
    b. his role in bringing the conflict to a successful conclusion would guarantee him the office of president as long as he wanted it.
    c. his postwar burdens would weigh almost as heavily as those of wartime.
    d. Democrats would eagerly support Republican policies.

50. The Civil War affected the United States by
    a. establishing the sovereignty of the federal government and the dominance of industrial capitalism.
    b. slowing down business activity in both the North and the South.
    c. assuring the equality of all Americans.
    d. greatly weakening national loyalty in the North.

Terminology Matching   Select the word or phrase from the Terms section that best matches the definition or example provided in the Definitions section. Some terms may be used more than once; some may not be used at all.

TERMS

a. Andersonville, Georgia

b. Antietam Creek

c. Beauregard, P. G. T.

d. "contraband of war"

e. Emancipation Proclamation

f. *Ex parte Milligan*

g. Gorgas, Josiah

h. Grant, Ulysses S.

i. Homestead Act

j. ironclad warship

k. McClellan, George B.

l. Morrill Act

m. *Our American Cousin*

n. Shiloh Church

o. substitute

p. *Trent*

q. Union naval blockade

r. writ of habeas corpus

DEFINITIONS

1. Little did Abraham Lincoln know as he sat watching this production that it would be the last one he would ever see. _____

2. If you were drafted into the Union army and had some money put away, you could hire one of these and stay home. _____

3. The battle waged here turned out to be the bloodiest day of the Civil War. _____

4. President Lincoln's suspension of this landed more than a few Northerners in jail because they were thought to be participating in activities subversive of the U.S. war effort. _____

5. President Lincoln reacted to criticism of this military commander by commenting, "I can't spare this man. He fights." _____

6. This general gave the command to fire on Fort Sumter, South Carolina, and in the process started the Civil War. _____

7. When a Union warship stopped this ship, it almost involved the United States in a war with England right in the middle of fighting the Confederate States of America. _____

8. Anything but a sentimental statement about the South's institution of slavery, Abraham Lincoln wrote this out of pure military necessity. _____

9. While this decision came a little too late to help those whose constitutional rights were violated by the U.S. government's efforts to defeat the Confederacy, it ensured that civilians would be tried by civilian courts as long as such courts were in operation. _____

10. Hailed as something of a miracle worker by Southerners, his efforts as head of the Confederacy's Ordnance Bureau put the South's war effort on a much more solid footing than many thought possible. _____

11. Passed in 1862 after the departure from Congress of recalcitrant Democrats, this legislation guaranteed land to farmers heading west if they would simply live on it and improve it. _____

12. This new maritime design was used by both the Union and Confederate navies in the Civil War. _____

13. General Benjamin Butler used this term to refer to slaves who escaped to Union lines in 1862. _____

14. The U.S. government authorized this protective measure early in the Civil War to make sure that the Confederacy could not play the cotton card to secure any foreign aid in its bid for independence. _____

15. Irked because this general was reluctant to employ his gargantuan army against the Confederates, President Lincoln diagnosed him with "the slows." _____

Chronology   Place the events in chronological order.

SET ONE

A. Confederate Congress passes first draft law in American history.

B. General George McClellan's forces are defeated during peninsula campaign in Virginia.

C. Ulysses S. Grant is appointed general in chief of all Union armies.

D. Confederate forces bombard Fort Sumter, South Carolina, thus beginning the Civil War.

E. President Lincoln is shot by John Wilkes Booth at Ford's Theatre in Washington, D.C., and dies the next day.

First _____

Second _____

Third _____

Fourth _____

Fifth _____

SET TWO

A. Emancipation Proclamation frees slaves in areas still in rebellion against the United States.

B. Battle of Gettysburg results in a Confederate defeat and General Lee's last offensive into the North.

C. Lee surrenders to Grant at Appomattox Court House, Virginia, essentially ending Confederate resistance.

D. Atlanta falls to Union forces under General William T. Sherman.

E. General Grant's forces engage Confederates in Virginia in the bloodiest fighting of the war, from the Wilderness to the beginnings of the siege of Petersburg.

First _____

Second _____

Third _____

Fourth _____

Fifth _____

Short Answer   Write a paragraph in response to each question.

1. Describe Abraham Lincoln's basic approach to the secession crisis when he became president on March 4, 1861.

2. Explain why nonslaveholding white Southerners were willing to risk their lives fighting in the Civil War.

3. Identify at least four key reasons why Southerners believed they could win the Civil War.

4. Describe General U. S. Grant's somewhat unorthodox — at least for his day — approach to defeating the Confederates.

5. Outline the fundamental northern Democratic argument for not turning the Civil War into a war for black liberation.

6. How did the participation of black men in the U.S. army during the Civil War speed up the destruction of slavery?

7. What role did slaves play in destroying slavery during the Civil War?

8. Identify three areas in which northern women contributed to the Union war effort.

9. What can the New York draft riots of 1863 tell us about the reaction of some Northerners to the new direction of the war by that period?

10. Cite three common causes of death among Civil War soldiers.

Essay   Respond to each of the following questions in an essay of three to four paragraphs. Your responses should include specific evidence and your interpretation of the significance of historical events and concepts.

1. In many respects, Americans in the North and South believed that they were fighting a war to uphold identical principles. What were those principles, and how did they allow people from both sections of the nation to view themselves as true "Americans"?

2. Leaders in the Confederate States of America believed they could employ King Cotton diplomacy to enlist the aid of powerful European nations in their struggle for independence. Why were Southerners so confident that this strategy would work? What had they failed to understand about the world situation? Why do you think England was more interested in staying out of a war with the United States than in aiding the Confederacy?

3. Compare and contrast Abraham Lincoln and Jefferson Davis as wartime leaders. Did their backgrounds and experience prepare them for the tasks they assumed? Whose leadership was more surprising? Why?

4. Almost as soon as the Confederacy came into existence its government began compromising most of what southerners had removed themselves from the Union to preserve. How were states' rights, individual freedom, and the institution of slavery weakened by the Confederate government's exertions to win the war?

Map Questions   Answer the questions below using Map 14.1, Secession, 1860–1861 (p. 496).

READING THE MAP

1. Which seven states left the Union in the first wave of secession? Which four left in the second wave of succession?

2. Which slave states did not secede from the Union?

3. What state seceded first? Which seceded last?

CONNECTIONS

1. What was President Lincoln's logic in not allowing Maryland to secede from the Union?

2. Why did leaders in Delaware show little interest in seceding from the Union?

3. Which slave states were the most difficult for the U.S. navy to blockade during the Civil War? Why was this so?

RECONSTRUCTION

1863–1877

Multiple Choice   Choose the letter of the best answer.

1. In the view of the majority of southern ex-slaveholders, emancipation meant that
   a. they would be free of the burden of caring for blacks.
   b. the economy of the South would collapse, and southern society would be thrown into chaos.
   c. they would need to change from an agricultural economy to a commercial economy.
   d. the freedmen should move out of the South.

2. When Union General Carl Schurz undertook a fact-finding mission to the ex-Confederate states in the summer of 1865, he determined that newly freed blacks would need
   a. federal protection, land of their own, and voting rights.
   b. jobs, access to an unbiased judicial system, and voting rights.
   c. military protection, employment contracts, and social equality.
   d. economic, social, and political equality.

3. The Union victory in the Civil War resolved the issues of
   a. slavery and secession but left unresolved the issues of compensation for ex-slaveholders and the conversion of Confederate currency to legal U.S. currency.
   b. slavery and secession but left undetermined the standing of the defeated ex-Confederate states within the Union and the place of freedmen in American society.
   c. citizenship and freedom for ex-slaves but left unresolved the issues of secession and states' rights.
   d. slavery and secession but left unresolved the issue of presidential and congressional term limits.

4. In attempting to establish a reconstruction policy after the Civil War,
   a. Lincoln's primary goal was to extend full political rights to ex-slaves.
   b. Lincoln rejected the "10 percent plan."
   c. Congress and the president disagreed about who had authority to devise a plan of reconstruction.
   d. Congress wanted to ensure the return to power of the former southern ruling class.

5. Pardons granted to rebels under the terms of Lincoln's Proclamation of Amnesty and Reconstruction were important in that they
   a. permitted the rebels to return home with limited currency.
   b. restored property (except slaves) and political participation.
   c. kept ex-Confederate leaders from returning to political power.
   d. granted voting rights and forgave debt incurred during the war.

6. Congress hoped Lincoln would not veto the Wade-Davis Bill because legislators desired to
   a. guarantee freedmen equal protection before the law.
   b. confiscate the property of ex-Confederates.
   c. punish ex-Confederates by refusing to convert the useless Confederate currency into U.S. dollars.
   d. grant forty acres and a mule to every ex-slave who was the head of a household.

7. The army's system of "compulsory free labor" in the South during and after the Civil War differed from the slave labor system in that
   a. wages were to be paid, and employers were prohibited from using physical punishment, though the army could discipline blacks who refused to work.
   b. wages were to be paid, and rudimentary workers' unions were set up to protect the rights of ex-slaves.
   c. wages were to be paid, and physical punishment by anyone was strictly prohibited.
   d. wages were to be paid, and only the local sheriff could physically punish a worker.

8. Ex-slaves believed that ownership of land
   a. meant social equality with white landowners.
   b. would give them income equity with white workers.
   c. was a moral right and was linked to black freedom.
   d. would mean economic and social equality.

9. "Sherman land" and the establishment of the Bureau of Refugees, Freedmen, and Abandoned Lands
   a. satisfied a majority of ex-slaves and encouraged them to form the Southern Republican Party.
   b. showed the freedmen that they would have to work for their land.
   c. lent validity to the ex-slaves' expectation of landownership and their sense of a "moral right" to that land.
   d. established a clear congressional policy regarding the importance of private ownership of property for the ex-slave.

10. Some ex-slaves who had formerly worshiped in biracial Methodist churches joined the African Methodist Episcopal Church, an all-black church from the North, because
   a. ex-slaves disagreed with the major theological teachings of the Methodist Church.
   b. ex-slaves desired religious autonomy and escape from white oversight.
   c. the Methodist Church rejected the newly freed black person.
   d. the African Methodist Episcopal Church denied entrance to whites.

11. Who might have opposed President Andrew Johnson's reconstruction plan because they felt that he "acted as midwife to the rebirth of the Old South"?
   a. Democratic legislators
   b. southern newspapers
   c. Republican legislators
   d. southern planters

12. Reformers were shocked by President Andrew Johnson's quick reconstruction of ex-Confederate states because
    a. Johnson's lenient terms for the reconstruction belied his earlier states' rights stance.
    b. his reconstruction plan seemed to contradict his earlier statements of willingness to destroy the southern planter aristocrats.
    c. his harsh terms for reconstruction belied his earlier statements of leniency.
    d. his civil rights legislation failed to follow through on his promise to grant the freedmen voting rights.

13. Abraham Lincoln's and Andrew Johnson's reconstruction plans shared the following points of emphasis:
    a. reconciliation, rapid restoration of civil government in the South, full amnesty to ex-rebels, and ratification of the Thirteenth Amendment.
    b. rapid restoration of civil government in the South, reconciliation, and limited black voting.
    c. rapid restoration of civil government in the South, reconciliation, confiscation of rebel property, and full amnesty to ex-Confederates.
    d. reconciliation, rapid restoration of civil government in the South, pardons for most ex-rebels, and ratification of the Thirteenth Amendment.

14. Andrew Johnson had crossed over from the Democratic Party to the Republican Party before becoming president, but he seemed to be more of a Democrat than a Republican as president because of
    a. his advocacy of states' rights and of limitations on federal power, especially in the economic realm.
    b. his veto of the Wade-Davis bill and his position on federal subsidies.
    c. his racism toward non-whites and his unwillingness to support any aspect of Lincoln's reconstruction plans.
    d. his vetoes of civil rights legislation and his attempt to empower the Freedmen's Bureau.

15. After President Andrew Johnson did not stand up to Mississippi's rejection of the legislation that outlawed slavery or to South Carolina's refusal to renounce secession,
    a. southern states saw their opportunity to shape Reconstruction, and southern resistance was rekindled.
    b. he decisively intervened against newly enacted "black codes."
    c. he refused to pardon planters and Confederate officials.
    d. the other southern states backed down on states' rights issues.

16. During the Reconstruction era, the southern black codes
    a. guaranteed freedmen full political and civil rights.
    b. re-established slavery.
    c. desegregated southern society.
    d. restricted freedmen's economic opportunities and civil rights.

17. The black codes were essentially an attempt to
    a. subordinate blacks to whites and regulate the labor supply.
    b. extend rights, although limited, to the freedmen.
    c. extend to blacks the same rights that whites enjoyed.
    d. provide economic equality but restrict social and political equality.

18. The U. S. congressional elections of 1865, combined with the black codes and with President Andrew Johnson's vetoes of key civil rights legislation,
    a. strengthened the South's position in its attempt to shape reconstruction policies.
    b. forged unity among moderate Democrats and moderate Republicans.
    c. forged unity among moderates and the Radicals within the Republican Party.
    d. forced President Johnson to denounce the legality of the new southern state constitutions.

19. In 1865, moderate Republicans and Republican Radicals differed in that
    a. moderates championed black equality, while Radicals sought limited rights for the black American.
    b. moderates supported states' rights and limited federal involvement in the economy, while Radicals sought expanded federal powers.
    c. moderates supported Andrew Johnson's reconstruction plan, while Radicals wanted to write their own.
    d. moderates did not actively support black voting rights and distribution of confiscated lands to the freedmen, while Radicals did.

20. The Civil Rights Act of 1866
    a. required the end of legal discrimination in state laws.
    b. declared martial law in the South.
    c. expanded a state's ability to write its own civil rights laws.
    d. prolonged the life of the Freedmen's Bureau and extended its jurisdiction over civil rights cases.

21. How did the Fourteenth Amendment deal with voting rights for blacks?
    a. The amendment explicitly granted all adult blacks the right to vote.
    b. The amendment gave Congress the right to reduce a state's representation in Congress if the state refused to give all of its adult male population, including ex-slaves, the right to vote.
    c. The amendment granted the vote to black males in all states.
    d. The amendment created a five-year phasing-in period during which blacks would gradually gain rights, culminating in the right to vote.

22. The factors that led to the inclusion of a guarantee of black suffrage in the Military Reconstruction Act of 1867 were
    a. the impeachment of Andrew Johnson and the disunity of the Republican Party.
    b. Johnson's open hostility to expanding civil rights for blacks, the sheer persistence of the Republican Radicals to structure a "moral" reform, and continuous pressure from African Americans.
    c. the Fourteenth Amendment and the failure of martial law in the South.
    d. Johnson's final acceptance of the Fourteenth Amendment and the pressure he put on southern states to ratify this amendment.

23. The one provision in the Reconstruction Acts of 1867 that could be said to have initiated "radical reconstruction" is
    a. the imposition of martial law.
    b. the confiscation of lands.
    c. the freeing of all slaves.
    d. black suffrage.

24. The impeachment trial of President Andrew Johnson
    a. found Johnson guilty of violation of the Tenure of Office Act.
    b. found Johnson guilty of misuse and abuse of constitutional powers.
    c. effectively ended Johnson's interference in reconstruction.
    d. found Johnson innocent of the misuse and abuse of constitutional powers.

25. The Fifteenth Amendment
    a. defined citizenship.
    b. prohibited state laws from infringing upon the civil rights of citizens.
    c. extended black male suffrage to the entire nation.
    d. outlawed slavery.

26. The constitutional amendment that prohibited states from depriving citizens of the right to vote on the basis of their "race, color, or previous condition of servitude"
    a. effectively restructured political power in the South until 1900.
    b. was undermined by literacy and property qualifications in Southern states.
    c. failed to deal adequately with the grandfather clauses imposed by southern states.
    d. made the United States the first nation with universal adult suffrage.

27. The Republican Party in the South in the late 1800s was made up of
    a. freedmen, "carpetbaggers," and small farmers.
    b. freedmen, landlords, and owners of small businesses.
    c. freedmen, "carpetbaggers," and ex-Confederates who had been pardoned.
    d. freedmen, "scalawags," and immigrants.

28. The Ku Klux Klan developed into a paramilitary organization, but it began as
    a. a social club for Confederate veterans who wanted to destroy southern Radicals.
    b. a fraternity at the University of Tennessee that wanted to intimidate blacks.
    c. an elitist order of the Sons of the South that wanted to destroy the Republican Party by lynching blacks.
    d. a social club for Confederate veterans who wanted to defeat Reconstruction and restore white supremacy.

29. The new southern state constitutions required by the Reconstruction Acts introduced
    a. universal male suffrage, prison reform, state responsibility for the care of orphans and the insane, and mandatory education.
    b. universal male suffrage, debtor relief for home mortgages, prison reforms, abolition of the property qualification for holding an elected office, and state responsibility for the care of orphans and the insane.
    c. black male suffrage, prison reforms, land redistribution, and mandatory education.
    d. black male suffrage, asylums for the insane, orphanages, mandatory education, and redistribution of property.

30. The southern Democrats claimed that the local and state governments created because of the Reconstruction Acts were under "Negro domination"; this claim was
    a. invalid in that four out of five Republican officeholders were white, despite black majorities in the populations of several states.
    b. valid for a short time period when blacks briefly held a majority in the state legislatures.
    c. invalid in that, while blacks could vote, they could not hold elected office.
    d. valid in that four out of five Republican officeholders were black despite white majorities in the populations of six states.

31. As new constitutions were ratified in the South in the late 1860s, local and state Republican governments focused on
    a. providing public education, full civil rights for blacks, and the reestablishment of a thriving economy based on agriculture.
    b. full black equality, public education, and redistribution of property.
    c. defense of civil rights, desegregation, black employment opportunity, and the restoration of a cotton economy.
    d. public education, defense of civil rights, abolition of racial discrimination, and the creation of a diversified economy.

32. The private ownership of land was critical to the successful integration of freedmen into the mainstream of American society, because owning land
    a. could give them economic independence and personal autonomy from whites.
    b. was necessary in order to hold public office and to vote.
    c. permitted them to act like white men and women.
    d. reduced their dependency on their extended families.

33. The system of agricultural labor that emerged after 1865 frequently pitted ex-slaves and their expectations for freedom against former slave masters who sought to restore the old plantation system; in this struggle
    a. ex-slaves lost to ex-masters because of lack of capital.
    b. ex-masters lost to ex-slaves because of lack of capital.
    c. no one won because of the failure of the army and the Freedmen's Bureau to intervene.
    d. ex-slaves resisted their ex-masters by rejecting wage labor, going on strike, and walking away from the worst employers.

34. The system under which farmers rented small amounts of land, paid their rent with a share of their crops, and were provided mules and tools by the landlord was known as
    a. a crop lien.
    b. a lend-lease.
    c. sharecropping.
    d. a Farm Bureau.

35. Ulysses S. Grant, the Republican presidential candidate in the election of 1868.
    a. was a former Union general who supported congressional reconstruction and was noted as a decisive president.
    b. was a former Union general who supported congressional reconstruction but did not have a deep moral commitment to the equality of African Americans.
    c. was a former member of Lincoln's cabinet who came to support congressional reconstruction and displayed decisive behavior.
    d. represented the Republican Party's attempt to entice southern Democrats over to the Republican Party.

36. During Ulysses S. Grant's administration, U.S. foreign policy demonstrated
    a. isolationism.
    b. a large measure of success.
    c. a failure to resolve problems with foreign powers.
    d. imperialism.

37. President Ulysses S. Grant's administration saw
    a. a severe economic recession, numerous incidents of corruption, and enormous success for railroads.
    b. widespread criticism for Grant's part in the Civil War, labor violence, and a satisfactory resolution of the dispute over war damages owed by Great Britain.
    c. corruption at all levels of government, a severe economic depression, labor violence, and an attempt to annex Santo Domingo to provide the freedmen with a new home.
    d. labor violence, civil service reform, little corruption, and a major depression.

38. When southern Republicans pleaded with Congress for federal protection from Ku Klux Klan violence and racial discrimination, Congress
    a. responded by passing the Ku Klux Klan Act and the Civil Rights Act of 1875.
    b. failed to respond out of a sense that it had done all it could do for southern blacks under the Constitution.
    c. ignored the request for fear that Democrats would not support the Republican economic agenda.
    d. responded by passing the Compromise of 1877.

39. The role of the Supreme Court in reconstruction could be summarized as
    a. an important agent in the Republican Radicals' agenda for civil rights.
    b. a decisive agent for the expansion of civil rights and federal power.
    c. a reactionary agent which undermined reconstruction.
    d. a progressive, but objective, arbitrator over civil rights issues.

40. After the Supreme Court's rulings in the *Slaughterhouse* cases (1873), if a South Carolina African American were to sue a South Carolina county because a law denied him the right to move to another county as long as he owed money to creditors where he lived, a federal court might decide
    a. it had no authority over the case because the power of the federal courts was limited when it came to the civil rights of state citizenship.
    b. it had no authority because the Fourteenth Amendment's due process clause did not extend to the issue of mobility.
    c. it would hear the case because it involved the Fourteenth Amendment's clause granting equal protection under the law.
    d. it would hear the case because it involved the civil rights of national citizenship.

41. In the *Slaughterhouse* cases (1873) and in *United States v. Cruikshank* (1876), the Supreme Court
    a. expanded its role in protecting civil rights.
    b. restricted the ability of the federal government and Congress to protect individuals from discrimination by other individuals.
    c. dimmed the hopes of conservatives that they could halt the rapid expansion of civil rights.
    d. greatly broadened the "due process" and "equal protection" clauses of the Fourteenth Amendment to include businesses.

42. By the early 1870s, the congressional reconstruction goals of 1866
    a. had essentially been met.
    b. had essentially been abandoned by Northerners.
    c. had been greatly expanded to women's suffrage.
    d. were still the nation's first priority.

43. "Redeemers" were
    a. reformers who hoped to establish public education in the South.
    b. economic reformers who believed Confederate dollars should be redeemed in U.S. dollars to revitalize the southern economy.
    c. evangelical reformers who hoped to heal the breach between northern and southern churches of the same denomination.
    d. southern Democrats who wished to restore white southern control in the South.

44. By the early 1870s, Democrats adopted a two-pronged strategy to defeat the Republicans of
    a. polarizing the political parties on the issue of color while relentlessly intimidating black voters.
    b. playing the race "card" and exposing the corruption within Grant's administration.
    c. giving free rein to the Ku Klux Klan and restoring all confiscated property.
    d. relentlessly intimidating officeholders and politicians who would not support a tax cut and who would not work to destroy the Republican Party.

45. In the presidential election of 1876,
    a. the Democratic candidate won the popular vote but fell one vote short of victory in the electoral college, while the Republican candidate initially fell nineteen electoral votes short of victory.
    b. Tilden defeated Hayes.
    c. the Republican Party went to court to challenge the popular vote in Florida, South Carolina, and Louisiana.
    d. the Democratic candidate lost the popular vote but won the electoral college, thus becoming president.

46. In the Compromise of 1877,
    a. the Republican Party was promised majority rule in Congress, and the Democratic Party was promised complete home rule in the South and lower taxes.
    b. southern Democrats accepted Republican rule in the White in exchange for federal monies for internal improvements and the removal of federal troops from the South.
    c. Republicans accepted Democratic rule in the White House as long as the Republicans obtained majority rule in Congress and the Democratic president would protect the southern Republican Party members.
    d. Democrats would regain control of Florida, South Carolina, and Louisiana and would in return support a Republican presidency and approve appropriations for internal improvements in the North.

47. The Compromise of 1877 essentially
    a. spelled the end of reconstruction and of the Republican commitment to the civil rights of African Americans.
    b. destroyed the efforts of the Redeemers and helped rebuild the southern economy.
    c. shifted the racist political strategies from the Democratic Party to the Republican Party.
    d. had little impact on southern blacks.

48. In 1877, the United States averted a second civil war, but this "victory" was at the expense of
    a. blacks, as southern Democrats gained a free hand in dealing with racial matters.
    b. yeoman farmers, who had fewer rights than black sharecroppers.
    c. Rutherford B. Hayes, who lost the disputed election.
    d. South Carolina, Louisiana, and Florida, which had to revise their constitutions.

49. The best evidence that presidential and congressional reconstruction efforts failed to reach their original goals is
    a. the assassination of Abraham Lincoln, the weak presidency of Andrew Johnson, the Compromise of 1877, and the greed of northern capitalists.
    b. the failure to provide freedmen with their own land, the Supreme Court's retrenchment of federal powers to protect civil rights, the corruption of Grant's administration, and Lincoln's assassination.
    c. the failure to redistribute land to the freedmen, the role of the Supreme Court in undermining Republican reform efforts, the Compromise of 1877, ongoing racism, and the evolving conservatism of the nation after the war.
    d. the failure to distribute land to freedmen, the presidential election of 1876, Johnson's reconstruction policies, and the failure of the Redeemers to sufficiently desegregate the South.

50. Congressional reconstruction did not meet all of its goals, but it did achieve some successes; critical evidence to support this statement includes
    a. the *Slaughterhouse* decisions, the Compromise of 1877, the Thirteenth and Fourteenth Amendments, and the Civil Rights Act of 1866.
    b. the Supreme Court's role in expanding the federal powers, the Fourteenth and Fifteenth Amendments, the congressional elections of 1865, and the black codes.
    c. the legacy of the Thirteenth, Fourteenth, and Fifteenth Amendments, the Civil Rights Act of 1875, and the establishment of public schools.
    d. the legacy of the Fourteenth, Fifteenth, and Sixteenth Amendments, the Civil Rights Act of 1875, and the *United States v. Cruikshank* decision.

Terminology Matching   Select the word or phrase from the Terms section that best matches the definition or example provided in the Definitions section. Some terms may be used more than once; some may not be used at all.

TERMS

a. bayonet rule

b. black codes

c. carpetbaggers

d. Civil Rights Act of 1866

e. Civil Rights Act of 1875

f. compulsory free labor

g. Confiscation Acts

h. Democratic Party

i. Emancipation Proclamation

j. Fifteenth Amendment

k. Fourteenth Amendment

l. Freedmen's Bureau

m. Grant, Ulysses

n. Hayes, Rutherford

o. home rule

p. Johnson, Andrew

q. Lincoln, Abraham

r. Proclamation of Amnesty and Reconstruction

s. reconstructed

t. Republican Party

u. scalawags

v. sharecropping

w. Tilden, Samuel

x. Wade-Davis bill

y. yeomen

DEFINITIONS

1. He said, "Let us strive on . . . to bind up the nation's wounds . . . to do all which may achieve and cherish a just, and a lasting peace." _____

2. 1863 act in which Lincoln offered a full pardon to Confederates willing to renounce slavery and to accept the abolition of slavery. _____

3. This threw out Lincoln's "10 percent plan" for readmitting ex-Confederate states to the Union. _____

4. Means of taking legal title to southern lands occupied by the Union army. _____

5. The establishment of this in 1865 significantly raised ex-slaves' hopes of owning their own land. _____

6. Label applied to an ex-Confederate state eligible to be readmitted to the Union. _____

7. Term applied to hybrid system that evolved during the Civil War when the northern military command required that planters enter into work contracts with ex-slaves and pay them wages. _____

8. Person that ex-slaves claimed as their Moses. _____

9. This president presided over the most corrupt administration during the Reconstruction era. _____

10. This president staunchly defended states' rights. _____

11. This president pardoned thousands of wealthy ex-Confederates despite a proclaimed hatred for southern aristocrats. _____

12. This president's thinking about black suffrage evolved from not even considering giving blacks the vote to advocating some form of limited voting. _____

13. This president was a defender of slavery. _____

14. This category of legislation passed by many southern state governments severely limited the economic, social, and political opportunities of freedmen. _____

15. This federal legislation outlawed racial discrimination in transportation, public accommodations, and juries. _____

16. This federal legislation granted blacks "full and equal benefit of all laws and proceedings for the security of person and property as is enjoyed by white citizens" and was passed after Congress overrode a presidential veto. _____

17. This political party is associated with goals to ensure fair treatment of blacks during Reconstruction. _____

18. This political party gained power in the South during the latter days of Reconstruction and is associated with the white supremacy of that time. _____

19. In order to govern in the South, this political party needed the assistance of military rule. _____

20. This is a defamatory term applied to southern-born white Republicans. _____

21. This term was used by conservative white southerners to describe northern whites who migrated to the South. _____

22. These farmers accounted for the vast majority of white Republicans in the South. _____

23. This economic system offered a way to resume agricultural production but forced many blacks to remain dependent on white landlords. _____

24. This president presided over the United States' most severe economic depression to that time during Reconstruction, which contributed to the rise of the southern Democratic Party. _____

25. *Redeemer* is a term associated with this political party. _____

26. Term used by southerners in reference to federal troops stationed in the South during Reconstruction. _____

27. Term associated with white southern jurisdictional control. _____

28. This amendment to the U.S. Constitution extended black voting to the entire nation. _____

29. This amendment to the U.S. Constitution granted blacks American citizenship. _____

30. The Ku Klux Klan committed hundreds of murders of southern Republicans to intimidate voters who supported this presidential candidate. _____

Chronology   Place the events in chronological order.

SET ONE

A. The passage of legislation defining citizenship.

B. The passage of legislation removing color as a voting barrier.

C. The passage of legislation prohibiting slavery.

First _____

Second _____

Third _____

SET TWO

A. President Abraham Lincoln is assassinated.

B. Southern local and state governments write black codes.

C. Andrew Johnson avoids impeachment in the Senate by one vote.

D. Congress approves Fifteenth Amendment.

First _____

Second _____

Third _____

Fourth _____

Short Answer   Write a paragraph in response to each question.

1. Explain the reason for the appointment of a special presidential electoral commission in 1877 and state the outcome of its vote, and identify the effect of the informal understanding known as the Compromise of 1877 on reconstruction.

2. Explain the following statement: By 1870, Northerners had begun a retreat from the ideals of reconstruction.

3. Cite differences in the perspectives of moderate Republicans and the Radical Republicans in Congress during the middle-to-late 1860s.

4. The Reconstruction Acts required southern states to draw up new constitutions. Identify the two general categories of extensive change in southern life that resulted from these constitutions and cite two examples of each category.

5. Identify the positive and negative results of ambitious economic development programs launched by Republican governments in the South.

6. From the perspective of white Southerners, what were the stated purpose and unstated actual goal of the black codes?

7. After emancipation, what did freedom mean to ex-slaves as far as their work lives, family lives, religious independence, and education?

8. Identify three important provisions of the Fourteenth Amendment.

9. Explain why leaders of the Equal Rights Association, such as Susan B. Anthony and Elizabeth Cady Stanton, were unhappy with the wording of the Fifteenth Amendment.

10. Identify two Supreme Court cases that essentially undermined reconstruction, and briefly explain the decisions.

Essay   Respond to each of the following questions in an essay of three to four paragraphs. Your responses should include specific evidence and your ability to interpret the significance of historical events and concepts.

1. According to the textbook, none of the many shortcomings of reconstruction disappointed ex-slaves more than the failure of the U.S. government to provide them with land of their own. Write an essay in which you discuss events and legislation that occurred during the latter part of the Civil War and immediately following the Union victory (1864–1865) and explain how they indicated to freedmen that the federal government intended to make some form of land ownership available to ex-slaves. Contrast those early promises with the later realities of the Reconstruction era that in effect placed land ownership beyond the reach of all but a small fraction of blacks.

2. The textbook states that the collapse of reconstruction began in 1868 when Grant was elected president. Write an essay that explains how Grant's inept administration, his lack of political willpower, and the economic depression that occurred during his administration empowered southern Democrats to gain "home rule" and end the experiment of Reconstruction.

3. Chapter 15 offers a series of insights into the perspective of white Southerners during Reconstruction. Write an essay in which you identify the viewpoints of white Southerners and explain how and why they were able to shape the transition in the South from slavery to freedom. Include their opinions about the behavior of ex-slaves and the impact of Republican reconstruction on their way of life.

4. The textbook identifies significant differences among the goals for reunification of the Confederate and Union states and the assumptions that guided the formation of different plans to reconstruct the South advanced by Abraham Lincoln, Congress, and President Andrew Johnson. In an essay, identify and compare the goals for reconstruction and specific actions taken by Lincoln, Johnson, and Congress. In addition, discuss the strengths and weaknesses of each of these plans.

Map Questions   Answer the questions below using Map 15.1, A Southern Plantation in 1860 and 1881 (p. 561).

READING THE MAP Explain the difference in location of the slave quarters in the 1860 map and the houses of former slaves in the 1881 map. Where are the service and farm buildings in relation to the slave quarters and the master's house?

CONNECTIONS Why do a church and a school appear in the 1881 map but not in the 1860 map? Why are there more houses of former slaves in the 1881 map than there are slave quarters in the 1881 map?

ANSWER KEY

Prologue: Ancient America, before 1492

Multiple Choice

1. a; medium; chapter introduction (pp. P-1–P-2)
2. a; easy; Archaeology and History (pp. P-2–P-5)
3. c; easy; The First Americans introduction (p. P-5)
4. c; medium; Asian Origins (p. P-5)
5. b; easy; Asian Origins (p. P-5)
6. a; medium; Paleo-Indian Hunters (pp. P-6–P-7)
7. b; medium; Paleo-Indian Hunters (pp. P-6–P-7)
8. d; difficult; Paleo-Indian Hunters (pp. P-6–P-7)
9. a; medium; Archaic Hunters and Gatherers introduction (pp. P-7–P-9)
10. c; medium; Archaic Hunters and Gatherers introduction (pp. P-7–P-9)
11. b; easy; Great Plains Bison Hunters (p. P-9)
12. d; medium; Great Basin Cultures (pp. P-9–P-10)
13. c; medium; Great Basin Cultures (pp. P-9–P-10)
14. a; medium; Great Basin Cultures (pp. P-9–P-10)
15. b; medium; Pacific Coast Cultures (pp. P-10–P-11)
16. c; easy; Pacific Coast Cultures (pp. P-10–P-11)
17. a; medium; Pacific Coast Cultures (pp. P-10–P-11)
18. c; medium; Pacific Coast Cultures (pp. P-10–P-11)
19. b; easy; Eastern Woodland Cultures (p. P-11)
20. a; medium; Eastern Woodland Cultures (p. P-11)
21. d; medium; Eastern Woodland Cultures (p. P-11)
22. d; medium; Southwestern Cultures (pp. P-13–P-15)
23. c; medium; Southwestern Cultures (pp. P-13–P-15)
24. a; easy; Southwestern Cultures (pp. P-13–P-15)
25. c; medium; Southwestern Cultures (pp. P-13–P-15)
26. b; easy; Burial Mounds and Chiefdoms (pp. P-16–P-17)
27. c; difficult; Burial Mounds and Chiefdoms (pp. P-16–P-17)
28. a; easy; Native Americans in 1492 (pp. P-17–P-19)
29. d; medium; Native Americans in 1492 (pp. P-17–P-19)
30. b; medium; Native Americans in 1492 (pp. P-17–P-19)
31. c; easy; Native Americans in 1492 (pp. P-17–P-19)
32. d; medium; Native Americans in 1492 (pp. P-17–P-19)
33. b; difficult; The Mexica: A Meso-American Culture (pp. P-19–P-22)
34. c; medium; Historical Question (pp. P-20–P-21)
35. a; medium; The Mexica: A Meso-American Culture (pp. P-19–P-22)

Terminology Matching

1. x		8. o	
2. k		9. d	
3. h		10. z	
4. a		11. e	
5. n		12. s	
6. u		13. b	
7. c		14. i	

15. y

16. m

17. r

18. g

19. r

20. j

21. f

22. w

23. q

24. w

25. j

Chronology

Set One: C, B, A, D

Set Two: C, D, A, B

Short Answer

1. medium; Archaeology and History (pp. P-2–P-5)

2. easy; Asian Origins (p. P-5)

3. medium; Paleo-Indian Hunters (pp. P-6–P-7)

4. easy; Great Plains Bison Hunters (p. P-9)

5. medium; Southwestern Cultures (pp. P-13–P-15)

6. difficult; Burial Mounds and Chiefdoms (pp. P-16–P-17)

7. medium; Native Americans in 1492 (pp. P-17–P-19)

8. medium; The Mexica: A Meso-American Culture (pp. P-19–P-22)

Essay

1. medium; chapter introduction (pp. P-1–P-2), Archaeology and History (pp. P-2–P-5), The First Americans introduction (p. P-5), Asian Origins (p. P-5), Paleo-Indian Hunters (pp. P-6–P-7)

2. difficult; The Mexica: A Meso-American Culture (pp. P-19–P-22)

Chapter 1: Europeans and the New World, 1492–1600

Multiple Choice

1. c; easy; chapter introduction (pp. 3–4)

2. a; easy; chapter introduction (pp. 3–4)

3. c; medium; chapter introduction (pp. 3–4)

4. a; difficult; chapter introduction (pp. 3–4)

5. c; difficult; The Geographic Revolution and the Columbian Exchange (pp. 9–12)

6. b; medium; Mediterranean Trade and European Expansion (pp. 5–6)

7. a; easy; Mediterranean Trade and European Expansion (pp. 5–6)

8. d; easy; A Century of Portuguese Exploration (pp. 6–7)

9. c; medium; A Century of Portuguese Exploration (pp. 6–7)

10. a; easy; A Century of Portuguese Exploration (pp. 6–7)

11. c; difficult; A Century of Portuguese Exploration (pp. 6–7)

12. d; easy; A Century of Portuguese Exploration (pp. 6–7)

13. c; difficult; A Century of Portuguese Exploration (pp. 6–7)

14. d; medium; The Explorations of Columbus (pp. 8–9)

15. a; medium; The Explorations of Columbus (pp. 8–9)

16. d; easy; The Explorations of Columbus (pp. 8–9)

17. a; medium; The Explorations of Columbus (pp. 8–9)

18. c; difficult; The Explorations of Columbus (pp. 8–9)

19. a; easy; The Explorations of Columbus (pp. 8–9)

20. a; difficult; The Explorations of Columbus (pp. 8–9)

21. b; easy; The Geographic Revolution and the Columbian Exchange (pp. 9–12)

22. d; medium; The Geographic Revolution and the Columbian Exchange (pp. 9–12)

23. d; medium; The Geographic Revolution and the Columbian Exchange (pp. 9–12)

24. b; difficult; The Geographic Revolution and the Columbian Exchange (pp. 9–12)

25. c; medium; The Geographic Revolution and the Columbian Exchange (pp. 9–12)

26. b; medium; The Geographic Revolution and the Columbian Exchange (pp. 9–12)

27. d; difficult; The Geographic Revolution and the Columbian Exchange (pp. 9–12)

28. a; medium; The Conquest of Mexico (pp. 13–14)

29. d; easy; The Conquest of Mexico (pp. 13–14)

30. b; medium; The Search for Other Mexicos (pp. 14–18)

31. d; easy; New Spain in the Sixteenth Century (pp. 18–25)

32. b; medium; New Spain in the Sixteenth Century (pp. 18–25)

33. a; medium; New Spain in the Sixteenth Century (pp. 18–25)

34. c; easy; New Spain in the Sixteenth Century (pp. 18–25)

35. b; medium; New Spain in the Sixteenth Century (pp. 18–25)

36. c; easy; New Spain in the Sixteenth Century (pp. 18–25)

37. a; medium; New Spain in the Sixteenth Century (pp. 18–25)

38. b; medium; New Spain in the Sixteenth Century (pp. 18–25)

39. d; easy; New Spain in the Sixteenth Century (pp. 18–25)

40. d; medium; New Spain in the Sixteenth Century (pp. 18–25)

41. b; easy; New Spain in the Sixteenth Century (pp. 18–25)

42. c; easy; New Spain in the Sixteenth Century (pp. 18–25)

43. c; difficult; New Spain in the Sixteenth Century (pp. 18–25)

44. a; medium; The Toll of Spanish Conquest and Colonization (pp. 25–27)

45. c; medium; The Toll of Spanish Conquest and Colonization (pp. 25–27)

46. d; easy; Northern Outposts in Florida and New Mexico (pp. 27–28)

47. b; medium; The New World and Europe introduction (p. 28)

48. a; difficult; The Protestant Reformation and the European Order (pp. 28–29)

49. b; medium; Europe and the Spanish Example (pp. 29–31)

50. d; medium; Europe and the Spanish Example (pp. 29–31)

Terminology Matching

1. t	11. m
2. i	12. j
3. b	13. d
4. a	14. q, s
5. n	15. k
6. o	16. f
7. c	17. p
8. m	18. m
9. e	19. r
10. l	20. h

Chronology

Set One: B, C, D, A

Set Two: B, A, C

Short Answer

1. medium; Mediterranean Trade and European Expansion (pp. 5–6)

2. easy; A Century of Portuguese Exploration (pp. 6–8)

3. medium; A Century of Portuguese Exploration (pp. 6–8)

4. easy; The Explorations of Columbus (pp. 8–9)

5. medium; The Conquest of Mexico (pp. 13–14)

6. medium; New Spain in the Sixteenth Century (pp. 18–25)

7. difficult; New Spain in the Sixteenth Century (pp. 18–25)

8. medium; New Spain in the Sixteenth Century (pp. 18–25)

9. easy; Northern Outposts in Florida and New Mexico (pp. 27–28)

10. easy; Europe and the Spanish Example (pp. 29–31)

Essay

1. medium; Mediterranean Trade and European Expansion (pp. 5–6), A Century of Portuguese Exploration (pp. 6–8)

2. easy; A Century of Portuguese Exploration (pp. 6–8), The Explorations of Columbus (pp. 8–9)

3. difficult; The Geographic Revolution and the Columbian Exchange (pp. 9–12)

4. medium; The Geographic Revolution and the Columbian Exchange (pp. 9–12)

Chapter 2: The Southern Colonies in the Seventeenth Century, 1601–1700

Multiple Choice

1. c; medium; chapter introduction (pp. 37–39)

2. a; easy; chapter introduction (pp. 37–39)

3. c; easy; An English Colony on the Chesapeake (pp. 40–45)

4. b; medium; An English Colony on the Chesapeake (pp. 40–45)

5. a; medium; An English Colony on the Chesapeake (pp. 40–45)

6. a; medium; The Fragile Jamestown Settlement (pp. 40–41)

7. a; easy; Encounters between Natives and Newcomers (pp. 41–44)

8. b; difficult; Encounters between Natives and Newcomers (pp. 41–44)

9. a; medium; chapter introduction (pp. 37–39), The Fragile Jamestown Settlement (pp. 40–41), Encounters Between Natives and Newcomers (pp. 41–44)

10. a; medium; Encounters between Natives and Newcomers (pp. 41–44)

11. b; difficult; Encounters between Natives and Newcomers (pp. 41–44)

12. c; medium; From Private Company to Royal Government (pp. 44–45)

13. d; medium; From Private Company to Royal Government (pp. 44–45)

14. b; easy; A Tobacco Society (pp.45–52)

15. b; easy; Tobacco Agriculture (pp. 45–48)

16. a; medium; Tobacco Agriculture (pp. 45–48)

17. d; easy; Tobacco Agriculture (pp. 45–48)

18. a; medium; A Servant Labor System (pp. 48–52)

19. b; easy; A Servant Labor System (pp. 48–52)

20. a; medium; A Servant Labor System (pp. 48–52)

21. b; difficult; A Servant Labor System (pp. 48–52)

22. c; difficult; A Servant Labor System (pp. 48–52)

23. d; medium; A Servant Labor System (pp. 48–52)

24. a; easy; A Servant Labor System (pp. 48–52)

25. c; easy; A Servant Labor System (pp. 48–52)

26. b; medium; Life, Faith, and Labor (pp. 53–56)

27. a; easy; A Servant Labor System (pp. 48–52)

28. b; medium; Life, Faith, and Labor (pp. 53–56)

29. a; medium; Life, Faith, and Labor (pp. 53–56)

30. b; easy; Life, Faith, and Labor (pp. 53–56)

31. a; medium; Life, Faith, and Labor (pp. 53–56)

32. a; medium; Life, Faith, and Labor (pp. 53–56)

33. c; difficult; Government, Politics, and Polarization (pp. 56–58)

34. a; difficult; Government, Politics, and Polarization (pp. 56–58)

35. d; easy; Government, Politics, and Polarization (pp. 56–58)

36. a; medium; Government, Politics, and Polarization (pp. 56–58)

37. a; medium; Bacon's Rebellion (pp. 58–59)

38. a; medium; Bacon's Rebellion (pp. 58–59)

39. b; easy; Bacon's Rebellion (pp. 58–59)

40. b; medium; Bacon's Rebellion (pp. 58–59)

41. c; easy; Toward a Slave Labor System (pp. 59–65)

42. c; easy; The West Indies: Sugar and Slavery (pp. 59–62)

43. b; easy; Carolina: A West Indian Frontier (pp. 62–63)

44. d; easy; Carolina: A West Indian Frontier (pp. 62–63)

45. a; difficult; Carolina: A West Indian Frontier (pp. 62–63)

46. c; medium; The Chesapeake: Tobacco and Slaves (pp. 63–65)

47. b; medium; The Chesapeake: Tobacco and Slaves (pp. 63–65)

48. b; easy; The Chesapeake: Tobacco and Slaves (pp. 63–65)

49. b; medium; The Chesapeake: Tobacco and Slaves (pp. 63–65)

50. b; medium; The Chesapeake: Tobacco and Slaves (pp. 63–65)

Terminology Matching

1. m	9. j
2. l	10. i
3. r	11. n
4. b	12. a
5. b	13. t
6. h	14. q
7. f	15. o
8. g	16. e

Chronology

C, D, B, A

Short Answer

1. easy; From Private Company to Royal Government (pp. 44–45)

2. easy; Life, Faith, and Labor (pp. 53–56)

3. medium; Government, Politics, and Polarization (pp. 56–58)

4. medium; Government, Politics, and Polarization (pp. 56–58)

5. medium; Bacon's Rebellion (pp. 58–59)

6. medium; Bacon's Rebellion (pp. 58–59)

7. medium; A Servant Labor System (pp. 48–52)

8. difficult; Carolina: A West Indian Frontier (pp. 62–63)

9. easy; The Chesapeake: Tobacco and Slaves (pp. 63–65)

10. difficult; The Chesapeake: Tobacco and Slaves (pp. 63–65)

Essay

1. difficult; chapter introduction (pp. 37–39), The Fragile Jamestown Settlement (pp. 40–41), Encounters between Natives and Newcomers (pp. 41–44)

2. medium; An English Colony on the Chesapeake introduction (p. 40), From Private Company to Royal Government (pp. 44–45)

3. medium; A Servant Labor System (pp. 48–52)

4. medium; Life, Faith, and Labor (pp. 53–56)

Chapter 3: The Northern Colonies in the Seventeenth Century, 1601–1700

Multiple Choice

1. b; medium; chapter introduction (pp. 71–72)

2. b; difficult; Puritan Origins: The English Reformation (pp. 72–74)

3. c; medium; Puritan Origins: The English Reformation (pp. 72–74)

4. d; easy; Puritan Origins: The English Reformation (pp. 72–74)

5. a; difficult; The Pilgrims and Plymouth Colony (pp. 74–76)

6. d; easy; The Pilgrims and Plymouth Colony (pp. 74–76)

7. b; medium; The Founding of Massachusetts Bay Colony (pp. 76–79)

8. c; medium; The Founding of Massachusetts Bay Colony (pp. 76–79)

9. b; difficult; The Founding of Massachusetts Bay Colony (pp. 76–79)

10. c; medium; The Founding of Massachusetts Bay Colony (pp. 76–79)

11. d; easy; The Founding of Massachusetts Bay Colony (pp. 76–79)

12. c; difficult; Documenting the American Promise: King Philip Considers Christianity (pp. 80–81)

13. a; easy; The Founding of Massachusetts Bay Colony (pp. 76–79)

14. b; difficult; The Founding of Massachusetts Bay Colony (pp. 76–79)

15. d; medium; Church, Covenant, and Conformity (pp. 82–83)

16. a; medium; Church, Covenant, and Conformity (pp. 82–83)

17. c; medium; Church, Covenant, and Conformity (pp. 82–83)

18. b; medium; Church, Covenant, and Conformity (pp. 82–83)

19. b; medium; Church, Covenant, and Conformity (pp. 82–83)

20. a; medium; Government by Puritans for Puritanism (pp. 83–84)

21. d; medium; Government by Puritans for Puritanism (pp. 83–84)

22. b; medium; The Splintering of Puritanism (pp. 84–85)

23. c; medium; The Splintering of Puritanism (pp. 84–85)

24. c; medium; The Splintering of Puritanism (pp. 84–85)

25. d; easy; Growth, Change, and Controversy (pp. 85–88)

26. b; medium; Growth, Change, and Controversy (pp. 85–88)

27. d; medium; Growth, Change, and Controversy (pp. 85–88)

28. c; difficult; Growth, Change, and Controversy (pp. 85–88)

29. b; difficult; Growth, Change, and Controversy (pp. 85–88)

30. d; medium; Growth, Change, and Controversy (pp. 85–88)

31. b; easy; Growth, Change, and Controversy (pp. 85–88)

32. a; difficult; Historical Question: Why Were Some New Englanders Accused of Being Witches? (pp. 90–91)

33. b; difficult; Historical Question: Why Were Some New Englanders Accused of Being Witches? (pp. 90–91)

34. c; medium; From New Netherland to New York (pp. 88–92)

35. a; medium; From New Netherland to New York (pp. 88–92)

36. b; easy; From New Netherland to New York (pp. 88–92)

37. c; medium; From New Netherland to New York (pp. 88–92)

38. d; easy; New Jersey and Pennsylvania (pp. 92–93)

39. a; medium; New Jersey and Pennsylvania (pp. 92–93)

40. d; medium; Toleration and Diversity in Pennsylvania (pp. 93–95)

41. d; medium; Toleration and Diversity in Pennsylvania (pp. 93–95)

42. c; medium; Toleration and Diversity in Pennsylvania (pp. 93–95)

43. b; medium; Royal Regulation of Colonial Trade (p. 95)

44. c; medium; Royal Regulation of Colonial Trade (p. 95)

45. b; medium; Consolidation of Royal Authority (pp. 95–98)

46. c; easy; Consolidation of Royal Authority (pp. 95–98)

47. d; medium; Consolidation of Royal Authority (pp. 95–98)

48. a; easy; Consolidation of Royal Authority (pp. 95–98)

49. c; medium; Consolidation of Royal Authority (pp. 95–98)

50. c; difficult; Conclusion: The Seventeenth-Century Legacy of English North America (pp. 98–99)

Terminology Matching

1. f
2. a
3. e
4. p
5. g
6. c
7. s
8. n
9. h
10. r
11. p
12. q

13. t	17. i
14. u	18. l
15. b	19. o
16. d	20. k

Chronology

Set One: B, A, E, D, C

Set Two: B, D, A, C, E

Short Answer

1. easy; The Colonies and the British Empire (pp. 76–79), The Founding of the Middle Colonies (pp. 88–95)

2. medium; Royal Regulation of Colonial Trade (p. 95)

3. medium to difficult; Consolidation of Royal Authority (pp. 95–98)

4. medium; Consolidation of Royal Authority (pp. 95–98)

5. medium; Historical Question: Why Were Some New Englanders Accused of Being Witches? (pp. 90–91)

6. medium to difficult; chapter introduction (pp. 71–72), The Evolution of New England Society (pp. 79–88), The Splintering of Puritanism (pp. 84–85)

7. medium; The Pilgrims and Plymouth Colony (pp. 74–76)

8. medium; The Founding of Massachusetts Bay Colony (pp. 76–79)

9. easy to medium; The Founding of Massachusetts Bay Colony (pp. 76–79)

10. medium; Growth, Change, and Controversy (pp. 85–88), New Jersey and Pennsylvania (pp. 92–93)

Essay

1. difficult; Puritan Origins: The English Reformation (pp. 72–74)

2. medium; Puritans and the Settlement of New England (pp. 74–79)

3. easy; From New Netherland to New York (pp. 88–92)

4. difficult; Toleration and Diversity in Pennsylvania (pp. 93–95)

Chapter 4: Colonial America in the Eighteenth Century, 1701–1770

Multiple Choice

1. a; medium; A Growing Population and Expanding Economy (pp. 107–8)

2. d; medium; A Growing Population and Expanding Economy (pp. 107–8)

3. c; medium; A Growing Population and Expanding Economy (pp. 107–8)

4. b; difficult; A Growing Population and Expanding Economy (pp. 107–8)

5. a; difficult; New England: From Puritan Settlers to Yankee Traders introduction (p. 108)

6. b; medium; Natural Increase and Land Distribution (pp. 108–9)

7. a; medium; Farms, Fish, and Trade (pp. 109–12)

8. b; medium; Farms, Fish, and Trade (pp. 109–12)

9. d; easy; Farms, Fish, and Trade (pp. 109–12)

10. c; difficult; Farms, Fish, and Trade (pp. 109–12)

11. a; medium; Farms, Fish and Trade (pp. 109–12)

12. c; medium; German and Scots-Irish Immigrants (pp. 112–13)

13. b; medium; German and Scots-Irish Immigrants (pp. 112–13)

14. a; easy; German and Scots-Irish Immigrants (pp. 112–13)

15. a; medium; Pennsylvania: "The Best Poor [White] Man's Country" (pp. 113–18)

16. d; medium; Pennsylvania: "The Best Poor [White] Man's Country" (pp. 113–18)

17. d; difficult; Pennsylvania: "The Best Poor [White] Man's Country" (pp. 113–18)

18. b; easy; Pennsylvania: "The Best Poor [White] Man's Country" (pp. 113–18)

19. a; medium; Pennsylvania: "The Best Poor [White] Man's Country" (pp. 113–18)

20. b; easy; Pennsylvania: "The Best Poor [White] Man's Country" (pp. 113–18)

21. c; difficult; Pennsylvania: "The Best Poor [White] Man's Country" (pp. 113–18)

22. a; easy; The Southern Colonies: Land of Slavery introduction (p. 118), The Atlantic Slave Trade and the Growth of Slavery (pp. 118–23)

23. b; medium; The Atlantic Slave Trade and the Growth of Slavery (pp. 118–23)

24. b; easy; The Atlantic Slave Trade and the Growth of Slavery (pp. 118–23)

25. b; medium; The Atlantic Slave Trade and the Growth of Slavery (pp. 118–23)

26. a; easy; The Atlantic Slave Trade and the Growth of Slavery (pp. 118–23)

27. a; medium; The Atlantic Slave Trade and the Growth of Slavery (pp. 118–23)

28. b; medium; The Atlantic Slave Trade and the Growth of Slavery (pp. 118–23)

29. b; medium; The Atlantic Slave Trade and the Growth of Slavery (pp. 118–23)

30. d; medium; Slave Labor and African American Culture (pp. 123–26)

31. b; medium; Slave Labor and African American Culture (pp. 123–26)

32. b; medium; Documenting the American Promise: Regulating Slavery (pp. 124–25)

33. a; difficult; Slave Labor and African American Culture (pp. 123–26)

34. b; medium; Tobacco, Rice, and Prosperity (pp. 126–27)

35. b; medium; Tobacco, Rice, and Prosperity (pp. 126–27)

36. c; easy; Tobacco, Rice, and Prosperity (pp. 126–27)

37. c; medium; Tobacco, Rice, and Prosperity (pp. 126–27)

38. a; difficult; Unifying Experiences introduction (p. 127)

39. c; difficult; Commerce and Consumption (pp. 127–30)

40. a; easy; The Promise of Technology: The Printing Press: "The Spring of Knowledge" (pp. 130–31)

41. d; difficult; Commerce and Consumption (pp. 127–30)

42. b; easy; Religion, Enlightenment, and Revival (pp. 131–34)

43. b; easy; Religion, Enlightenment, and Revival (pp. 131–34)

44. c; medium; Religion, Enlightenment, and Revival (pp. 131–34)

45. b; medium; Religion, Enlightenment, and Revival (pp. 131–34)

46. a; difficult; Religion, Enlightenment, and Revival (pp. 131–34)

47. b; easy; Religion, Enlightenment, and Revival (pp. 131–34)

48. d; medium; Bonds of Empire (pp. 134–36)

49. a; difficult; Bonds of Empire (pp. 134–36)

50. a; medium; Conclusion: The Dual Identity of British North American Colonists (p. 136)

Terminology Matching

1. g	12. r
2. n	13. c
3. k	14. q
4. l	15. h
5. m	16. b
6. l	17. a
7. l	18. d
8. o	19. g
9. p	20. f
10. s	21. i
11. j	

Chronology

Set One: E, C, D, B, A

Set Two: D, A, B, C

Short Answer

1. easy; A Growing Population and Expanding Economy (pp. 107–8)

2. medium; New England: From Puritan Settlers to Yankee Traders introduction (p. 108), Farms, Fish, and Trade (pp. 109–12)

3. easy; German and Scots-Irish Immigrants (pp. 112–13)

4. medium; The Atlantic Slave Trade and the Growth of Slavery (pp. 118–23)

5. medium; The Atlantic Slave Trade and the Growth of Slavery (pp. 118–23)

6. easy; Slave Labor and African American Culture (pp. 123–26), Documenting the American Promise: Regulating Slavery (pp. 124–25)

7. medium; Unifying Experiences (p. 127)

8. difficult; Bonds of Empire (pp. 134–36)

9. difficult; Bonds of Empire (pp. 134–36)

10. medium; The Promise of Technology: The Printing Press: "The Spring of Knowledge" (pp. 130–31)

Essay

1. medium; A Growing Population and Expanding Economy (pp. 107–8), New England: From Puritan Settlers to Yankee Traders (pp. 108–12)

2. medium; The Middle Colonies: Immigrants, Wheat, and Work (pp. 112–13)

3. difficult; The Southern Colonies: Land of Slavery (pp. 118–27)

4. difficult; Religion, Enlightenment, and Revival (pp. 131–34)

Chapter 5: The British Empire and the Colonial Crisis, 1754–1775

Multiple Choice

1. a; medium; French-English Rivalry in the Ohio Valley (pp. 144–46)

2. b; medium; The Albany Congress and Intercolonial Defense (p. 146)

3. d; medium; The Albany Congress and Intercolonial Defense (p. 146)

4. a; medium; The Albany Congress and Intercolonial Defense (p. 146)

5. c; easy; The War and Its Consequences (pp. 146–51)

6. b; medium; The War and Its Consequences (pp. 146–51)

7. d; medium; The War and Its Consequences (pp. 146–51)

8. a; medium; British Leadership and the Indian Question (pp. 151–52)

9. a; medium; British Leadership and the Indian Question (pp. 151–52)

10. d; easy; British Leadership and the Indian Question (pp. 151–52)

11. c; difficult; British Leadership and the Indian Question (pp. 151–52)

12. b; medium; British Leadership and the Indian Question (pp. 151–52)

13. b; medium; Growing Resentment of British Authority (pp. 152–54)

14. b; difficult; Growing Resentment of British Authority (pp. 152–54)

15. a; difficult; Growing Resentment of British Authority (pp. 152–54)

16. d; medium; Taxation and Consent (pp. 154–55)

17. b; medium; Taxation and Consent (pp. 154–55)

18. c; medium; Taxation and Consent (pp. 154–55)

19. c; difficult; Taxation and Consent (pp. 154–55)

20. b; easy; Resistance Strategies and Crowd Politics (pp. 155–58)

21. d; medium; Resistance Strategies and Crowd Politics (pp. 155–58)

22. a; medium; Resistance Strategies and Crowd Politics (pp. 155–58)

23. d; medium; Liberty and Property (pp. 158–59)

24. d; medium; Liberty and Property (pp. 158–59)

25. a; easy; Liberty and Property (pp. 158–59)

26. a; difficult; The Townshend Acts and Economic Retaliation, 1767–1770 introduction (p. 159)

27. b; medium; The Townshend Duties (pp. 159–60)

28. b; difficult; The Townshend Duties (pp. 159–60)

29. c; easy; The Townshend Duties (pp. 159–60)

30. d; difficult; Nonconsumption and the Daughters of Liberty (pp. 160–62)

31. a; medium; Nonconsumption and the Daughters of Liberty (pp. 160–62)

32. c; easy; Military Occupation and "Massacre" in Boston (pp. 162–63)

33. d; easy; Military Occupation and "Massacre" in Boston (pp. 162–63)

34. d; difficult; Military Occupation and "Massacre" in Boston (pp. 162–63)

35. a; difficult; The Calm before the Storm (p. 164)

36. c; medium; The Calm before the Storm (p. 164)

37. c; easy; The Calm before the Storm (p. 164)

38. d; medium; Tea in Boston Harbor (pp. 164–66)

39. b; easy; Tea in Boston Harbor (pp. 164–66)

40. a; difficult; The Coercive Acts (pp. 166–67)

41. d; difficult; The Coercive Acts (pp. 166–67)

42. a; difficult; The Coercive Acts (pp. 166–67)

43. b; difficult; The First Continental Congress (pp. 167, 171)

44. c; difficult; The First Continental Congress (pp. 167, 171)

45. c; medium; Lexington and Concord (pp. 171, 174)

46. d; difficult; Lexington and Concord (pp. 171, 174)

47. d; easy; Lexington and Concord (pp. 171, 174)

48. a; difficult; Another Rebellion against Slavery (pp. 174–76)

49. b; medium; Another Rebellion against Slavery (pp. 174–76)

50. a; difficult; Another Rebellion against Slavery (pp. 174–76)

Terminology Matching

1. o	11. d
2. s	12. e
3. h	13. p
4. a	14. m
5. j	15. b
6. n	16. f
7. t	17. g
8. u	18. c
9. i	19. k
10. l	20. r

Chronology

Set One: B, A, D, C, E

Set Two: D, B, A, C

Short Answer

1. medium; The French and Indian War, 1754–1763 (pp. 144–51)

2. medium; British Leadership and the Indian Question (pp. 151–52)

3. difficult; Growing Resentment of British Authority (pp. 152–54)

4. medium; Taxation and Consent (pp. 154–55)

5. difficult; Liberty and Property (pp. 158–59)

6. medium; The Townshend Acts and Economic Retaliation, 1767–1770 (pp. 159–63)

7. medium; The Calm before the Storm (p. 164)

8. easy; Tea in Boston Harbor (pp. 164–66)

9. medium; The First Continental Congress (pp. 167, 171)

10. medium; Domestic Insurrections, 1774–1775 introduction (p. 171), Lexington and Concord (pp. 171, 174)

Essay

1. difficult; The War and Its Consequences (pp. 146–51), Tightening the Bonds of Empire (pp. 151–54)

2. medium; Growing Resentment of British Authority (pp. 152–54), The Stamp Act Crisis, 1765 (pp. 154–59), The Townshend Acts and Economic Retaliation, 1767–1770 (pp. 159–63), The Coercive Acts (pp. 166–67)

3. medium; Resistance Strategies and Crowd Politics (pp. 155–58), Liberty and Property (pp. 158–59), Nonconsumption and the Daughters of Liberty (pp. 160–62), Tea in Boston Harbor (pp. 164–66)

4. easy; Historical Question: Who Got Tarred and Feathered, and Why? (pp. 172–73)

Chapter 6: The War for America, 1775–1783

Multiple Choice

1. c; easy; The Second Continental Congress introduction (p. 184)

2. b; medium; The Second Continental Congress introduction (p. 184)

3. b; medium; Assuming Political and Military Authority (pp. 184–86)

4. d; difficult; Assuming Political and Military Authority (pp. 184–86)

5. c; medium; Assuming Political and Military Authority (pp. 184–86)

6. d; medium; Pursuing Both War and Peace (pp. 186–88)

7. b; easy; Pursuing Both War and Peace (pp. 186–88)

8. b; difficult; Pursuing Both War and Peace (pp. 186–88)

9. a; medium; Thomas Paine and the Case for Independence (pp. 188–92)

10. c; difficult; Thomas Paine and the Case for Independence (pp. 188–92)

11. d; easy; Thomas Paine and the Case for Independence (pp. 188–92)

12. a; difficult; Thomas Paine and the Case for Independence (pp. 188–92)

13. b; difficult; Thomas Paine and the Case for Independence (pp. 188–92)

14. c; medium; The First Year of War, 1775–1776 introduction (p. 192)

15. d; medium; The First Year of War, 1775–1776 introduction (p. 192)

16. a; difficult; The American Military Forces (pp. 192–94)

17. c; medium; The American Military Forces (pp. 192–94)

18. b; medium; The American Military Forces (pp. 192–94)

19. a; easy; The American Military Forces (pp. 192–94)

20. c; medium; The British Strategy (p. 194)

21. b; medium; The British Strategy (p. 194)

22. a; medium; Quebec, New York, and New Jersey (pp. 194–95)

23. b; medium; Quebec, New York, and New Jersey (pp. 194–95)

24. a; difficult; Quebec, New York, and New Jersey (pp. 194–95)

25. c; easy; Quebec, New York, and New Jersey (pp. 194–95)

26. c; difficult; Quebec, New York, and New Jersey (pp. 194–95)

27. d; medium; Patriotism at the Local Level (p. 197)

28. b; medium; The Loyalists (pp. 197–200)

29. a; medium; Who Is a Traitor? (pp. 200–2)

30. b; medium; Who Is a Traitor? (pp. 200–2)

31. c; difficult; Financial Instability and Corruption (p. 202)

32. b; medium; Financial Instability and Corruption (p. 202)

33. a; easy; The Campaigns of 1777–1779: Highs and Lows introduction (p. 203)

34. b; medium; Burgoyne's Army and the Battle of Saratoga (pp. 204–5), The French Alliance (p. 208)

35. c; difficult; Burgoyne's Army and the Battle of Saratoga (pp. 204–5)

36. d; medium; Burgoyne's Army and the Battle of Saratoga (pp. 204–5)

37. a; medium; The War in Indian Country (p. 205)

38. a; difficult; The French Alliance (p. 208)

39. b; medium; The Southern Strategy and the End of the War (pp. 208–14)

40. d; difficult; Georgia and South Carolina (p. 209)

41. b; medium; Georgia and South Carolina (p. 209)

42. c; easy; Benedict Arnold's Treason (pp. 209–11)

43. d; difficult; Benedict Arnold's Treason (pp. 209–11)

44. a; medium; The Other Southern War: Guerrillas (pp. 211–12)

45. b; medium; Surrender at Yorktown (pp. 212–13)

46. c; medium; Surrender at Yorktown (pp. 212–13)

47. a; easy; The Losers and the Winners (pp. 213–14)

48. a; medium; The Losers and the Winners (pp. 213–14)

49. c; difficult; Conclusion: Why the British Lost (pp. 214–15)

50. a; easy; Conclusion: Why the British Lost (pp. 214–15)

Terminology Matching

1. r	11. o
2. q	12. j
3. t	13. m
4. p	14. s
5. g	15. d
6. k	16. i
7. e	17. u
8. b	18. a
9. l	19. p
10. h	20. t

Chronology

Set One: B, E, C, D, A

Set Two: A, D, B, C

Short Answer

1. medium; Thomas Paine and the Case for Independence (pp. 188–92)

2. medium; Thomas Paine and the Case for Independence (pp. 188–92)

3. easy; The First Year of War, 1775–1776 (pp. 192–95)

4. easy; The First Year of War, 1775–1776 (pp. 192–95)

5. medium; The Loyalists (pp. 197–200)

6. medium; Financial Instability and Corruption (p. 202)

7. difficult; The French Alliance (p. 208)

8. medium; The Southern Strategy and the End of the War (pp. 208–14)

9. easy; Surrender at Yorktown (pp. 212–13)

10. medium; The Losers and the Winners (pp. 213–14)

Essay

1. medium; The Second Continental Congress (pp. 184–92)

2. difficult; Documenting the American Promise: The Issue of Independence (pp. 190–91)

3. medium; The American Military Forces (pp. 192–94), Patriotism at the Local Level (p. 197)

4. difficult; Conclusion: Why the British Lost (pp. 214–15)

Chapter 7: Building a Republic, 1775–1789

Multiple Choice

1. a; medium; Congress and Confederation (p. 223)

2. b; medium; Congress and Confederation (p. 223)

3. d; difficult; Congress and Confederation (p. 223)

4. c; difficult; The Problem of Western Lands (p. 224)

5. a; medium; Running the New Government (pp. 224–26)

6. b; medium; The State Constitutions (pp. 226–27)

7. c; difficult; The State Constitutions (pp. 226–27)

8. d; difficult; The State Constitutions (pp. 226–27)

9. d; difficult; The State Constitutions (pp. 226–27)

10. b; medium; Who Are "the People"? (pp. 227–28)

11. a; medium; Who Are "the People"? (pp. 227–28)

12. a; difficult; Equality and Slavery (pp. 228–33)

13. c; difficult; Equality and Slavery (pp. 228–33)

14. b; medium; Equality and Slavery (pp. 228–33)

15. d; easy; Financial Chaos and Paper Money (pp. 233–35)

16. b; difficult; Financial Chaos and Paper Money (pp. 233–35)

17. a; medium; Financial Chaos and Paper Money (pp. 233–35)

18. a; medium; Land Ordinances and the Northwest Territory (pp. 235–38)

19. c; medium; Land Ordinances and the Northwest Territory (pp. 235–38)

20. d; medium; Land Ordinances and the Northwest Territory (pp. 235–38)

21. a; easy; Land Ordinances and the Northwest Territory (pp. 235–38)

22. b; medium; Shays's Rebellion, 1786–1787 (pp. 239–40)

23. a; easy; Shays's Rebellion, 1786–1787 (pp. 239–40)

24. a; difficult; Shays's Rebellion, 1786–1787 (pp. 239–40)

25. c; difficult; Shays's Rebellion, 1786–1787 (pp. 239–40), The United States Constitution (pp. 240–43)

26. b; medium; From Annapolis to Philadelphia (p. 240)

27. a; medium; From Annapolis to Philadelphia (p. 240)

28. b; medium; From Annapolis to Philadelphia (p. 240)

29. c; difficult; The Virginia and New Jersey Plans (pp. 240–42)

30. d; easy; The Virginia and New Jersey Plans (pp. 240–42)

31. a; medium; The Virginia and New Jersey Plans (pp. 240–42)

32. d; medium; The Virginia and New Jersey Plans (pp. 240–42)

33. b; difficult; The Virginia and New Jersey Plans (pp. 240–42)

34. a; easy; The Virginia and New Jersey Plans (pp. 240–42)

35. c; medium; The Virginia and New Jersey Plans (pp. 240–42)

36. a; easy; The Virginia and New Jersey Plans (pp. 240–42)

37. a; medium; The Virginia and New Jersey Plans (pp. 240–42)

38. b; difficult; Democracy versus Republicanism (pp. 242–43)

39. a; easy; Democracy versus Republicanism (pp. 242–43)

40. d; medium; Democracy versus Republicanism (pp. 242–43)

41. d; medium; Democracy versus Republicanism (pp. 242–43)

42. b; medium; Ratification of the Constitution introduction (p. 243)

43. c; easy; The Federalists (pp. 243–45)

44. a; easy; The Federalists (pp. 243–45)

45. c; medium; The Antifederalists (pp. 245, 248)

46. d; medium; The Antifederalists (pp. 245, 248)

47. b; medium; The Big Holdouts: Virginia and New York (pp. 248–49)

48. c; medium; The Big Holdouts: Virginia and New York (pp. 248–49)

49. a; medium; The Big Holdouts: Virginia and New York (pp. 248–49)

50. c; difficult; The Big Holdouts: Virginia and New York (pp. 248–49)

Terminology Matching

1. b	11. q
2. c	12. f
3. m	13. e
4. k	14. h
5. o	15. a
6. p	16. j
7. l	17. s
8. r	18. c
9. n	19. g
10. i	

Chronology

Set One: C, E, D, B, A

Set Two: B, A, C

Short Answer

1. medium; Congress and Confederation (p. 223)

2. medium; The Problem of Western Lands (p. 224)

3. difficult; The State Constitutions (pp. 226–27)

4. medium; Equality and Slavery (pp. 228–33)

5. medium; Financial Chaos and Paper Money (pp. 233–35)

6. easy; Land Ordinances and the Northwest Territory (pp. 235–38)

7. easy; From Annapolis to Philadelphia (p. 240)

8. easy; The Virginia and New Jersey Plans (pp. 240–42)

9. difficult; The Federalists (pp. 243–45), The Antifederalists (pp. 245, 248)

10. medium; The Big Holdouts: Virginia and New York (pp. 248–49)

Essay

1. medium; Land Ordinances and the Northwest Territory (pp. 235–38)

2. medium; Shays's Rebellion, 1786–1787 (pp. 239–40)

3. difficult; Ratification of the Constitution (pp. 243–49)

4. easy; The Big Holdouts: Virginia and New York (pp. 248–49)

Chapter 8: The New Nation Takes Form, 1789–1800

Multiple Choice

1. c; difficult; chapter introduction (pp. 255–57)

2. c; medium; The Search for Stability introduction (p. 257)

3. a; medium; Washington's Cabinet (pp. 257–58)

4. d; easy; Washington's Cabinet (pp. 257–58)

5. b; medium; Washington's Cabinet (pp. 257–58)

6. a; medium; The Bill of Rights (p. 258)

7. b; easy; The Bill of Rights (p. 258)

8. a; medium; The Republican Wife and Mother (pp. 259–60)

9. b; difficult; The Republican Wife and Mother (pp. 259–60)

10. c; easy; Commercial Agriculture (p. 260)

11. b; medium; Transportation (pp. 260–61)

12. a; difficult; Merchants and Capital (pp. 261–62)

13. d; medium; Hamilton's Political Economy introduction (p. 263)

14. d; difficult; The Public Debt and Taxes (pp. 263, 266)

15. a; easy; The Public Debt and Taxes (pp. 263, 266)

16. a; medium; The First Bank of the United States and the *Report on Manufactures* (p. 267)

17. b; difficult; The First Bank of the United States and the *Report on Manufactures* (p. 267)

18. b; medium; The First Bank of the United States and the *Report on Manufactures* (p. 267)

19. c; medium; The First Bank of the United States and the *Report on Manufactures* (p. 267)

20. d; easy; The Whiskey Rebellion (pp. 267–69)

21. c; medium; The Whiskey Rebellion (pp. 267–69)

22. b; difficult; The Whiskey Rebellion (pp. 267–69)

23. a; medium; To the West: The Indians (pp. 269–71)

24. b; medium; To the West: The Indians (pp. 269–71)

25. c; medium; To the West: The Indians (pp. 269–71)

26. c; easy; To the West: The Indians (pp. 269–71)

27. d; easy; Across the Atlantic: France and England (pp. 271–73)

28. d; difficult; Across the Atlantic: France and England (pp. 271–73)

29. b; medium; The Jay Treaty (p. 273)

30. c; medium; To the South: The Haitian Revolution (p. 274)

31. a; medium; Federalists and Republicans introduction (p. 275)

32. a; easy; The Election of 1796 (pp. 275–76)

33. d; medium; The Election of 1796 (pp. 275–76)

34. b; easy; The Election of 1796 (pp. 275–76)

35. c; medium; The Election of 1796 (pp. 275–76), The XYZ Affair (pp. 276–77)

36. a; easy; The XYZ Affair (pp. 276–77)

37. b; easy; The XYZ Affair (pp. 276–77)

38. c; difficult; The XYZ Affair (pp. 276–77)

39. b; medium; The Alien and Sedition Acts (pp. 277–81)

40. c; difficult; The Alien and Sedition Acts (pp. 277–81)

41. a; difficult; The Alien and Sedition Acts (pp. 277–81)

42. b; medium; The Alien and Sedition Acts (pp. 277–81)

43. a; difficult; The Alien and Sedition Acts (pp. 277–81)

44. b; medium; The Alien and Sedition Acts (pp. 277–81)

45. d; medium; The Alien and Sedition Acts (pp. 277–81)

46. b; medium; The Alien and Sedition Acts (pp. 277–81)

47. b; medium; The Alien and Sedition Acts (pp. 277–81)

48. d; difficult; Conclusion Parties Nonetheless (p. 282)

49. c; medium; Conclusion: Parties Nonetheless (p. 282)

50. b; medium; Conclusion: Parties Nonetheless (p. 282)

Terminology Matching

1. q		10. l	
2. h		11. o	
3. f		12. i	
4. u		13. k	
5. t		14. g	
6. d		15. b	
7. j		16. r	
8. m		17. s	
9. v			

Chronology

Set One: E, A, B, D, C

Set Two: A, C, B, D

Short Answer

1. difficult; The Bill of Rights (p. 258)

2. medium; Sources of Economic Change (pp. 260–62)

3. difficult; Historical Question: How Did Washington, D.C., Become the Federal Capital? (pp. 264–65)

4. medium; The Public Debt and Taxes (pp. 263, 266)

5. difficult; The Whiskey Rebellion (pp. 267–69)

6. medium; To the West: The Indians (pp. 269–71)

7. medium; The Jay Treaty (p. 273)

8. easy; To the South: The Haitian Revolution (p. 274)

9. medium; The XYZ Affair (pp. 276–77), The Alien and Sedition Acts (pp. 277–81)

10. medium; Conclusion: Parties Nonetheless (p. 282)

Essay

1. difficult; The Public Debt and Taxes (pp. 263, 266), The First Bank of the United States and the *Report on Manufactures* (p. 267)

2. medium; To the West: The Indians (pp. 269–71)

3. difficult; Across the Atlantic: France and England (pp. 271–73), The Jay Treaty (p. 273), The XYZ Affair (pp. 276–77), The Alien and Sedition Acts (pp. 277–81)

4. difficult; The Alien and Sedition Acts (pp. 277–81)

Chapter 9: Republican Ascendancy, 1800–1824

Multiple Choice

1. a; medium; Jefferson's Presidency introduction (p. 289)

2. c; medium; The Election of 1800 (pp. 289–90)

3. c; difficult; Gabriel's Rebellion (pp. 290–91)

4. d; medium; Gabriel's Rebellion (pp. 290–91)

5. b; easy; The Jefferson Vision of Republican Simplicity (pp. 291–93)

6. b; medium; The Jefferson Vision of Republican Simplicity (pp. 291–93)

7. a; easy; The Jefferson Vision of Republican Simplicity (pp. 291–93)

8. c; medium; The Jefferson Vision of Republican Simplicity (pp. 291–93)

9. b; difficult; The Judiciary and the Midnight Judges (p. 293)

10. d; difficult; The Judiciary and the Midnight Judges (p. 293)

11. b; easy; The Promise of the West: The Louisiana Purchase and the Lewis and Clark Expedition (pp. 293–96)

12. d; medium; The Promise of the West: The Louisiana Purchase and the Lewis and Clark Expedition (pp. 293–96)

13. c; medium; The Promise of the West: The Louisiana Purchase and the Lewis and Clark Expedition (pp. 293–96)

14. c; medium; Historical Question: How Could a Vice President Get Away with Murder? (pp. 298–99)

15. b; medium; Troubles at Sea and the Embargo Act of 1807 (pp. 296–97, 300)

16. b; medium; Troubles at Sea and the Embargo Act of 1807 (pp. 296–97, 300)

17. c; medium; Troubles at Sea and the Embargo Act of 1807 (pp. 296–97, 300)

18. d; easy; Troubles at Sea and the Embargo Act of 1807 (pp. 296–97, 300)

19. a; difficult; Indian Troubles in the West (pp. 301–3)

20. a; easy; Indian Troubles in the West (pp. 301–3)

21. b; easy; Indian Troubles in the West (pp. 301–3)

22. a; medium; Madison Gets Entangled (pp. 300–1), The War Begins (pp. 303–4)

23. b; difficult; The War Begins (pp. 303–4)

24. c; easy; The British Offensives of 1814 (pp. 304–5)

25. b; medium; The British Offensives of 1814 (pp. 304–5)

26. b; easy; The British Offensives of 1814 (pp. 304–5)

27. d; medium; The War Ends (pp. 305–6)

28. b; difficult; The War Ends (pp. 305–6)

29. a; medium; The War Ends (pp. 305–6)

30. c; easy; Women and the Law (pp. 306–8)

31. b; medium; Women and the Law (pp. 306–8)

32. c; medium; Women and the Law (pp. 306–8)

33. b; medium; Women and the Law (pp. 306–8)

34. a; medium; Women and the Law (pp. 306–8)

35. b; easy; Women and Church Governance (pp. 308–9)

36. c; medium; Women and Church Governance (pp. 308–9)

37. d; difficult; Madison's Successors introduction (p. 309)

38. b; medium; The Missouri Compromise (pp. 309–12)

39. c; medium; The Missouri Compromise (pp. 309–12)

40. b; easy; The Monroe Doctrine (p. 312)

41. a; difficult; The Election of 1824 (pp. 312–15)

42. c; difficult; The Election of 1824 (pp. 312–15)

43. d; medium; The Election of 1824 (pp. 312–15)

44. b; easy; The Adams Administration (p. 315)

45. a; easy; The Adams Administration (p. 315)

46. c; medium; The Promise of Technology: Eli Terry's Clock (pp. 316–17)

47. b; medium; The Promise of Technology: Eli Terry's Clock (pp. 316–17)

48. d; medium; The Promise of Technology: Eli Terry's Clock (pp. 316–17)

49. b; easy; Conclusion: From Jefferson to Adams (pp. 315, 318)

50. c; medium; Conclusion: From Jefferson to Adams (pp. 315, 318)

Terminology Matching

1. i
2. j
3. o
4. q
5. m
6. l
7. g
8. b
9. e
10. p
11. h
12. c
13. r
14. n
15. a

Chronology

Set One: A, B, D, E, C

Set Two: D, F, E, B, A, C

Short Answer

1. difficult; chapter introduction (pp. 287–89)

2. easy; The Jefferson Vision of Republican Simplicity (pp. 291–93)

3. medium; The Promise of the West: The Louisiana Purchase and the Lewis and Clark Expedition (pp. 293–96)

4. medium; Troubles at Sea and the Embargo Act of 1807 (pp. 296–97, 300)

5. difficult; Indian Troubles in the West (pp. 301–3)

6. easy; Madison Gets Entangled (pp. 300–1), The War Begins (pp. 303–4)

7. medium; Women and the Law (pp. 306–8)

8. easy; The Monroe Doctrine (p. 312)

9. medium; The Election of 1824 (pp. 312–15)

10. easy; The Adams Administration (p. 315)

Essay

1. medium; Gabriel's Rebellion (pp. 290–91)

2. medium; The War Ends (pp. 305–6)

3. difficult; The War of 1812 (pp. 303–6)

4. difficult; The Missouri Compromise (pp. 309–12)

Chapter 10: The Expanding Republic, 1815–1840

Multiple Choice

1. b; difficult; chapter introduction (pp. 323–24)

2. a; medium; The Market Revolution (pp. 324–34)

3. d; easy; Improvements in Transportation (pp. 324–26)

4. c; easy; Improvements in Transportation (pp. 324–26), The Promise of Technology: Early Steamboats (pp. 328–30)

5. c; easy; Improvements in Transportation (pp. 324–26), The Promise of Technology: Early Steamboats (pp. 328–30)

6. b; medium; Improvements in Transportation (pp. 324–26)

7. b; medium; Improvements in Transportation (pp. 324–26)

8. d; medium; Improvements in Transportation (pp. 324–26)

9. b; medium; Factories, Workingwomen, and Wage Labor (pp. 326–27, 330–32)

10. c; medium; Factories, Workingwomen, and Wage Labor (pp. 326–27, 330–32)

11. b; medium; Factories, Workingwomen, and Wage Labor (pp. 326–27, 330–32)

12. c; medium; Bankers and Lawyers (pp. 332–34)

13. d; difficult; Bankers and Lawyers (pp. 332–34)

14. b; medium; Bankers and Lawyers (pp. 332–34)

15. c; difficult; Bankers and Lawyers (pp. 332–34)

16. b; medium; Booms and Busts (p. 334)

17. d; medium; The Spread of Democracy introduction (p. 334), Popular Politics and Partisan Identity (pp. 334–35)

18. b; easy; Popular Politics and Partisan Identity (pp. 334–35)

19. d; difficult; Popular Politics and Partisan Identity (pp. 334–35)

20. a; easy; The Election of 1828 and the Character Issue (pp. 335–36)

21. b; medium; The Election of 1828 and the Character Issue (pp. 335–36)

22. c; difficult; Jackson's Democratic Agenda (pp. 336–38)

23. b; easy; The Family and Separate Spheres (pp. 338–39)

24. d; difficult; The Family and Separate Spheres (pp. 338–39)

25. a; easy; The Education and Training of Youth (pp. 339–41)

26. c; medium; The Education and Training of Youth (pp. 339–41)

27. a; easy; The Education and Training of Youth (pp. 339–41)

28. c; easy; Public Life, the Press, and Popular Amusements (pp. 341–43)

29. b; easy; Public Life, the Press, and Popular Amusements (pp. 341–43)

30. d; medium; Public Life, the Press, and Popular Amusements (pp. 341–43)

31. b; easy; Democracy and Religion introduction (p. 343)

32. a; medium; The Second Great Awakening (pp. 343–44)

33. b; medium; The Temperance Movement and the Campaign for Moral Reform (pp. 344–47)

34. d; easy; The Temperance Movement and the Campaign for Moral Reform (pp. 344–47)

35. c; medium; The Temperance Movement and the Campaign for Moral Reform (pp. 344–47)

36. b; medium; Organizing against Slavery (pp. 347–49)

37. b; easy; Organizing against Slavery (pp. 347–49)

38. d; medium; Organizing against Slavery (pp. 347–49)

39. c; medium; Organizing against Slavery (pp. 347–49)

40. a; medium; Indian Policy and the Trail of Tears (pp. 349–52)

41. b; medium; Indian Policy and the Trail of Tears (pp. 349–52)

42. c; medium; Indian Policy and the Trail of Tears (pp. 349–52)

43. d; difficult; The Tariff of Abominations and Nullification (pp. 352–53)

44. a; difficult; The Tariff of Abominations and Nullification (pp. 352–53)

45. b; medium; The Bank War and the Panic of 1837 (pp. 353–55)

46. c; medium; The Bank War and the Panic of 1837 (pp. 353–55)

47. b; easy; The Bank War and the Panic of 1837 (pp. 353–55)

48. a; medium; The Bank War and the Panic of 1837 (pp. 353–55)

49. c; difficult; Van Buren's One-Term Presidency (pp. 355, 358)

50. b; medium; Conclusion: Democrats and Whigs (p. 359)

Terminology Matching

1. t	9. f
2. u	10. i
3. h	11. o
4. k	12. q
5. c	13. b
6. r	14. n
7. m	15. l
8. p	

Chronology

Set One: B, A, C, E, D

Set Two: A, D, C, B

Short Answer

1. medium; chapter introduction (pp. 323–24), The Spread of Democracy (pp. 334–38)

2. difficult; Improvements in Transportation (pp. 324–26), The Promise of Technology: Early Steamboats (pp. 328–30)

3. easy; Factories, Workingwomen, and Wage Labor (pp. 326–27, 330–32)

4. easy; Bankers and Lawyers (pp. 332–34), Booms and Busts (p. 334)

5. medium; The Spread of Democracy introduction (p. 334), Popular Politics and Partisan Identity (pp. 334–35)

6. medium; The Spread of Democracy introduction (p. 334), Popular Politics and Partisan Identity (pp. 334–35), The Election of 1828 and the Character Issue (pp. 335–36)

7. medium; Public Life, the Press, and Popular Amusements (pp. 341–43)

8. medium; The Second Great Awakening (pp. 343–44)

9. difficult; The Bank War and the Panic of 1837 (pp. 353–55)

10. easy; Van Buren's One-Term Presidency (pp. 355, 358)

Essay

1. medium; Bankers and Lawyers (pp. 332–34)

2. difficult; chapter introduction (pp. 323–24), The Spread of Democracy (pp. 334–38)

3. medium; The Market Revolution (324–34), Democracy and Religion introduction (p. 343), The Second Great Awakening (pp. 343–44)

4. medium; Organizing against Slavery (pp. 347–49)

Chapter 11: The Free North and West, 1840–1860

Multiple Choice

1. a; medium; Economic and Industrial Evolution introduction (pp. 366–67)

2. b; easy; Economic and Industrial Evolution introduction (pp. 366–67)

3. d; difficult; Economic and Industrial Evolution introduction (pp. 366–67)

4. d; easy; Agriculture and Land Policy (pp. 367–69)

5. b; medium; Agriculture and Land Policy (pp. 367–69)

6. a; medium; Agriculture and Land Policy (pp. 367–69)

7. d; difficult; Manufacturing and Mechanization introduction (p. 369)

8. c; medium; Railroads: Breaking the Bonds of Nature (pp. 369–72)

9. a; easy; The Promise of Technology: The Telegraph: "The Wonder Working Wire" (pp. 374–75)

10. b; difficult; The Promise of Technology: The Telegraph: "The Wonder Working Wire" (pp. 374–75)

11. b; medium; The Free-Labor Ideal: Freedom plus Labor (pp. 372–73)

12. b; medium; Economic Inequality (pp. 373–76)

13. c; easy; Immigrants and the Free-Labor Ladder (pp. 376–77)

14. a; medium; Immigrants and the Free-Labor Ladder (pp. 376–77)

15. c; medium; Immigrants and the Free-Labor Ladder (pp. 376–77)

16. d; medium; The Pursuit of Perfection: Transcendentalists and Utopians (pp. 378–80)

17. c; easy; The Pursuit of Perfection: Transcendentalists and Utopians (pp. 378–80)

18. a; medium; Women's Rights Activists (p. 380)

19. b; medium; Women's Rights Activists (p. 380)

20. c; easy; Abolitionists and the American Ideal (pp. 380–82)

21. b; medium; Abolitionists and the American Ideal (pp. 380–82)

22. a; difficult; Abolitionists and the American Ideal (pp. 380–82)

23. b; easy; Abolitionists and the American Ideal (pp. 380–82)

24. d; medium; Manifest Destiny (pp. 382–84)

25. c; medium; "Oregon Fever" and the Overland Trail (pp. 384–87)

26. b; medium; "Oregon Fever" and the Overland Trail (pp. 384–87)

27. b; medium; The Mormon Migration (pp. 387–89)

28. c; medium; The Mormon Migration (pp. 387–89)

29. c; easy; The Mexican Borderlands (pp. 389–92)

30. a; medium; The Mexican Borderlands (pp. 389–92)

31. c; easy; The Mexican Borderlands (pp. 389–92)

32. d; medium; The Mexican Borderlands (pp. 389–92)

33. c; easy; Tyler and the Whig Fiasco (pp. 392–93)

34. a; medium; Tyler and the Whig Fiasco (pp. 392–93)

35. a; difficult; Texas, Oregon, and the Election of 1844 (pp. 393–94)

36. a; medium; Texas, Oregon, and the Election of 1844 (pp. 393–94)

37. b; difficult; Texas, Oregon, and the Election of 1844 (pp. 393–94)

38. a; medium; Texas, Oregon, and the Election of 1844 (pp. 393–94)

39. d; difficult; Texas, Oregon, and the Election of 1844 (pp. 393–94)

40. a; medium; The Mexican War, 1846–1848 introduction (p. 394)

41. b; medium; "Mr. Polk's War" (pp. 394–97)

42. d; medium; "Mr. Polk's War" (pp. 394–97)

43. a; medium; "Mr. Polk's War" (pp. 394–97)

44. c; medium; "Mr. Polk's War" (pp. 394–97)

45. d; difficult; "Mr. Polk's War" (pp. 394–97)

46. b; medium; "Mr. Polk's War" (pp. 394–97)

47. c; easy; Victory in Mexico (pp. 397–402)

48. d; medium; Victory in Mexico (pp. 397–402)

49. b; easy; Historical Question: Who Rushed for California Gold? (pp. 400–1)

50. a; difficult; Victory in Mexico (pp. 397–402)

Terminology Matching

1. e	11. w
2. k	12. o
3. l	13. n
4. i	14. f
5. h	15. x
6. c	16. a
7. m	17. p
8. q	18. d
9. s	19. u
10. v	

Chronology

Set One: B, A, D, E, C

Set Two: D, B, A, C

Short Answer

1. medium; Economic and Industrial Evolution (pp. 366–72)

2. easy; Agriculture and Land Policy (pp. 367–69)

3. medium; Railroads: Breaking the Bonds of Nature (pp. 369–72)

4. medium; Immigrants and the Free-Labor Ladder (pp. 376–77)

5. medium; The Pursuit of Perfection: Transcendentalist and Utopians (pp. 378–80)

6. difficult; Women's Rights Activists (p. 380)

7. easy; Abolitionists and the American Ideal (pp. 380–82)

8. difficult; Manifest Destiny (pp. 382–84)

9. easy; The Mormon Migration (pp. 387–89)

10. medium; Tyler and the Whig Fiasco (pp. 392–93)

Essay

1. medium; Economic and Industrial Evolution (pp. 366–72), Immigrants and the Free-Labor Ladder (pp. 376–77), Women's Rights Activists (p. 380), Abolitionists and the American Ideal (pp. 380–82), Manifest Destiny (pp. 382–84)

2. medium; The Mexican Borderlands (pp. 389–92), "Mr. Polk's War" (pp. 394–97)

3. difficult; The Mexican Borderlands (pp. 389–92), The Politics of Expansion (pp. 392–94), The Mexican War, 1846–1848 (pp. 394–402)

4. easy; "Oregon Fever" and the Overland Trail (pp. 384–87), The Mexican Borderlands (pp. 389–92), Texas, Oregon and the Election of 1844 (pp. 393–94), The Mexican War, 1846–1848 (pp. 394–402)

Chapter 12: The Slave South, 1820–1860

Multiple Choice

1. c; easy; chapter introduction (pp. 409–11)
2. d; medium; chapter introduction (pp. 409–11)
3. a; medium; chapter introduction (pp. 409–11)
4. b; difficult; chapter introduction (pp. 409–11)
5. d; easy; The Southern Difference introduction (p. 411)
6. b; medium; Cotton Kingdom, Slave Empire (pp. 411–13)
7. d; medium; Cotton Kingdom, Slave Empire (pp. 411–13)
8. c; medium; Cotton Kingdom, Slave Empire (pp. 411–13)
9. b; easy; Cotton Kingdom, Slave Empire (pp. 411–13)
10. c; medium; The South in Black and White (pp. 413–15)
11. b; medium; The South in Black and White (pp. 413–15)
12. a; medium; The South in Black and White (pp. 413–15)
13. d; medium; The South in Black and White (pp. 413–15)
14. c; medium; The Plantation Economy (pp. 415–21)
15. a; easy; The Plantation Economy (pp. 415–21)
16. d; easy; The Plantation Economy (pp. 415–21)
17. d; medium; The Plantation Economy (pp. 415–21)
18. b; difficult; The Plantation Economy (pp. 415–21)
19. a; medium; The Plantation Economy (pp. 415–21)
20. b; difficult; The Plantation Economy (pp. 415–21)
21. b; medium; Plantation Masters (pp. 422–26)
22. a; medium; Plantation Masters (pp. 422–26)
23. c; easy; Plantation Masters (pp. 422–26)
24. a; medium; Plantation Masters (pp. 422–26)
25. d; medium; Plantation Masters (pp. 422–26)
26. b; difficult; Plantation Mistresses (pp. 426–28)
27. b; medium; Plantation Mistresses (pp. 426–28)
28. d; medium; Plantation Mistresses (pp. 426–28)
29. a; easy; Plantation Mistresses (pp. 426–28)
30. b; medium; Slaves and the Quarters introduction (p. 428)
31. d; medium; Work (pp. 428–31)
32. c; medium; Work (pp. 428–31)
33. d; medium; Work (pp. 428–31)
34. a; medium; Family, Religion, and Community (pp. 431–34)
35. c; difficult; Family, Religion, and Community (pp. 431–34)
36. a; difficult; Family, Religion, and Community (pp. 431–34)
37. c; medium; Resistance and Rebellion (pp. 434–35)
38. b; easy; Resistance and Rebellion (pp. 434–35)
39. a; medium; Resistance and Rebellion (pp. 434–35)
40. b; difficult; Black and Free: On the Middle Ground (pp. 435–37)
41. d; medium; Black and Free: On the Middle Ground (pp. 435–37)
42. c; medium; The Plain Folk introduction (p. 437)
43. a; easy; Plantation Belt Yeomen (pp. 437–38)
44. b; medium; Plantation Belt Yeomen (pp. 437–38)
45. b; medium; Upcountry Yeomen (pp. 438–40)
46. c; medium; Upcountry Yeomen (pp. 438–40)
47. b; difficult; Poor Whites (pp. 440–41)
48. a; easy; The Democratization of the Political Arena (pp. 441–42)
49. d; medium; Planter Power (pp. 442–44)
50. d; difficult; Planter Power (pp. 442–44)

Terminology Matching

1. v
2. i
3. n
4. u
5. m
6. t
7. r
8. l
9. q
10. q
11. w
12. g
13. p
14. o
15. d
16. c
17. h
18. f
19. x
20. e

Chronology

B, C, A, D

Short Answer

1. easy; Cotton Kingdom, Slave Empire (pp. 411–13)
2. easy; Cotton Kingdom, Slave Empire (pp. 411–13)
3. difficult; The South in Black and White (pp. 413–15)
4. medium; The South in Black and White (pp. 413–15)
5. medium; The Plantation Economy (pp. 415–21)
6. medium; The Plantation Economy (pp. 415–21)
7. medium; Slaves and the Quarters introduction (p. 428), Work (pp. 428–31)
8. medium; Free Blacks and the White Response (pp. 435–36)
9. difficult; The Plain Folk (pp. 437–41)
10. medium; Planter Power (pp. 442–44)

Essay

1. easy; Family, Religion, and Community
(pp. 431–34)

2. medium; Black and Free: On the Middle Ground
(pp. 435–37)

3. difficult; The Plain Folk (pp. 437–41)

4. medium; The Politics of Slavery (pp. 441–44)

Chapter 13: The House Divided, 1846–1861

Multiple Choice

1. c; easy; chapter introduction (pp. 449–50)

2. b; medium; chapter introduction (pp. 449–50)

3. d; easy; The Wilmot Proviso and the Expansion of Slavery (pp. 451–53)

4. a; medium; The Wilmot Proviso and the Expansion of Slavery (pp. 451–53)

5. c; easy; The Wilmot Proviso and the Expansion of Slavery (pp. 451–53)

6. b; medium; The Election of 1848 (pp. 453–54)

7. d; easy; Debate and Compromise (pp. 454–56)

8. a; medium; Debate and Compromise (pp. 454–56)

9. b; easy; Debate and Compromise (pp. 454–56)

10. c; medium; Debate and Compromise (pp. 454–56)

11. d; medium; The Fugitive Slave Act (pp. 457–59)

12. b; medium; Uncle Tom's Cabin (pp. 459–62)

13. c; difficult; The Election of 1852 (pp. 462–63)

14. c; easy; The Election of 1852 (pp. 462–63)

15. b; medium; The Kansas-Nebraska Act (pp. 463–64)

16. c; difficult; Realignment of the Party System
(pp. 464–69)

17. a; easy; The New Parties: Know-Nothings and Republicans (pp. 466–68)

18. d; medium; The New Parties: Know-Nothings and Republicans (pp. 466–68)

19. b; medium; The Election of 1856 (pp. 468–69)

20. c; medium; "Bleeding Kansas" (pp. 472–74)

21. a; medium; "Bleeding Kansas" (pp. 472–74)

22. c; medium; "Bleeding Kansas" (pp. 472–74)

23. d; easy; "Bleeding Kansas" (pp. 472–74)

24. b; difficult; "Bleeding Kansas" (pp. 472–74)

25. a; difficult; The *Dred Scott* Decision (pp. 474–76)

26. b; difficult; The *Dred Scott* Decision (pp. 474–76)

27. a; difficult; The *Dred Scott* Decision (pp. 474–76)

28. c; easy; Prairie Republican: Abraham Lincoln
(pp. 476–77)

29. d; medium; Prairie Republican: Abraham Lincoln
(pp. 476–77)

30. c; easy; Prairie Republican: Abraham Lincoln
(pp. 476–77)

31. b; easy; Prairie Republican: Abraham Lincoln
(pp. 476–77)

32. c; difficult; Prairie Republican: Abraham Lincoln
(pp. 476–77)

33. c; medium; The Lincoln-Douglas Debates
(pp. 477–79)

34. b; medium; The Lincoln-Douglas Debates
(pp. 477–79)

35. a; medium; The Lincoln-Douglas Debates
(pp. 477–79)

36. c; easy; The Lincoln-Douglas Debates (pp. 477–79)

37. d; easy; The Aftermath of John Brown's Raid
(p. 480)

38. b; medium; The Aftermath of John Brown's Raid
(p. 480)

39. c; easy; Republican Victory in 1860 (pp. 480–83)

40. b; medium; Republican Victory in 1860
(pp. 480–83)

41. d; easy; Republican Victory in 1860 (pp. 480–83)

42. b; medium; Republican Victory in 1860
(pp. 480–83)

43. c; medium; Republican Victory in 1860
(pp. 480–83)

44. d; difficult; Secession Winter (pp. 483–86)

45. a; difficult; Secession Winter (pp. 483–86)

46. c; easy; Secession Winter (pp. 483–86)

47. d; medium; Secession Winter (pp. 483–86)

48. b; medium; Secession Winter (pp. 483–86)

49. b; medium; Secession Winter (pp. 483–86)

50. a; medium; Secession Winter (pp. 483–86)

Terminology Matching

1. h	9. f
2. q	10. p
3. d	11. a
4. g	12. e
5. c	13. j
6. m	14. b
7. k	15. l
8. o	

Chronology

Set One: E, D, C, B, A

Set Two: A, C, E, D, B

Short Answer

1. difficult; chapter introduction (pp. 449–50), The Aftermath of John Brown's Raid (p. 480)

2. medium; The Wilmot Proviso and the Expansion of Slavery (pp. 451–53)

3. easy; Debate and Compromise (pp. 454–56)

4. medium; Debate and Compromise (pp. 454–56)

5. medium; The Fugitive Slave Act (pp. 457–59)

6. medium; The Kansas-Nebraska Act (pp. 463–64)

7. difficult; The Election of 1856 (pp. 468–69), Freedom under Siege introduction (pp. 469, 472)

8. easy; Prairie Republican: Abraham Lincoln (pp. 476–77)

9. difficult; Republican Victory in 1860 (pp. 480–83)

10. easy; Secession Winter (pp. 483–86)

Essay

1. difficult; The Fugitive Slave Act (pp. 457–59)

2. easy; The Promise of Technology: Daguerreo-types: The "Sunbeam Art" (pp. 458–59)

3. medium; Realignment of the Party System (pp. 464–69)

4. difficult; Prairie Republican: Abraham Lincoln (pp. 476–77), The Lincoln-Douglas Debates (pp. 477–79), The Aftermath of John Brown's Raid (p. 480), Secession Winter (pp. 483–86)

Chapter 14: The Crucible of War, 1861–1865

Multiple Choice

1. b; difficult; chapter introduction (pp. 493–94), Hardship Below (pp. 513–15)

2. c; easy; "And the War Came" (pp. 494–95)

3. d; easy; Attack on Fort Sumter (p. 495)

4. a; easy; Attack on Fort Sumter (p. 495), The Upper South Chooses Sides (pp. 495–97)

5. b; difficult; The Upper South Chooses Sides (pp. 495–97)

6. c; medium; What They Fought For (pp. 497–98)

7. a; medium; What They Fought For (pp. 497–98)

8. d; medium; How They Expected to Win (pp. 498–500)

9. c; difficult; Lincoln and Davis Mobilize (pp. 500–2)

10. b; medium; Stalemate in the Eastern Theater (pp. 502–4)

11. a; easy; Stalemate in the Eastern Theater (pp. 502–4)

12. d; medium; Stalemate in the Eastern Theater (pp. 502–4)

13. c; easy; Union Victories in the Western Theater (pp. 504–6)

14. b; medium; Union Victories in the Western Theater (pp. 504–6)

15. a; difficult; War and Diplomacy in the Atlantic Theater (pp. 506–7)

16. b; medium; From Slaves to Contraband (pp. 507–9)

17. a; medium; From Slaves to Contraband (pp. 507–9)

18. d; difficult; From Slaves to Contraband (pp. 507–9)

19. c; medium; From Contraband to Free People (pp. 509–10)

20. a; difficult; From Contraband to Free People (pp. 509–10)

21. d; medium; War of Black Liberation (pp. 510–11)

22. a; medium; Revolution from Above (pp. 512–13)

23. b; medium; Hardship Below (pp. 513–15)

24. a; medium; Hardship Below (pp. 513–15)

25. c; medium; Hardship Below (pp. 513–15)

26. b; medium; The Disintegration of Slavery (p. 515)

27. d; easy; The Disintegration of Slavery (p. 515)

28. d; medium; The Disintegration of Slavery (p. 515)

29. a; medium; The Government and the Economy (pp. 518–19)

30. b; medium; The Government and the Economy (pp. 518–19)

31. c; easy; Women and Work on the Home Front (pp. 519–20)

32. d; medium; Women and Work on the Home Front (pp. 519–20)

33. b; medium; Women and Work on the Home Front (pp. 519–20)

34. c; easy; Women and Work on the Home Front (pp. 519–20)

35. a; difficult; Politics and Dissent (pp. 520–22)

36. d; medium; Politics and Dissent (pp. 520–22)

37. c; medium; Politics and Dissent (pp. 520–22)

38. a; medium; Politics and Dissent (pp. 520–22)

39. b; medium; Politics and Dissent (pp. 520–22)

40. c; medium; Vicksburg and Gettysburg (pp. 522–24)

41. a; medium; Vicksburg and Gettysburg (pp. 522–24)

42. b; medium; Grant Takes Command (pp. 524–28)

43. d; medium; Grant Takes Command (pp. 524–28)

44. b; medium; Historical Question: Why Did So Many Soldiers Die? (pp. 526–28)

45. a; medium; The Election of 1864 (pp. 528–30)

46. b; medium; The Election of 1864 (pp. 528–30)

47. d; easy; The Confederacy Collapses (pp. 530–31)

48. b; medium; The Confederacy Collapses (pp. 530–31)

49. c; medium; The Confederacy Collapses (pp. 530–31)

50. a; difficult; Conclusion: The Second American Revolution (p. 532)

Terminology Matching

1. m	9. f
2. o	10. g
3. b	11. i
4. r	12. j
5. h	13. d
6. c	14. q
7. p	15. k
8. e	

Chronology

Set One: D, A, B, C, E

Set Two: A, B, E, D, C

Short Answer

1. medium; "And the War Came" (pp. 494–95)

2. medium; What They Fought For (pp. 497–98)

3. easy; How They Expected to Win (pp. 498–500)

4. medium; Union Victories in the Western Theater (pp. 504–6), Grinding out Victory, 1863–1865 introduction (p. 522), Grant Takes Command (pp. 524–28)

5. difficult; From Slaves to Contraband (pp. 507–9), From Contraband to Free People (pp. 509–10)

6. medium; War of Black Liberation (pp. 510–11)

7. medium; The Disintegration of Slavery (p. 515)

8. easy; Women and Work on the Home Front (pp. 519–20)

9. difficult; Politics and Dissent (pp. 520–22)

10. easy; Historical Question: Why Did So Many Soldiers Die? (pp. 526–28)

Essay

1. difficult; What They Fought For (pp. 497–98)

2. medium; How They Expected to Win (pp. 498–500), War and Diplomacy in the Atlantic Theater (pp. 506–7)

3. medium; Lincoln and Davis Mobilize (pp. 500–2)

4. difficult; The South at War (pp. 511–15), The Confederacy Collapses (pp. 530–31)

Chapter 15: Reconstruction, 1863–1877

Multiple Choice

1. b; medium; chapter introduction (pp. 537–38)

2. a; medium; chapter introduction (pp. 537–38)

3. b; medium; chapter introduction (pp. 537–38)

4. c; easy; Wartime Reconstruction introduction (pp. 538–39), "To Bind Up the Nation's Wounds" (pp. 539–40)

5. b; easy; "To Bind Up the Nation's Wounds" (pp. 539–40)

6. a; medium; "To Bind Up the Nation's Wounds" (pp. 539–40)

7. a; medium; Land and Labor (p. 540)

8. c; medium; Land and Labor (p. 540)

9. c; difficult; Land and Labor (p. 540)

10. b; medium; The African American Quest for Autonomy (pp. 541–45)

11. c; medium; Presidential Reconstruction introduction (p. 545)

12. b; difficult; Johnson's Program of Reconciliation (pp. 545–46)

13. d; medium; Johnson's Program of Reconciliation (pp. 545–46)

14. a; medium; Johnson's Program of Reconciliation (pp. 545–46)

15. a; medium; Southern Resistance and Black Codes (pp. 546–47)

16. d; easy; Southern Resistance and Black Codes (pp. 546–47)

17. a; medium; Southern Resistance and Black Codes (pp. 546–47)

18. c; difficult; Expansion of Black Rights and Federal Authority (pp. 547–49)

19. d; medium; Expansion of Black Rights and Federal Authority (pp. 547–49)

20. a; easy; Expansion of Black Rights and Federal Authority (pp. 547–49)

21. b; easy; The Fourteenth Amendment and Escalating Violence (pp. 549–51)

22. b; easy; Radical Reconstruction and Military Rule (pp. 551–52)

23. d; easy; Radical Reconstruction and Military Rule (pp. 551–52)

24. c. easy; Impeaching a President (pp. 552–53)

25. c; easy; The Fifteenth Amendment and Women's Demands (pp. 553–55)

26. b; medium; The Fifteenth Amendment and Women's Demands (pp. 553–55)

27. a; easy; Freedmen, Yankees, and Yeomen (pp. 555–56)

28. d; medium; Freedmen, Yankees, and Yeomen (pp. 555–56)

29. b; difficult; Republican Rule (pp. 556–57, 560)

30. a; easy; Republican Rule (pp. 556–57, 560)

31. d; medium; Republican Rule (pp. 556–57, 560)

32. a; medium; White Landlords, Black Sharecroppers (pp. 560–62)

33. d; difficult; White Landlords, Black Sharecroppers (pp. 560–62)

34. c; easy; White Landlords, Black Sharecroppers (pp. 560–62)

35. b; medium; The Grant Regime: Cronies, Corruption, and Economic Collapse (pp. 562–64)

36. d; difficult; The Grant Regime: Cronies, Corruption, and Economic Collapse (pp. 562–64)

37. c; medium; The Grant Regime: Cronies, Corruption, and Economic Collapse (pp. 562–64)

38. a; easy; Northern Resolve Withers (pp. 564–65)

39. c; easy; Northern Resolve Withers (pp. 564–65)

40. a; difficult; Northern Resolve Withers (pp. 564–65)

41. b; difficult; Northern Resolve Withers (pp. 564–65)

42. b; easy; Northern Resolve Withers (pp. 564–65)

43. d; easy; White Supremacy Triumphs (pp. 565–67)

44. a; easy; White Supremacy Triumphs (pp. 565–67)

45. a; medium; An Election and a Compromise (pp. 567–69)

46. b; medium; An Election and a Compromise (pp. 567–69)

47. a; easy; An Election and a Compromise (pp. 567–69)

48. a; medium; An Election and a Compromise (pp. 567–69)

49. c; difficult; Conclusion: "A Revolution but Half Accomplished" (p. 569)

50. c; difficult; Conclusion: "A Revolution but Half Accomplished" (p. 569)

Terminology Matching

1. q
2. r
3. x
4. i
5. l
6. s
7. f
8. q
9. m
10. p

11. p
12. q
13. p
14. b
15. e
16. d
17. t
18. h
19. t
20. u
21. c
22. y
23. v
24. m
25. h
26. a
27. o
28. j
29. k
30. m

Chronology

Set One: C, A, B

Set Two: A, B, C, D

Short Answer

1. medium; An Election and a Compromise (pp. 567–69)

2. medium; Northern Resolve Withers (pp. 564–65)

3. easy; Congressional Reconstruction (pp. 549–55)

4. medium; Republican Rule (pp. 556–57, 560)

5. medium; Republican Rule (pp. 556–57, 560)

6. easy; Southern Resistance and Black Codes (pp. 546–47)

7. medium; The African American Quest for Autonomy (pp. 541–45)

8. easy; The Fourteenth Amendment and Escalating Violence (pp. 549–51)

9. easy; The Fifteenth Amendment and Women's Demands (pp. 553–55)

10. medium; Northern Resolve Withers (pp. 564–65)

Essay

1. medium; Wartime Reconstruction (pp. 538–45), Presidential Reconstruction (pp. 545–49), Congressional Reconstruction (pp. 549–55), The Struggle in the South (pp. 555–62)

2. easy; Reconstruction Collapses (pp. 562–69)

3. difficult; Wartime Reconstruction (pp. 538–45), Presidential Reconstruction (pp. 545–49), The Struggle in the South (pp. 555–62)

4. medium; Wartime Reconstruction (pp. 538–45), Presidential Reconstruction (pp. 545–49), Congressional Reconstruction (pp. 549–55)

APPENDIX

LESSON 1: A WORLD APART

Multiple Choice   Choose the letter of the best answer.

1. According to historians cited in the video, the study of history should do all of the following EXCEPT
    a. provide a sense of who we are.
    b. include multiple stories.
    c. spark our curiosity.
    d. emphasize dates and battles.

2. In the Northwest, indigenous peoples used art on totem poles to
    a. give directions.
    b. stake out boundaries.
    c. commemorate clans.
    d. create items for trade.

3. The Chumash culture along the California coast was
    a. completely self-sufficient.
    b. connected to other cultures through trade.
    c. isolated from the interior.
    d. associated with elaborate burial mounds.

4. In the video, Professor Michael Adler states the view that the major cultural achievement of the ancestral pueblo peoples was the
    a. development of a community life.
    b. division of power among rulers.
    c. application of irrigation systems.
    d. avoidance of conflict with nearby tribes.

5. At Cahokia, Monk's Mound likely served as a site for
    a. burying women.
    b. the ruling chief.
    c. dispatching hunters.
    d. observing nearby tribes.

6. In the video, Professor Alex Barker notes that the indigenous peoples of the Southeast
   a. lived in fixed tribal units.
   b. had access to very limited resources.
   c. were politically complex.
   d. looked to the ocean for trade.

7. Among the pre-Columbian indigenous peoples of the Northeast,
   a. single-family housing prevailed.
   b. Iroquois and Algonquian people seldom mingled.
   c. men concentrated on village life.
   d. women cultivated food crops.

8. The legacy of pre-Columbian indigenous peoples includes lessons about
   a. relationships with the environment.
   b. spirituality.
   c. cultural diversity.
   d. all of the above.

Short Answer   Your answers should specifically address the points indicated in one or two paragraphs.

1. Explain the following statement in reference to archaic Americans: The absence of written sources means that ancient human beings remain anonymous.

2. What were the similarities of the cultures of indigenous peoples in America in 1492, and how did they differ from the culture of Europe at the time?

3. What were the main features of the Mexica culture prior to European contact?

Essay Question   Your response should be several paragraphs long. Your answer should elaborate on the points indicated in a manner that expresses understanding of the material.

1. Describe and explain the characteristics of the pre-Columbian indigenous cultures that existed in the Pacific Northwest, the California coastal region, the Southwest, the Mississippi Valley, the Southeast, and the Northeast. What is the legacy of these cultures?

ANSWER KEY

Multiple Choice

1. d; easy; video segment 1
2. c; medium; pp. P-10–P-11; video segment 2
3. b; medium; pp. P-10–P-11; video segment 3
4. a; medium; pp. P-13–P-15; video segment 4
5. b; easy; pp. P-16–P-17; video segment 5
6. c; medium; video segment 6
7. d; medium; pp. P-17–P-18; video segment 7
8. d; difficult; pp. P-17–P-19; video segment 8

Short Answer

1. medium; (pp. P-2–P-5)
    *   How do we learn about cultures that did not use written languages?
    *   What can we learn about those cultures?
    *   What elements do written sources bring to our knowledge about people?

2. difficult; (pp. P-6–P-7)
    *   Consider the adaptations to the environment in order to survive.
    *   Are social and political organizations similar? How did various cultures communicate?
    *   Contrast indigenous cultures with European technology and domesticated animals, etc.

3. medium; (pp. P-19–P-22)
    *   What was the extent of their empire in the Americas?
    *   How was their society structured?
    *   What role did tribute play in their empire?

Essay

1. medium; (pp. P-7–P-8, P-10–P-11, P-13–P-19); video segments 2–7
    *   Consider how the environment affected the economy of each culture.
    *   How did they organize their communities?
    *   Identify at least one feature of each culture.
    *   What can we learn from them?

LESSON 2:
WORLDS TRANSFORMED

Multiple Choice   Choose the letter of the best answer.

1. Some historians believe that because of the effects of the Columbian exchange, the so-called discovery of America was
   a. beneficial to the indigenous peoples.
   b. the most important event in the history of the world.
   c. of little benefit to Europe and Asia.
   d. all of the above.

2. Cortés' entry into Tenochtitlan was a unique moment in world history because
   a. two incredible civilizations previously unknown to each other made contact.
   b. Montezuma immediately converted to Catholicism.
   c. Cortés realized how superior the Aztecs really were in technology.
   d. European brutality shocked Aztec sensibilities.

3. Cabeza de Vaca differed from other Spanish conquistadores in the respect that he
   a. appreciated the Indian world that he entered.
   b. refused to allow missionaries to travel with him.
   c. found great wealth in Mexico.
   d. applied technological advantages to subdue the natives.

4. Santa Fe was founded in the early seventeenth century because
   a. Acoma Indians needed refuge from the Spanish.
   b. Spain wanted to use the slave labor in the mines there.
   c. the Spanish could establish an identity separate from the Pueblo communities.
   d. missionaries had already converted the local Indians.

5. In the video, Professor David Weber reminds us that in frontier regions
   a. people tend to develop a new culture.
   b. democracy always emerges among settlers.
   c. indigenous culture is totally destroyed.
   d. expansion moves almost invariably from east to west.

Short Answer   Your answers should specifically address the points indicated in one or two paragraphs.

1.   How and why was Cortés able to conquer Mexico?

2.   Explain the role Portugal played in the age of European exploration.

3.   How and why did a geographic revolution take place in the sixteenth century?

4.   Why did Spain become the dominant European power in the New World in the sixteenth century?

5.   Why did Spain establish settlements in areas that became Florida and New Mexico?

Essay Question   Your response should be several paragraphs long. Your answer should elaborate on the points indicated in a manner that expresses understanding of the material.

1.   Describe and explain the meaning of the Columbian exchange. How did both the Old and New Worlds experience gains and losses because of the exchange? Which world benefited the most? Why? In what ways does the exchange continue today?

2.   During the sixteenth century, Spain became the most powerful country in both Europe and the Americas. How and why did this happen? How did Spain transform America? How is the Spanish influence still visible in the United States today?

ANSWER KEY

Multiple Choice

1.   b; medium; pp. 11–12; video segment 2
2.   a; medium; video segment 3
3.   a; medium; video segment 3
4.   c; medium; pp. 27–28; video segment 4
5.   a; medium; p. 26; video segment 5

Short Answer

1.   medium; pp. 13–14, 16–17; video segment 3
     - What technological advantages did Cortés have?
     - How and why was he able to get help from some of the indigenous peoples?

2.   medium; pp. 6–7
     - Where was Portugal located?
     - Why did Portugal encourage voyages around Africa?
     - What technological advances are associated with Portugal's efforts?

3.   medium; pp. 9–11
     - How did mapmakers depict the world prior to this time?
     - How did Martin Waldseemüller map the world? What information did he have?
     - What effect did the European "discovery" of the Pacific Ocean have?

4.   medium; pp. 28–31
   - What areas did Spain colonize? By what authority?
   - What resources in the Americas did Spain use to its advantage?
   - How were they able to control and use the native peoples?

5.   easy; pp. 27–28; video segment 4
   - How would a colony in Florida solidify its claim and protect its ships?
   - What were the Spanish seeking in New Mexico? What did they end up doing there?

Essay

1.   medium; pp. 11–12, 26, 28–31; video segments 2, 5
   - What is the Columbian exchange?
   - How did New World food products, crops, and mineral resources affect Europe and Asia?
   - How did diseases affect both areas?
   - Did the New World gain anything from Europe? What?
   - How does the exchange of organisms continue?

2.   medium; pp. 4–6, 10–31; video segments 2–5
   - What geographic advantages did Spain have?
   - How did Spain use the resources it gained in the Americas?
   - Why was Spain able to establish its empire? What parts of their culture did they impose?
   - How is the influence reflected in people, language, religion, architecture, etc.?

LESSON 3: SETTLING THE SOUTHERN COLONIES

Multiple Choice Choose the letter of the best answer.

1. In the video, Professor Karen Kupperman points out that the British painter John White depicted American Indians in the vicinity of Roanoke as
   a. agriculturalists.
   b. savages.
   c. warriors.
   d. hunters.

2. In the video, Professor Karen Kupperman speculates that the "lost" colonists of Roanoke likely
   a. were killed by Indians.
   b. melded in with the Indian population in the area.
   c. abandoned the island to go to the West Indies.
   d. starved due to laziness.

3. In the video, Professor Karen Kupperman observes that Powhatan initially saw the Jamestown colonists as
   a. capable and organized.
   b. a major military threat.
   c. a source for obtaining trade goods.
   d. allies against hostile tribes.

4. Relations between Jamestown colonists and Indians changed by 1622 because
   a. Powhatan was losing power.
   b. Virginia became a royal colony.
   c. John Smith took over as Governor.
   d. expansion of the settlement now encroached on Indian land.

5. When the first Africans arrived in Virginia, they were considered
   a. slaves for life.
   b. a source of labor.
   c. knowledgeable about tobacco production.
   d. potential allies with the Indians.

6. The life of Anthony Johnson illustrated how
   a. Africans could obtain freedom and land in the Chesapeake region.
   b. British settlers could prosper in one generation.
   c. Virginians moved westward beyond the fall line by 1650.
   d. all of the above.

7. One consequence of Bacon's Rebellion was
   a. diminishing power of the planter aristocracy in Virginia.
   b. peace between settlers and Indians of the frontier.
   c. greater efforts to divide poor whites from poor blacks.
   d. a more even distribution of property among classes.

8. In the video, Professor Dan Littlefield observes that the shift in seventeenth century Virginia away from indentured servant labor was accompanied by
   a. increasing tobacco production.
   b. slowing rates of population growth.
   c. accelerating movement toward democracy.
   d. using race as a dividing line among the poor.

9. In the video, Professor Karen Kupperman refers to property ownership in colonial Virginia as a "double-edged sword" because it
   a. applied to both land and labor.
   b. guaranteed both whites and blacks the right to vote.
   c. tended to destroy a sense of community.
   d. gave women a cause to complain about.

Short Answer   Your answers should specifically address the points indicated in one or two paragraphs.

1. Why was John Smith a critical person in the survival of Jamestown?

2. How did Nathaniel Bacon justify his rebellion in 1676?

3. In what ways was seventeenth century South Carolina, a frontier outpost for Barbados?

Essay Question   Your response should be several paragraphs long. Your answer should elaborate on the points indicated in a manner that expresses understanding of the material.

1. Why did the British establish colonies in the Chesapeake and Carolina? How and why did life and labor in these colonies change during the 17th century? What developments occurred then that continued to shape America for generations?

ANSWER KEY

Multiple Choice

1. a; easy; p. 31; video segment 1
2. b; medium; p. 31; video segment 1
3. c; medium; pp. 41–44; video segment 2
4. d; medium; pp. 41–44; video segment 2
5. b; medium; video segment 4
6. a; medium; video segment 4
7. c; difficult; pp. 58–59; video; document; video segment 4
8. d; difficult; pp. 62–65; video segment 7
9. a; medium; pp. 62–65, 36-39; video segment 1–7

Short Answer

1. easy; pp. 37–43; video segment 2
    - Why was the initial settlement suffering from a leadership void?
    - What did he force the settlers to do?
    - How did he get along with the Indians in the area?

2. medium; pp. 58–59; document, video segment 4
    - What is Bacon complaining about?
    - Who does he blame for the troubles?
    - Was he guilty of treason?

3. medium; pp. 59–63; video segment 6
    - Who settled the Carolina region?
    - What socioeconomic system was put in place in Carolina?
    - What products were traded between Barbados and Carolina?

Essay

1. medium; pp. 40, 44–45, 47–56, 58–63; document; video segments 2–4, 6
    - Consider the economic motives for each region. What adaptations were made economically?
    - What social system developed? How was land parceled out?
    - Why did a servant labor system change to a slave labor system?
    - How would you characterize these colonies by the late seventeenth century? What were the long-term economic, social, and political patterns established?

LESSON 4:
SETTLING IN NEW ENGLAND

Multiple Choice   Choose the letter of the best answer.

1. Prior to the Pilgrims' arrival in the New England area, American Indians in that region had
   a. suffered the effects of an epidemic.
   b. formed an alliance to trade with Europeans.
   c. converted to Christianity because of earlier missionaries.
   d. abandoned the region because of the climate.

2. In the video, Historian Jim Baker observes that American Indians in the area of Plymouth colony signed a treaty of friendship with the Pilgrims because they
   a. realized the military superiority of the Pilgrims.
   b. sought allies against neighboring Indian tribes.
   c. wanted to acquire agricultural products from the Pilgrims.
   d. all of the above.

3. In the video, Historian Jim Baker observes that the Pilgrim story has been mythologized in America because
   a. New Englanders wrote most of the history books.
   b. the nation needed a past separate from England.
   c. it was an empathetic story about families.
   d. all of the above.

4. In the video, Professor Curtis Thomas describes the Puritans as
   a. perfectionists.
   b. Utopians.
   c. earthy people trying to be holy.
   d. hypocritical regarding sinfulness.

5. Ann Hutchinson was banished from Massachusetts Bay for all of the following reasons EXCEPT
   a. Puritans had no process to deal with dissenters.
   b. she was operating out of the norm for women.
   c. Ann challenged the teachings of ministers.
   d. men joined in meetings to hear her views.

6. In the video, Professor John Demos points out that when settlers were taken captive by the Indians, it raised the fundamental issue of
   a. ransom to be paid.
   b. which culture was civilizing the other.
   c. military rescue operations.
   d. treaty provisions covering prisoners of war.

7. Metacomet (King Philip) leads a war against New England settlers in the 1670s because
   a. trade was declining between the settlers and Indians.
   b. Puritan missionaries had become too aggressive.
   c. settlers continued to encroach upon Indian lands.
   d. he needed to divert attention away from internal problems.

8. In the video, Professor Jon Butler maintains that the witchcraft episode in Salem in 1692 resulted in part from
   a. outside religious missionaries disrupting the Puritan community.
   b. infiltration of local Indian religious traditions into the community.
   c. an attempt to control religious dissenters.
   d. a need to explain the decline of the original Puritan society.

9. In the video, Professor John Demos states his opinion that the Salem witchcraft episode is comparable to the
   a. Red Scare of the 1940s and 1950s.
   b. Boston Massacre of 1770.
   c. race riots of the 1910s and 1920s.
   d. anti-war protests of the 1960s and 1970s.

10. In the video, Professor Curtis Thomas observes that the Puritan influence on Americans can still be seen in their tendency to assume
    a. religion controls their lives
    b. people are basically evil
    c. economic forces determine how communities organize
    d. government will provide for them

11. In the video, Professor Jon Butler says that we tend to overemphasize the Puritan legacy in regard to
    a. economic development of the country.
    b. shaping our political system.
    c. the foundation of religion in America.
    d. the importance of community building.

Short Answer   Your answers should specifically address the points indicated in one or two paragraphs.

1. Why did the Pilgrim story become mythological in America?

2. How was the Pueblo Revolt similar to King Philip's War?

3. How and why were the New England colonies different from the southern colonies in the 17th century?

Essay Question   Your response should be several paragraphs long. Your answer should elaborate on the points indicated in a manner that expresses understanding of the material.

1. Describe the Puritan "city upon a hill" envisioned by John Winthrop. Analyze the ways in which the Puritans attempted to realize this vision in New England. What tensions and conflicts did this bring about? To what extent did Puritan influences shape America, and how is this reflected today?

ANSWER KEY

Multiple Choice

1. a; medium; pp. 75–76; video segments 1, 2
2. b; medium; pp. 75–76; video segments 1, 2
3. d; medium; video segment 2
4. c; medium; pp. 76–84; video segment 3
5. a; medium; pp. 71–72, 84–85; video segment 3
6. b; difficult; video segment 4
7. c; difficult; pp. 95–97; video segment 4
8. d; difficult; pp. 90–92; video segment 6
9. a; easy; pp. 90–92; video segment 6
10. b; medium; video segment 7
11. c; medium video segment 7

Short Answer

1. medium; video segment 7
   - Who told the story?
   - Why was a story needed?
   - Why was the story empathetic?

2. medium; video segment 5
   - What prompted the two episodes?
   - What were the results?

3. easy; pp. 76–77, 79, 82–88, 95–99
   - Consider the geography of each region and its effects on people and the economy.
   - What role did religion and community play in each area?

Essay

1. medium; pp. 71–72, 76–88, 90–92, 95–97; video segments 3, 4, 6, 7
   - What ideals were expressed by Winthrop?
   - What role did community play in upholding the vision?
   - How were settlements organized and governed?
   - Why did dissent occur and how did they deal with it?
   - What explains the Salem witchcraft episode?
   - How do we see Puritan influences in our society?

LESSON 5:
DIVERSIFYING BRITISH AMERICA

Multiple Choice   Choose the letter of the best answer.

1. The trial of journalist John Peter Zenger was significant because the verdict
    a. found the defendant guilty.
    b. became a foundation stone for freedom of the press.
    c. established freedom of religion for Jews in America.
    d. set a precedent for requiring a jury of peers.

2. Ethnic groups sustained their identity in colonial New York by
    a. preventing intermarriage with other groups.
    b. refusing to work with members of other faiths.
    c. maintaining familiar language and religious affiliations.
    d. moving to the frontier regions.

3. One result of the multiplicity of religions in colonial America was the
    a. persecution of the Jews.
    b. tightening of the affiliation with colonial governments.
    c. marked improvement in relations with American Indians.
    d. growing sense of toleration for different faiths.

4. Conrad Weiser and Shikellamy were important persons in colonial Pennsylvania because they
    a. served as go-betweens to bridge cultural differences.
    b. shared farm land in the Susquahanna river valley.
    c. joined the Ephrata Cloister in search of spiritual guidance.
    d. signed the treaty preserving Indian rights in Pennsylvania Dutch country.

5. Toward the end of the colonial period, American Indians and European colonists
    a. agreed to respect the other's culture.
    b. realized that the French posed a common threat to their interests.
    c. engaged in a series of wars along the Atlantic coast.
    d. had a greater sense of difference than earlier.

Short Answer   Your answers should specifically address the points indicated in one or two paragraphs.

1. Explain how and why New York became a diverse community in the colonial period. How was this diversity reflected? How was ethnic identity maintained?

2. Why did Pennsylvania become "the best poor [white] man's country" in colonial America?

3. Describe the role of go-betweens on the frontier. How did they help maintain some degree of stability?

4. By 1700, how and why were the British colonies in North America different from those established by Spain?

Essay Question   Your response should be several paragraphs long. Your answer should elaborate on the points indicated in a manner that expresses understanding of the material.

1. How and why did the middle colonies become more diverse than the southern and New England colonies? What are the short- and long-term economic, social, and political consequences of this diversity?

ANSWER KEY

Multiple Choice

1. b; easy; video segment 3
2. c; medium; video segment 3
3. d; medium; video segment 6
4. a; easy; video segment 5
5. d; difficult; video segment 6

Short Answer

1. medium; pp. 92–93; video segments 2–4
    -   What effect did the Dutch origins of the colony have?
    -   Why did commerce attract diverse peoples? What ethnic groups and religions were reflected?
    -   What roles did religion and neighborhood settlement play in identity?

2. medium; pp. 113–118
    -   What geographic advantages did Pennsylvania have?
    -   How did the attitude of its founders encourage opportunity? What types of people settled there?
    -   How did it blend agriculture with commerce?

3. medium; video segment 5
    -   What types of problems did these people deal with?
    -   What skills did they have that helped resolve conflicts?
    -   How were they able to establish respect and understanding?

4. medium; pp. 99–100
    -   What role did geography play?
    -   How were the people different? How were their relations with Indian peoples different?
    -   How was the economy different? Religion? Politics?

Essay

1. medium; pp. 92–95, 105–108, 112–118; video segments 2–5
    - What role did geography play?
    - Who founded these colonies? How tolerant were the founders and early settlers?
    - What types of people settled there? What religions and talents did they bring?
    - How did these colonies blend agriculture and commerce?
    - How did diversity contribute toward further toleration and freedom?
    - How did diversity help shape an American identity?

LESSON 6:
A DISTINCTIVE SOCIETY

Multiple Choice   Choose the letter of the best answer.

1. Among the factors which led to an increase in the importation of African slaves in the eighteenth century was the
   a. population decline among white colonists.
   b. breaking up of the plantation system.
   c. improvement in survival rates for blacks and whites.
   d. improvement in living and working conditions for slaves.

2. In the video, Professor Dan Littlefield makes the point that Africans being sold in Africa were
   a. shipped out according to a specific order of preference.
   b. not always exactly what slave traders and buyers preferred.
   c. most often people with royal heritage.
   d. willing to leave Africa since conditions were so bad there.

3. Some scholars suggest that African American culture began when Africans
   a. were sold on the auction blocks.
   b. were thrown together on slave ships.
   c. had children born in America.
   d. refused to adapt their traditions to new surroundings.

4. In the video, Professor James O. Horton suggests that one way Africans affected the colony of South Carolina was in the
   a. production of rice.
   b. growing of tobacco.
   c. invention of the cotton gin.
   d. introduction of new varieties of wheat.

5. "Gullah" refers to a language which
   a. traces its roots to Africa.
   b. is still alive in South Carolina.
   c. became a primary means of communication among slaves.
   d. all of the above.

6. Slavery changed the accustomed class system in the southern colonies in the respect that it
    a. unified whites in thinking they were supposed to be on top.
    b. led to a more level distribution of wealth.
    c. split whites between those who owned slaves and those who did not.
    d. made the area a more desirable place for poor whites to live.

7. The South was a distinctive society by 1750 because of its commitment to slavery and that
    a. religious diversity was more widespread there.
    b. most of the people lived in booming port cities.
    c. an emerging middle class dominated political life.
    d. the British considered it to be the most valuable part of North America.

Short Answer   Your answers should specifically address the points indicated in one or two paragraphs.

1. Describe the process known as "seasoning" in the African slave trade. Why did this process help make slaves more valuable to planters?

2. To what extent was an African American culture emerging in colonial America? How was this culture expressed?

Essay Questions   Your response should be several paragraphs long. Your answers should elaborate on the points indicated in a manner that expresses understanding of the material.

1. How and why had the southern colonies become a distinctive society by 1760? What were the short- and long-term consequences of this distinctiveness.

2. Compare and contrast the northern, middle, and southern colonies by 1760. What experiences were unifying the colonies? How were the British colonies different from Spain's colonies?

3. How and why were the British colonists becoming "American" by 1760? What characterized this society?

ANSWER KEY

Multiple Choice

1. c; difficult; video segment 1
2. b; medium; pp. 118–119; video segment 2
3. b; medium; pp. 120–123, 126; video segments 2, 3
4. a; easy; video segments 3, 4
5. d; medium; pp. 126–127; video segment 5video segments 3, 4
6. a; medium; pp. 124–125
7. d; medium; pp. 124–125

Short Answer

1. medium; pp. 120–122; video segment 2
   - How was the physical condition of the slaves arriving from Africa restored?
   - What sort of cultural changes had to take place?
   - How would a healthier and more communicative slave population benefit planters?

2. medium; 123, 126; video segments 3, 4
   - How important were kin networks to the slaves? How were they expressed?
   - How did names and language reflect a new culture?
   - How did food crops and music fit into this scheme?

Essay

1. medium; 123–127; video segments 3–5
   - What role did geography play?
   - What crops were developed?
   - Why did a slave labor system develop?
   - How did the slave labor system affect race relations? How did slavery influence the class system and politics?
   - How would slavery ultimately affect relations with other colonies and eventually states (after the Revolution)?

2. medium; pp. 127–136
   - What role did geography play?
   - How were the economy and diversity issues different?
   - How did commerce and consumption unify them?
   - What role did religion play?
   - What did it mean that they were all British subjects?
   - How did they differ from Spain regarding geography, religion, agriculture, and types of people present?

3. difficult; p. 136; video segment 6
   - How had the encounters with Indian peoples forged an identity?
   - To what extent was freedom becoming associated with America?
   - How and why was diversity shaping a different identity?
   - To what extent had an "American" economic and political identity emerged?

LESSON 7:
MAKING A REVOLUTION

Multiple Choice   Choose the letter of the best answer.

1. In the video, Professors Sheila Skemp and Jon Butler indicate that the American colonies were ripe for revolution prior to 1776 for all of the following reasons EXCEPT that they
   a. had developed a new political order.
   b. had a clear blueprint for a new national government.
   c. were steeped in the English tradition of rights.
   d. lived in diverse social and economic communities.

2. James Otis argued that the writs of assistance violated
   a. a natural right of privacy.
   b. the Fourth Amendment to the Constitution.
   c. British court orders.
   d. colonial provisions for trial by jury.

3. In the video, Professor Edward Countryman points out that as a result of the Stamp Act crisis, the prime issue for Americans shifted to the question of
   a. troops on the western frontier.
   b. preparation of a declaration of independence.
   c. propaganda about British abuses.
   d. who is in charge of taxing policy.

4. In the video, Professors Patricia Cline Cohen and Sheila Skemp maintain that tea became invested with a lot of political meaning in the 1760s and 1770s because
   a. taxes on it were exorbitant.
   b. it was a reminder that Britain maintained its right to tax the colonials.
   c. boycotts of tea were ineffective.
   d. colonial social customs demanded that it be served with dinner.

Short Answer   Your answers should specifically address the points indicated in one or two paragraphs.

1. After listening to and reflecting upon James Otis' arguments against the writs of assistance, John Adams observed that "then and there, the child of independence was born." Explain why Adams made this statement. Do you agree with him? Why or why not? (LO 3; FP 5; video segment 5)

Essay Question   Your response should be several paragraphs long. Your answer should elaborate on the points indicated in a manner that expresses understanding of the material.

1. Describe and explain the evolution of American political thought and tactics in opposing British policies between 1754 and 1774. Why and how had the revolutionary movement brought the colonies to the brink of declaring independence? Do you think that the American Revolution was inevitable by 1774? Why or why not?

ANSWER KEY

Multiple Choice

1. b; difficult; video segment 1
2. a; medium; video segment 3
3. d; medium; p. 158; video segment 4
4. b; medium; pp. 163–166; video segment 6

Short Answer

1. medium; video segment 3
    *   What was Otis' central argument?
    *   How could Otis' argument be applied to other issues in the 1760s and 1770s?
    *   How does Otis' argument connect to a right of revolution? How does Otis' argument connect to the Declaration of Independence?

Essay

1. difficult; pp. 144–173; video segments 1–7
    *   Consider the ingredients necessary to make a revolution.
    *   What was the status of colonial political union in 1754?
    *   How did the Americans begin to apply natural rights to their situation?
    *   Why and how did the Americans connect ideas of liberty and property? Why would this connection lead them toward more revolutionary positions?
    *   Describe the various tactics the Americans used to express their disagreement with the British. How and why did their tactics and actions coalesce into a revolutionary movement?
    *   What was the status of colonial political union in 1774?
    *   Take a position on the inevitability question and defend it.

LESSON 8:
DECLARING INDEPENDENCE

Multiple Choice Choose the letter of the best answer.

1. Professor Edward Countryman states in the video that he thinks Thomas Jefferson's vision of equality at the time of the writing of the Declaration of Independence meant
   a. the American people were equal to other people.
   b. the west was equal to the east.
   c. women were equal to men.
   d. free blacks were equal to slaves.

2. Thomas Jefferson's initial draft of the Declaration of Independence blamed the King for the slave trade because
   a. records showed that the profits went to the British treasury.
   b. that was a popular position in Virginia at that time.
   c. he wanted to discourage slaves from joining the British army.
   d. he believed in equality of the races.

3. Congress excised the passage in the Declaration of Independence condemning George III for slavery because
   a. they wanted stronger language used.
   b. they were still awaiting a response to the olive branch petition.
   c. the issue itself was too divisive and controversial.
   d. slaves had already joined the British army.

4. Professor James Oliver Horton believes that Thomas Jefferson's position on slavery illustrates
   a. the hypocrisy of the entire Declaration of Independence.
   b. the American conflict in trying to live up to principles.
   c. that Virginia would soon abolish slavery.
   d. the unanimity among the delegates at the Second Continental Congress.

5. Professor Joseph Ellis points out that, on the whole, Congress' editing of the Declaration of Independence
   a. weakened the document considerably.
   b. clearly made George III the target.
   c. made for a more cogent and stately document.
   d. illustrated the ineffectiveness of committees for such a task.

6. The signing of the Declaration of Independence was difficult and meaningful at the time because the signers were
   a. in a position of committing treason.
   b. sure to become rich and famous.
   c. now obligated to join Washington's army.
   d. not sure of exact wording of the document.

7. In the video, Professors Cohen, Ellis, and Countryman maintain that the Declaration of Independence has become part of the American creed partly because it has been used by all of the following EXCEPT
   a. women's rights advocates.
   b. Abraham Lincoln.
   c. the gay population.
   d. corporate executives.

8. In the video, Professor James Oliver Horton says that for African Americans the Declaration of Independence
   a. is a living document.
   b. should be amended.
   c. is meaningless.
   d. applies only to the nineteenth century.

Short Answer   Your answers should specifically address the points indicated in one or two paragraphs.

1. What were the contradictory tasks of the Second Continental Congress in 1775? How did they pursue each one?

2. Why was Thomas Jefferson chosen to be the primary author of the Declaration of Independence? What was important about that?

3. Explain the key points of political philosophy contained in the Declaration of Independence.

Essay Question   Your response should be several paragraphs long. Your answer should elaborate on the points indicated in a manner that expresses understanding of the material.

1. Describe and explain the background, purpose, and meaning of the Declaration of Independence. Why did this document become part of the American creed?

ANSWER KEY

Multiple Choice

1. a; easy; video segment 3
2. b; medium; video segment 3
3. c; medium; video segment 3
4. b; medium; video segment 3
5. c; medium; video segment 4
6. a; easy; p. 192; video segments 4, 5
7. d; medium; video segments 5, 6
8. a; medium; video segments 5, 6

Short Answer

1. medium; pp. 184–186, 187–188
   - Consider the situation when the Congress convened.
   - What steps did they take to prepare for war?
   - How did they continue to pursue peace with King George?

2. medium; video segment 3
   - Who were the likely authors?
   - What role did Jefferson play in the Congress?
   - Why did others turn down the job?
   - What talents did Jefferson have? How did he see the world?
   - Why was it important that he was from Virginia?

3. medium; pp. 189, A-1–A3; video segments 2, 3
   - How are natural rights expressed in the document?
   - What is the purpose of government?
   - What do the people have a right to do in case the government falls short?

Essay

1. medium; pp. 171, 174–178, 183–189, A-1–A-3; video segments 1–6
   - Consider the significant events and actions that brought the delegates to consider a formal declaration of independence.
   - What are some of the key grievances in the document?
   - How does the document justify revolution?
   - What did the document mean in 1776?
   - Why did the statement about equality change over time?
   - What key individuals and groups have applied the Declaration to pursue principles stated in the document?
   - Why does the document have meaning today?

LESSON 9:
WINNING INDEPENDENCE

Multiple Choice   Choose the letter of the best answer.

1. All of the following were advantages of the British at the beginning of the Revolutionary War EXCEPT
    a. Americans were poorly armed.
    b. a majority of the American people were loyal to Britain
    c. Americans lacked adequate financing.
    d. the British Army and Navy were considered among the best in the world.

2. All of the following were advantages of the Americans at the beginning of the Revolutionary War EXCEPT
    a. they were fighting a defensive war.
    b. their cause was more compelling.
    c. they were supported by most of the Iroquois Confederacy.
    d. General Washington understood what it took to win.

3. Between 1776-1778, much of the Revolutionary War was fought in New York and New Jersey because
    a. the British were trying to cut off New England from the rest of America.
    b. the American forces were weakest there.
    c. the British already controlled the South.
    d. the French were blockading the Chesapeake region.

4. Washington's victory at Trenton was important because it
    a. crushed British General Howe's forces.
    b. proved that fighting would go on during the winter.
    c. illustrated the vital roles of blacks and women in the military.
    d. boosted morale and assured reenlistments.

5. Slaves in South Carolina and Georgia could achieve freedom during the Revolutionary War by joining
    a. the militia.
    b. Continental Army.
    c. British forces.
    d. all of the above.

6. At Oriskany, New York, in August, 1777, America Indians
   a. ambushed British forces.
   b. fought on both sides.
   c. helped the British take Fort Stanwix.
   d. signed a peace treaty with the Americans.

7. At Valley Forge during the winter of 1777-1778, Baron von Steuben
   a. served as a negotiator with the American Indians in the area.
   b. offered to spy on German mercenaries.
   c. procured needed food from the Pennsylvania countryside.
   d. helped turn American forces into a professional army.

8. In the video, Professor Calvin L. Christman observes that, at Valley Forge, most American soldiers remained committed because of
   a. promise of higher pay at the end of the war.
   b. an almost mystical bond to cause and comrades.
   c. British atrocities in the region.
   d. assurances that the war was almost over.

9. After the Battle of Monmouth,
   a. British forces never faced Washington's army again in the North.
   b. American forces retreated in disgrace.
   c. women were accepted as regular combat troops.
   d. the French agreed to become allies.

10. At the Battle of Monmouth, Molly Ludwig Hayes
    a. served as a spy for the British.
    b. saw combat duty.
    c. provided refuge for retreating Americans.
    d. burned her house to avoid surrendering it.

11. In the video, Professor Sheila Skemp observes that loyalists in the South were
    a. firmly opposed to slavery.
    b. quickly joining the regular British Army.
    c. mostly recent immigrants from Barbados.
    d. less numerous than the British thought.

Short Answer   Your answers should specifically address the points indicated in one or two paragraphs.

1. Who were the loyalists in the Revolutionary War? Why were they the "true losers" in the war?

2. How and why did the Battle of Oriskany affect the outcome of the Battle of Saratoga?

3. Who were the "Molly Pitchers" of the war? How did women support the war effort?

4. What effect did the French alliance have on the outcome of the Revolutionary War?

Essay Question   Your response should be several paragraphs long. Your answer should elaborate on the points indicated in a manner that expresses understanding of the material.

1. Describe and explain the roles played by loyalists, African Americans, women, and American Indians during the Revolutionary War. How did the outcome of the war affect them?

2. Describe and explain why the British lost and the Americans won the Revolutionary War. In your answer, cite key military battles as well as other factors.

ANSWER KEY

Multiple Choice

1. b; medium; pp. 192–194; document; video segments 1, 2
2. c; medium; pp. 192–194; document; video segments 1, 2
3. a; medium; pp. 194–196
4. d; medium; p. 195; video segments 1, 2
5. c; medium; video segment 2
6. b; medium; p. 205; video segment 3
7. d; easy; document, video segment 4
8. b; medium; document; video segment 4
9. a; medium; video segment 5
10. b; medium; video segment 5
11. d; medium; pp. 208–212; video segment 6

Short Answer

1. medium; pp. 197–202, 213–215; video segments 6, 7
   • Consider the economic status, political positions, and location of the loyalists.
   • What did they have at stake in the Revolution? What happened to them at the end of the war?

2. difficult; p. 205; video segment 3
   • What happened at Oriskany, particularly in reference to the American Indians' role?
   • What did the British army do after Oriskany?
   • How did lack of reinforcement affect Burgoyne at Saratoga?

3. medium; p. 197; video segment 5
   • What does the term *pitcher* indicate about what these women were doing?
   • How were some of these women drawn into combat?
   • What roles did women play on the home front? How did they help the military?

4. easy; pp. 208, 214–215; video segments 3, 6
   • What types of support did the French provide?
   • Why would the French alliance give concern to Britain?
   • How did Yorktown illustrate the French effect?

Essay

1. medium; pp. 213–215; video segment 7
   • Who were the loyalists? How did they help the British? What happened to them?
   • How were African Americans pursuing freedom? What happened to them?
   • What did women do during the war? How did this affect post-war conditions?
   • How and why were American Indians caught in the middle of the war? Why was the outcome of the war likely to cause them more problems?

2. medium; pp. 192–215; all video segments
   • Consider the British task and mistakes: Could they conquer the countryside? Did they take the Americans seriously? Did they overestimate the loyalist support? Did they have a cause which would sustain the fight?
   • Consider American strengths: How important was George Washington? How critical was French help? How committed were American troops and political leaders? How compelling was the American cause?
   • Consider the battles of Long Island, Trenton, Oriskany, Saratoga, Monmouth, and Yorktown.

LESSON 10:
INVENTING A NATION

Multiple Choice   Choose the letter of the best answer.

1. At Newburgh, New York, in 1783, disgruntled army officers
   a. discussed threatening Congress if their demands were not met.
   b. advocated removing George Washington from his commander-in-chief position.
   c. established a military academy later relocated to West Point.
   d. refused to support ongoing treaty negotiations with the British.

2. The threatened Newburgh Mutiny illustrated that
   a. loyalty to Britain was still strong at the end of the revolutionary war.
   b. anxiety and instability existed in the new United States of America.
   c. Congress was ignoring the concerns of the military.
   d. George Washington was losing his influence among military officers.

3. In the video, Professor Jack Rakove observes that a basic problem of the government under the Articles
   of Confederation was the
   a. location of the capitol.
   b. weak representation of the states.
   c. lack of a means of enforcement for Congress.
   d. dominance of the central government.

4. In the video, Professor Mel Yazawa offers the view that the proceedings of the Constitutional
   Convention were kept secret so that members could
   a. speak without fear of retribution.
   b. cover up their true feelings.
   c. more easily skip the meetings.
   d. escape the scrutiny of the media.

5. All of the following were associated with James Madison at the Constitutional Convention EXCEPT that
   he
   a. kept notes of the proceedings.
   b. believed fundamental change was needed.
   c. prepared to control the agenda.
   d. presided at the meeting.

6. In the video, Professor Jack Rakove points out that the 3/5ths compromise was
   a. was unfair to the South.
   b. was probably necessary at the time to assure that slave states would join the Union.
   c. gave slaves some assurance of future rights.
   d. was going to be overturned during the ratification process.

7. The Preamble to the Constitution
   a. gives the President executive powers.
   b. protects the individual from the government.
   c. describes the purposes of the government.
   d. indicates the states are sovereign.

8. In the video, Professor Jack Rakove notes that the most important change the framers of the Constitution made in the national government was
   a. adopting a bill of rights to protect individuals.
   b. devising an amendment process that facilitated changing the document.
   c. empowering the Congress to issue currency.
   d. creating a national government that would enact, execute, and adjudicate its own laws.

9. In the video, Professor Rakove observes that James Madison believed that a bill of rights would become effective when
   a. people internalized the principles enunciated.
   b. the Supreme Court was able to clarify the meaning.
   c. states were bound by the same principles.
   d. the President enforced the law.

10. Both Professors Gordon Wood and Jack Rakove think that the meaning of the Constitution
   a. was fixed by the framers.
   b. has been overrated by historians.
   c. has been enhanced by experience.
   d. is relatively easy to determine.

Short Answer   Your answers should specifically address the points indicated in one or two paragraphs.

1. Why was the decade of the 1780s a "critical period" for the United States?

2. What features of the Land Ordinance of 1785 and the Northwest Ordinance of 1787 had long-term significance in the shaping of America?

3. Why is James Madison called the "Father of the Constitution"?

4. Why is it difficult to determine the "original meanings" of the Constitution? In what ways do we know more about what the Constitution means than the people who wrote the document?

Essay Question   Your response should be several paragraphs long. Your answer should elaborate on the points indicated in a manner that expresses understanding of the material.

1. During the 1780s, the revolutionary generation made fundamental changes in the framework of the national government. In a well-developed essay, address the following questions: (1) Why was the Articles of Confederation replaced by the Constitution? (2) How did the Constitution alter the structure and operation of the national government? (3) What does the Constitution mean to America?

ANSWER KEY

Multiple Choice

1. a; medium; video segment 1
2. b; difficult; video segment 1
3. c; medium; pp. 222–226; video segment 2
4. a; medium; pp. 239–240; video segment 3
5. d; medium; pp. 240–242; video segment 3
6. b; medium; pp. 241–242; video segment 3
7. c; medium; p. a-8; video segments 2, 3
8. d; medium; pp. 242–243; video segment 3
9. a; difficult; pp. a-14–a-17; video segment 5
10. c; difficult; video segment 20

Short Answer

1. medium; pp. 222–240; video segments 1, 2, 3
    - Consider the financial difficulties at the time.
    - What problems with foreign countries existed?
    - How were the state and central governments dealing with pressing issues?

2. medium; pp. 233–238; video segment 2
    - What pattern of survey and sale of land was established?
    - What precedents were set by the Northwest Ordinance?
    - How did these laws affect the future of the United States?

3. medium; pp. 240–249, 258; video segments 3–5
    - What role did Madison play at the Convention?
    - How did he influence the ratification process?
    - What effect did he have on the Bill of Rights?
    - How did he affect our historical record of the times?

4. difficult; video segment 6
    - Whose "original meanings" are at issue?
    - What records do we have?
    - To what degree were the framers experimenting at the time?
    - What has experience taught us about the meaning?

Essay

1. difficult; pp. 222–249, 258, A8; video segments 1–6
    - What were the fundamental problems with the Articles?
    - Who was pushing for change and why?
    - Describe the major changes brought about by the Constitution in the operations of the national government.
    - What effect does the Constitution have on stabilizing government?
    - What effect does it have on national identity? How does the average citizen use the Constitution?

LESSON 11:
SEARCHING FOR STABILITY

Multiple Choice   Choose the letter of the best answer.

1. Alexander Hamilton's vision for America differed from Thomas Jefferson's in the respect that
   a. Jefferson wanted to foster manufacturing.
   b. Hamilton admired the British model.
   c. Jefferson favored a hierarchical system.
   d. Hamilton encouraged rural development.

2. By 1790, New York City
   a. had banned slavetraders from its boundaries.
   b. was the nation's commercial hub.
   c. lost its position a the nation's capital.
   d. was benefiting from the Erie Canal.

3. Even though a wealthy elite dominated Charleston, South Carolina, by 1790,
   a. African Americans were playing key roles in the community.
   b. back-country farmers controlled state politics.
   c. Indian peoples in the region posed a threat to the city.
   d. the rich were reluctant to display their wealth.

4. In 1790, St. Louis
   a. was the capital of Spanish Louisiana.
   b. had established itself as a major urban center.
   c. had a rather open, free-wheeling society.
   d. was linked to the east by a series of canals.

5. In 1790, Santa Fe
   a. suffered from a major indian revolt.
   b. banned pueblo people from the city.
   c. became the capital of Spanish New Mexico.
   d. experienced a developing trading network between pueblo peoples and Spanish colonists.

6. In 1790, San Francisco
   a. had yet to be discovered by the Spanish.
   b. illustrated the on-going missionary activity of the Spanish.
   c. forced Indian villages to move east.
   d. began to develop trade with Santa Fe.

7. In 1790, the Willamette Valley
   a. attracted American settlers from the east.
   b. was dominated by Spanish landowners.
   c. provided refuge for ship-wrecked sailors.
   d. was very much a contested part of the world.

8. Alexander Hamilton was uniquely qualified for the position of Secretary of Treasury because he
   a. grew up in an urban commercial environment.
   b. was Washington's top aide during the revolutionary war.
   c. had been director of the Bank of America.
   d. knew the value of maintaining his inherited wealth.

9. When opposing Hamilton's proposal to establish a national bank, Jefferson interpreted the Constitution in a manner referred to as
   a. the doctrine of implied powers.
   b. strict construction.
   c. nullification.
   d. liberal.

10. In the video, Historian Richard Brookhiser observes that for George Washington, the Whiskey Rebellion
    a. involved the question of who best understood the revolution.
    b. offered an opportunity to bolster his reputation.
    c. did not merit his attention.
    d. illustrated Hamilton's grab for power.

11. In the video, Historian Richard Brookhiser states that, as a leader, George Washington was
    a. arrogant and pompous.
    b. humorless and anti-social.
    c. intellectual and philosophical.
    d. dependable and realistic.

Short Answer   Your answers should specifically address the points indicated in one or two paragraphs.

1. What problems faced Alexander Hamilton as he took the office of secretary of the treasury?

2. Why was Washington, D.C., an area not controlled by any state, chosen as the location of the permanent federal capital?

3. How can the Whiskey Rebellion be seen as more than just a revolt of unhappy farmers?

Essay Question   Your response should be several paragraphs long. Your answer should elaborate on the points indicated in a manner that expresses understanding of the material.

1. Why is George Washington considered to be one of the United States' greatest presidents? In your answer, be sure to consider the times, his personal qualities, and his legacy. How and why does Washington live on in the American memory?

2. Describe and explain Alexander Hamilton's three-part economic program for the new nation, and analyze the success of each of the three components. To what extent do you think Hamilton's vision of America has prevailed?

ANSWER KEY

Multiple Choice

1. b; medium; video segment 1
2. b; medium; video segment 2
3. a; medium; video segment 2
4. c; easy; video segment 2
5. d; medium; video segment 2
6. b; medium; video segment 2
7. d; medium; video segment 2
8. a; medium; video segment 3
9. b; medium; p. 267; document; video segment 3
10. a; medium; pp. 267–268; video segment 4
11. d; medium; video segment 5

Short Answer

1. medium; pp. 263–267; document; video segment 3
    - What was the debt situation at the national and state level?
    - How much confidence did people have in the national government's ability to deal effectively with economic issues?
    - What revenue could the government count on?
    - What was the banking situation in the country?

2. medium; pp. 264–265; video segment 3
    - What does the Constitution say about a capital?
    - How was the location connected to the assumption of the state debts?
    - What role did George Washington play in selecting the site?

3. difficult; pp. 267–268; video segment 4
    - How did Hamilton view the rebellion?
    - Why did Washington connect the rebellion to the meaning of the American Revolution?
    - What would have happened if the rebellion had been successful?

Essay

1. medium; pp. 254–258; video segment 1
    - What made the 1790s a particularly important period in American history?
    - Describe Washington's strengths as a leader.
    - What precedents did Washington establish? What was important about his giving up power?
    - Why is it important that the nation have a history, and that Washington plays an important role in that?
    - Where do we see Washington memorialized today?

2. difficult; pp. 263–269; video segments 1, 3, 4, 6
    - What was the state of the nation economically when Hamilton came to the treasury?
    - How did he propose to deal with the debt issues? What were the results?
    - Why did Hamilton favor a national bank? What did it do? How effective was it?
    - What taxes did Hamilton favor? Why?
    - What were the overall effects of his program?
    - How does the United States mirror "Hamilton's Republic"?

LESSON 12:
A PEACEFUL TRANSFER OF POWER

Multiple Choice   Choose the letter of the best answer.

1. As a result of the defeat of General Arthur St. Clair in 1791,
    a. Indians in the region signed the Treaty of Greenville.
    b. the United States sought British help to expel Indians from the Ohio Valley.
    c. troops were withdrawn from the Great Lakes region.
    d. General Anthony Wayne made careful preparations for the next battle.

2. As a result of the Treaty of Greenville (1795),
    a. the British evacuated their forts in the Old Northwest.
    b. U.S. military forces withdrew from Ohio.
    c. American Indians lost their struggle to preserve the Ohio River as a boundary to white settlement.
    d. the United States agreed to respect Indian tribal customs.

3. As a result of the Treaty of Greenville (1795),
    a. the Cherokee Indians agreed to removal west of the Mississippi River.
    b. the United States gained rights to establish forts within Indian country.
    c. Indians were assured of citizenship rights.
    d. the Northwest Ordinance was repealed.

4. In the video, Professor Richard White refers to the Treaty of Greenville (1795) as an
    a. absolute disaster for Indian peoples.
    b. opportunity for Indian peoples to regain lost territory.
    c. illegal action, since Indian peoples did not understand the language used.
    d. example of Britain's continued influence in the Ohio Valley.

5. One long-term benefit for Indians of treaties between the United States and Indian peoples is that
    a. Indian lifestyles showed marked improvement in the 19th century.
    b. liquor was specifically banned as a part of the goods shipped to Indians.
    c. states could assert legal authority on reservations.
    d. treaties became the basis of Indian rights within the United States.

6. The Oneida Indians' land claims against the state of New York illustrates
    a. the futility of Indian attempts to gain compensation for lost lands.
    b. the primacy of states' rights in our federal system.
    c. how treaties can be used to protect Indian interests.
    d. how violent protest by minorities can work in the United States.

7. President George Washington announced a policy of neutrality in the 1790s because
   a. the Franco-American Alliance was no longer binding under the new government.
   b. United States' interests were served by avoiding war.
   c. Britain agreed to lower tariffs on United States' products.
   d. Hamilton favored an even-handed approach in dealing with Europe.

8. In the video, Professor Joseph Ellis observes that the Alien and Sedition Acts were counterproductive for the Federalists because
   a. they helped Jefferson win the election of 1800.
   b. most new immigrants actually tend to support the Federalists.
   c. pro-Federalist newspapers were shut down.
   d. they could not reveal details of the XYZ affair.

9. In the video, Professor Joseph Ellis observes that by pursuing peace in the late 1790s, President John Adams
   a. gained votes in the 1800 election.
   b. went against the wishes of Thomas Jefferson.
   c. served the public interest while losing popularity.
   d. sought to placate Alexander Hamilton.

10. George Washington's neutrality policy and John Adams' pursuit of peace in the 1790s set a precedent for much of the 19th century that included
    a. partisan use of foreign policy.
    b. pursuit of isolationism abroad and expansionism at home.
    c. aggressive assertion of United States' treaty rights.
    d. application of foreign policy to favor big business interests.

11. When the electoral vote in the 1800 presidential election ended in a tie and the House of Representatives had to choose a winner,
    a. Alexander Hamilton helped Thomas Jefferson prevail.
    b. John Adams took his case to the Supreme Court.
    c. Aaron Burr challenged Alexander Hamilton to a duel.
    d. Thomas Jefferson persuaded Aaron Burr to withdraw before a vote had to be taken.

12. As a result of the 1800 presidential election results,
    a. a constitutional amendment set up separate electoral votes for president and vice-president.
    b. Hamilton's economic program was dismantled.
    c. John Adams joined the Republican Party.
    d. the Federalist Party gained power.

13. In the video, Professor Joseph Ellis observes that the creation of political parties allows
    a. the elite to control elections.
    b. political dissent to coexist without violence.
    c. minority groups to gain political leverage.
    d. incumbent politicians to maintain their offices.

14. One parallel between the presidential elections of 1800 and 2000 is that
    a. the electoral vote ended in a tie.
    b. impeachment proceedings hurt the incumbent's chances.
    c. the eventual winner was determined well after the initial votes were counted.
    d. the Supreme Court had to decide the outcome in each case.

15. In the video, Professor Eric Foner observes that during the revolutionary era, the idea of freedom
    a. narrowed in definition after 1776.
    b. was contradicted by Indian Removal.
    c. applied only to particular groups of people.
    d. became universalized and democratized.

16. In the video, Professor James O. Horton observes that, from the standpoint of African Americans, the revolutionary era
    a. offered hope that a racially egalitarian America was possible.
    b. was a period of betrayal.
    c. led to the emergence of a black middle class.
    d. should have resulted in a redistribution of loyalist property to slaves.

Short Answer   Your answers should specifically address the points indicated in one or two paragraphs.

1. In your opinion, was the Sedition Act of 1798 constitutional? Why or why not?

2. What were the differences between Federalists and Republicans in 1800?

3. Cite three precedents established in the 1790s. What were the long-term effects?

Essay Question   Your response should be several paragraphs long. Your answer should elaborate on the points indicated in a manner that expresses understanding of the material.

1. Analyze the presidential election of 1800 in respect to the candidates, issues, campaign, and results. Why was a peaceful transfer of power significant in American history?

2. Describe and explain how the revolutionary era (1760–1801) shaped America. In your answer, consider the major changes that took place, particularly relating to American identity and the concepts of freedom and equality. How does that era continue to affect us today?

ANSWER KEY

Multiple Choice

1. d; medium; p. 271; video segment 2
2. c; medium; p. 271; video segment 2
3. b; medium; p. 271; video segment 2
4. a; easy; p. 271; video segment 2
5. d; medium; video segments 2, 3
6. c; medium; video segments 2, 3
7. b; medium; pp. 272–273; video segment 4
8. a; difficult; pp. 277–281; video segment 4
9. c; medium; pp. 280–281; video segment 4
10. b; medium; video segment 4
11. a; medium; pp. 289–290; video segment 5
12. a; medium; pp. 289–290; video segment 5
13. b; difficult; pp. 281–282, 289; video segment 5
14. c; medium; video segment 6
15. d; medium; video segment 7
16. a; medium; video segment 7

Short Answer

1. medium; pp. 277–281; video segment 4
   - What did the Sedition Act say?
   - What part of the Constitution did it seem to contradict?
   - To what extent can the government restrict expression during times of crisis?

2. medium; pp. 281–282; 289; video segment 5
   - Consider the issues of the use of the central government versus states' rights, the Bank of the United States, excise taxes, Alien and Sedition Acts, foreign policy disagreements, etc.
   - Who supported each group? Who led each group?

3. difficult; pp. 272–273; video segments 2–5, 7
   - U.S.-Indian treaties; boundaries established, but usually broken; Indian rights eventually upheld.
   - Neutrality in foreign policy; the United States could concentrate on continentalism.
   - Censorship during "wartime"? How far can the government go?
   - A peaceful transfer of power; creation of a loyal opposition.
   - Functions of political parties; in addition to transfer of power, what else happens?

Essay

1. medium; pp. 289–290; video segments 5, 6
   - Candidates: Who was running for each party?
   - Issues: What separated the Federalists and the Republicans?
   - Campaign: How were campaigns done in those days?
   - Results: Jefferson and Burr end up in a tie; how is this dealt with? What did it mean to the parties? What did it mean to the nation?
   - Consider how the United States handles election results without violence; what is the role of the losing candidate and party? What are the alternatives?

2. difficult; video segment 8
   - How did the revolution, the Declaration of Independence, the Constitution, and the precedents set in the 1790s give America an identity?
   - What role did geography play in this identity?
   - How was the concept of freedom defined in this era? How had it changed?
   - How were minority groups fitting into the concept of American identity?
   - What are the most important elements of revolutionary America still present today?

LESSON 13:
JEFFERSON'S VISION OF AMERICA

Multiple Choice   Choose the letter of the best answer.

1. In the video, Professor Andrew Cayton observes that, in American history, the period from 1800 to 1850 has an "unfinished" quality to it because
   a. many young people living then had choices and opportunities.
   b. historians have not focused on those times.
   c. transportation systems were not keeping up with the growing market.
   d. political leadership seemed confused after the founding fathers died.

2. In the video, historian Dayton Duncan observes that, in American history, the West often represented
   a. desolate landscapes inhospitable to farming.
   b. an opportunity to start anew.
   c. dangerous territory due to hostile indigenous peoples.
   d. a place to solve problems.

3. For most of the first half of the nineteenth century, the West allowed the United States to
   a. avoid conflict with indigenous peoples.
   b. become a major world power.
   c. postpone reckoning with issues like slavery.
   d. lower its tariff rates.

4. In Thomas Jefferson's vision of America, the key element consisted of
   a. slave-holding planters.
   b. urban workers.
   c. business entrepreneurs
   d. independent farmers.

5. The purpose of the Lewis and Clark Expedition included all of the following objectives EXCEPT
   a. legitimizing a United States claim to California.
   b. opening up contact with Indian peoples.
   c. looking for a water route across the continent.
   d. gathering scientific information.

6. In the video, historian Dayton Duncan maintains that the diverse Corps of Discovery
   a. lacked a unity of purpose.
   b. succeeded because they worked together.
   c. treated American Indians too harshly.
   d. offended the sensibilities of St. Louis' high society.

7. Sacagawea's roles during the Lewis and Clark Expedition included
   a. journalist and map-maker.
   b. financier and manager.
   c. guide and mediator.
   d. all of the above.

8. One of the enduring lessons of the Lewis and Clark Expedition is captured in the phrase found in their journals:
   a. "go West, young man"
   b. "look homeward, angel."
   c. "never look back."
   d. "we proceeded on."

9. Tecumseh's approach to white expansion westward included the idea that American Indians should
   a. agree not to cede lands without the consent of all Indian peoples.
   b. convert to Christianity.
   c. use their highly trained armies to engage in sustained conflict.
   d. isolate themselves from any alliance with Europeans.

10. In the video, Professor Richard White observes that the War of 1812 was critical for American Indians because
    a. United States' boundaries were now extended to the Mississippi River.
    b. they lost the ability to negotiate a middle ground.
    c. Tecumseh's attempt to form an alliance with the United States collapsed.
    d. small pox began to spread west of the Appalachian Mountains.

11. As part of the Missouri Compromise,
    a. Kansas Territory was open to slavery.
    b. Missouri became a free state.
    c. a line was drawn to separate free and slave territory.
    d. American Indians were removed west of the Mississippi River.

12. Thomas Jefferson referred to the Missouri Compromise as "a fire-bell in the night" because
    a. fugitive slaves would now likely try to flee the South.
    b. slave rebellions would become more likely.
    c. plantation owners would have to free their slaves if they moved West.
    d. the union would be divided on the issue of slavery in the territories.

Short Answer   Your answers should specifically address the points indicated in one or two paragraphs.

1. How did the Louisiana Purchase and the Adams-Onis Treaty affect the boundaries of the United States?

2. What effect did the Lewis and Clark expedition have on the country? What can we learn from the Corps of Discovery?

Essay Question   Your response should be several paragraphs long. Your answer should elaborate on the points indicated in a manner that expresses understanding of the material.

1. Describe and explain why Thomas Jefferson looked to the West to fulfill his vision of America. How did he attempt to assure that the West would be accessible? What effects did movement to the West have on American Indians and the question of slavery?

2. Describe and explain the causes and consequences of the War of 1812. How did that war affect American Indians and the Federalist Party?

ANSWER KEY

Multiple Choice

1. a; medium; video segment 1
2. b; medium; video segment 1
3. c; difficult; video segment 1
4. d; easy; pp. 292–293; video segment 2
5. a; medium; pp. 294–296; video segment 2
6. b; medium; pp. 294–296; video segment 2
7. c; easy; pp. 294–296; video segment 2
8. d; easy; pp. 294–296; video segment 2
9. a; medium; pp. 287–289, 301–303; video segment 3
10. b; medium; pp. 305–306; video segment 3
11. c; medium; pp. 309–312; video segment 4
12. d; medium; pp. 309–312; video segment 4

Short Answer

1. medium; pp. 293–295, 309–312; video segments 2, 4
    *   Describe the area acquired from France in the Louisiana Purchase treaty; what areas were not included?
    *   How did the Adams-Onis Treaty affect Florida? What was significant about the transcontinental feature of the treaty?

2. medium; pp. 294–296; video segment 2
    *   Why did the expedition whet the appetite for further expansion westward?
    *   What did the Corps of Discovery illustrate about diversity? How did it create a sense of wonder about how westward expansion might have proceeded?

Essay

1. medium; pp. 287–289, 291–296, 301–303, 305–306, 309–312; video segments 2–4
    *   Why was the independent farmer a key to Jefferson's vision? How could an empire of liberty be maintained?
    *   How did the Louisiana Purchase fit into Jefferson's vision? How did the Lewis and Clark expedition facilitate movement westward?
    *   How did American Indians, particularly Tecumseh, respond? How did the War of 1812 affect Indians? Where would Indians go?
    *   How did having more land in the West affect debates on the future of slavery?

2. difficult; pp. 296–297, 300–301, 303–306, 309–312; video segments 3, 4
    *   What were the causes of the war? Consider the diplomatic breakdown, the expansionist desires, and the question of honor.
    *   What were the military highlights of the war? What did the treaty ending the war change?
    *   Why were American Indians big losers in the war?
    *   Why did the Federalist Party lose ground because of the war?
    *   Why did the United States have a surge of nationalism after the war?

LESSON 14:
THE MARKET REVOLUTION

Multiple Choice   Choose the letter of the best answer.

1. In the video, Professor Thomas Dublin points out that women entered the work force at Lowell for all of the following reasons EXCEPT to
   a. earn money for themselves
   b. be able to purchase consumer goods.
   c. enjoy a less structured life style.
   d. escape limited options in the country.

2. In the video, Professor Thomas Dublin expresses the view that women workers learned that they could
   a. hardly make enough to pay the boardinghouse rent.
   b. publicly protest ill treatment.
   c. usually find a future husband in the workforce.
   d. lose their paycheck if they remained single.

3. The effectiveness of the women's labor movement at Lowell was mainly undercut by
   a. adaptation of new technology.
   b. lower tariff rates.
   c. compassionate mill owners.
   d. plentiful immigrant workers.

4. In the video, Professor Joyce Appleby states that widespread use of print media led to enhanced
   a. literacy.
   b. unemployment.
   c. commitment to public service.
   d. standards of morality.

5. The completion of the Erie Canal
   a. necessitated the removal of the Iroquois Indians.
   b. held back railroad development in America.
   c. allowed New York City to have direct access to the West.
   d. all of the above.

6. Federal and state governments spurred movement westward in the first half of the nineteenth century by all of the following actions EXCEPT
   a. selling land cheaply.
   b. using the army to control indigenous peoples.
   c. building roads.
   d. tightening credit on businesses.

7. The career of John Deere illustrated the
   a. link between business and agriculture.
   b. boom and bust cycles in the economy.
   c. benefits of high tariff rates.
   d. necessity of government support for private enterprise.

8. The community of Jacksonville, Illinois, represented development on the northwestern frontier in all of the following ways EXCEPT
   a. railroad lines became increasingly important.
   b. surplus agricultural products were being shipped out of the area.
   c. religious conformity stifled disagreements.
   d. anti-slavery sentiment grew.

Short Answer   Your answers should specifically address the points indicated in one or two paragraphs.

1. What did the experience of the working women of Lowell indicate about labor and economic opportunities for women in the first half of the nineteenth century?

2. How did the building of the Erie Canal illustrate the confluence of a vision, public support, and the practical use of labor and technology?

Essay Question   Your response should be several paragraphs long. Your answer should elaborate on the points indicated in a manner that expresses understanding of the material.

1. Describe and explain the significant economic changes that took place in the north and west during the first half of the nineteenth century. How did these changes affect the development of a free-labor ideology in that region of the country? What were the short- and long-term effects of these developments?

ANSWER KEY

Multiple Choice

1. c; difficult; pp. 327, 330–332; document; video segment 2
2. b; medium; pp. 327, 330–332; document; video segment 2
3. d; medium; pp. 331–332, 376–377; video segment 2
4. a; easy; pp. 341–343; video segment 3
5. c; medium; p. 326; video segment 4
6. d; medium; pp. 367–368; video segments 5, 6
7. a; medium; pp. 367–368; video segments 5, 6
8. c; difficult; p. 369; video segment 6

Short Answer

1. medium; pp. 320–332, 376–377; document; video segment 2
   - Why were women recruited to the mills?
   - Why did the women go to work there?
   - What were the positive and negative sides to the experience?
   - What other types of opportunities were available?

2. difficult; p. 326; video segment 4
   - Explain the vision of DeWitt Clinton.
   - What type of public support became available?
   - Who provided the labor?
   - How did they overcome barriers?
   - What was the result?

Essay

1. difficult; pp. 316–317, 324–334, 366–377; video segments 1–7
   - What characterized the market revolution?
   - Beyond the market, what opportunities were opening up in the region? Why was this happening?
   - What is meant by a free-labor ideology? Why did this emerge?
   - What were the results of these changes? How would you describe the losses and benefits?
   - What was important about linking economic and political freedom in the North?

LESSON 15:
A WHITE MAN'S DEMOCRACY

Multiple Choice   Choose the letter of the best answer.

1. The changing market and economic conditions in the early nineteenth century
   a. caused more people to take a greater interest in politics.
   b. forced the Bank of the United States to lower interest rates.
   c. led to lower tariff rates.
   d. extended the life of the Federalist Party.

2. Part of Andrew Jackson's appeal as a political candidate was based on his
   a. consistent policy recommendations.
   b. rapport with a masculine electorate.
   c. polished oratorical and literary skills.
   d. compassion toward minority groups.

3. Jacksonian Democracy, as contrasted with Jeffersonian Democracy, held that
   a. campaigns needed to be less raucous.
   b. women should be given the right to vote.
   c. party politics was unnecessary.
   d. leaders should emerge from the mass electorate.

4. In the video, Professor Harry Watson observes that Andrew Jackson's presidential victory in 1828 helped create
   a. the need for greater security at the White House.
   b. greater emphasis on campaign finance reform.
   c. a dualism in American political culture between the elite and the common people.
   d. disillusionment with the corrupt bargains used to gain the presidency.

5. All of the following represented Andrew Jackson's core beliefs EXCEPT for his
   a. identification with the masses.
   b. respect for the governing elites.
   c. support for slavery.
   d. desire to gain access to Indian lands.

6. In the video, Professor Harry Watson observes that Andrew Jackson thought that John C. Calhoun's position on nullification
   a. would lead to anarchy.
   b. illustrated Calhoun's limited reasoning ability.
   c. was based on a Hamiltonian view of the Constitution.
   d. made Calhoun a viable presidential contender.

7. For President Jackson, the Bank of the United States represented
   a. Wall Street domination of the nation's finances.
   b. an elite threat to people's liberty.
   c. a logical way to control interest rates.
   d. a classic example of the spoils system.

8. In the video, Cherokee Chief Chad Smith notes that the removal of the Cherokee in the 1830s did all of the following EXCEPT
   a. disturb patterns of village and family life.
   b. leave a painful impression on Cherokee memory
   c. destroy the Cherokee ability to adapt and survive.
   d. cause about 4,000 deaths.

9. In the video, Professor Theda Perdue observes that Indian removal
   a. diminished President Jackson's popularity.
   b. angered the residents of Oklahoma.
   c. helped unify the Cherokee people behind a common cause.
   d. was another step toward making the United States a white man's country.

10. One result of Andrew Jackson's presidency was that from then on
    a. politicians had to appeal to the masses.
    b. the same two parties dominated the national political scene.
    c. states' rights lost credibility as a political argument.
    d. American Indians lost their tribal identity.

Short Answer   Your answers should specifically address the points indicated in one or two paragraphs.

1. How did President Andrew Jackson justify Indian removal?

2. What was at the basis of the nullification crisis? How did this episode escalate the ongoing debate about states' rights?

3. Why was Andrew Jackson so popular with the common man?

Essay Question   Your response should be several paragraphs long. Your answer should elaborate on the points indicated in a manner that expresses understanding of the material.

1. Describe and explain President Andrew Jackson's decisions and actions regarding Indian removal, the nullification crisis, and the bank war. What were the effects of his decisions? How would you rate Jackson as a president?

ANSWER KEY

Multiple Choice

1. a; difficult; pp. 312–314, 323; video segments 1, 2
2. b; medium; pp. 312–314, 323; video segments 1, 2
3. d; medium; pp. 312–314, 323; video segments 1, 2
4. c; difficult; pp. 335–336; video segment 2
5. b; medium; pp. 337–338; video segment 3
6. a; medium; p. 353; video segment 3
7. b; medium; pp. 353–355; video segment 3
8. c; medium; video segment 5
9. d; medium; video segment 5
10. a; medium; p. 359; video segment 6

Short Answer

1. medium; pp. 349–351; video segment 5
    - What were Jackson's views on Indian treaties?
    - What did he think of the "civilization" program?
    - How could it benefit both Indians and whites?

2. medium; pp. 351–353; video segment 3
    - How and why did nullification challenge federal authority?
    - What did President Jackson think about nullification?
    - What did Jackson propose to do about it?
    - What key idea now became linked to the states' rights ideology?

3. easy; pp. 312–314, 323, 335–336, 359; video segments 1, 2, 6
    - What elements of his personality appealed to and reflected the culture of the times?
    - Who generally benefited from Jackson's decisions and actions? Why?

Essay

1. difficult; pp. 334–338, 349–359; video segments 2–6
    - Present a clear explanation of each issue specified in the question.
    - Be sure to consider the short-term as well as long-term effects.
    - What was Jackson's legacy?
    - What is your opinion of Jackson?

LESSON 16:
THE SLAVE SOUTH

Multiple Choice   Choose the letter of the best answer.

1. Slavery benefited the North by
   a. opening up new jobs for immigrants.
   b. providing for growth in trade goods
   c. spurring westward expansion.
   d. all of the above.

2. Among the reasons non-slaveholding whites supported slavery was the
   a. psychological satisfaction of thinking themselves superior to any black.
   b. economic benefits that flowed their way.
   c. opportunity it provided for political advancement.
   d. evidence supporting the "positive good" argument.

3. In the video, Professor Larry Hudson points out that slaves became attached to the land for all of the following reasons EXCEPT
   a. rest and recuperation.
   b. burial grounds.
   c. supplemental crops for themselves.
   d. property rights gave them hope for equality.

4. The "Brer Fox" and "Brer Rabbit" folktales illustrate how
   a. slaves deferred to their masters' strength.
   b. owners used religion to support slavery.
   c. valuable lessons were taught in the slave community.
   d. literature gained fairly widespread use among slaves.

5. In the video, Professor Raymond Dobard relates a theory that quilts may have served as
   a. an expression of artistic development.
   b. a way to achieve personal comfort.
   c. an innovative approach to using cotton fabric.
   d. a means of communication.

6. Slaves ran away for all of the following reasons EXCEPT
   a. trouble with owners.
   b. realistic chances of making it out of the South.
   c. to see loved ones nearby.
   d. to pursue freedom.

7. In the video, Professor Loren Schweninger observes that the vast majority of slaves who ran away
   a. did not venture far beyond their immediate area.
   b. were accurately tabulated and reported by masters.
   c. used the Underground Railroad.
   d. were apprehended by northern bounty hunters.

Short Answer   Your answers should specifically address the points indicated in one or two paragraphs.

1. How did slaves create a culture that sustained their lives in meaningful ways? How and why did this culture survive the abolition of slavery?

2. Why did Nat Turner lead a slave rebellion in Virginia in 1831? What meaning did Turner and the rebellion have for both blacks and whites?

Essay Question   Your response should be several paragraphs long. Your answer should elaborate on the points indicated in a manner that expresses understanding of the material.

1. Describe and explain how slavery affected the economic, social, and political development of the South during the first half of the nineteenth century. Why did slavery become the essential difference between the North and the South? What are the long-term effects of slavery?

ANSWER KEY

Multiple Choice

1. b; medium; pp. 418–421; video segment 1
2. a; medium; pp. 413–415; documents; video segment 2
3. d; medium; pp. 431–434; video segment 3
4. c; difficult; pp. 434–435; video segment 3
5. d; medium; video segment 4
6. b; medium; p. 434; video segment 5
7. a; medium; p. 434; video segment 5

Short Answer

1. medium; pp. 431–434; video segment 4
   - Consider how slaves could "negotiate" work and living conditions, including use of land.
   - What roles did the family and religion play?
   - How did they use folktales and music?
   - Be sure to give a reasoned opinion on how and why elements of the slave's culture survived the abolition of slavery.

2. medium; pp. 409–410; video segment 5
   - Who was Nat Turner and what prompted his actions?
   - How did whites react to the immediate threat? What did they do to prevent future rebellions?
   - How did blacks view Turner?

Essay

1. medium; pp. 409–444; video segments 1–6
    - Consider how and why slavery spread across the South and what that meant to the southern economy.
    - What effects did slavery have on race relations and the class system in the South?
    - How and why did the plantation aristocracy dominate southern politics? What interests were they sure to support?
    - Consider how the South differed from the North. Why is slavery at the basis of these differences?
    - How has slavery affected America since its abolition?

LESSON 17:
PERFECTING AMERICA

Multiple Choice   Choose the letter of the best answer.

1. Sarah and Angelina Grimke reflected the spirit of the times in which they lived by
   a. having a passion for religion and reform.
   b. becoming members of the Shaker community.
   c. advocating slave rebellions in Charleston.
   d. leading camp meeting revivals in New York.

2. In the video, Professor Jon Butler points out that during the Second Great Awakening, religion became
   a. too removed from the common people.
   b. central to the development of American culture.
   c. state-supported in most regions.
   d. infused with rationalist philosophy.

3. Those who believed in the millennium thought that they should
   a. attempt to abolish slavery immediately.
   b. endorse legislation to guarantee women's rights.
   c. perfect their lives in preparation for the coming of Christ.
   d. restore Old Testament teachings in the public schools.

4. The Shaker communities practiced
   a. complex marriage.
   b. discrimination toward women.
   c. polygamy.
   d. celibacy.

5. In the video, Professor Jon Butler observes that part of Joseph Smith's success in establishing the Mormon movement stemmed from
   a. his ability to cut through some of the religious confusion of the era.
   b. widespread support for practicing polygamy.
   c. the availability of free land in Utah.
   d. all of the above.

6. Dorothea Dix illustrates the role of women in the reform efforts concerning
   a. prisons.
   b. public education.
   c. care for the insane.
   d. temperance.

7. In the video, Professor Kathryn Sklar observes that what made the American Anti-Slavery Society so radical was its support for
   a. colonization of freed slaves.
   b. immediate emancipation.
   c. the underground railroad.
   d. Denmark Vesey's Rebellion.

8. Within the antislavery movement, what made immediate emancipation so radical was that it
   a. rejected Christian teachings.
   b. sought funding from overseas.
   c. endorsed imprisonment for slaveowners.
   d. accepted African Americans as fully equal humans.

9. In the video, Professor Richard Blackett maintains that the abolitionist Frederick Douglass had all of the following attributes EXCEPT
   a. a willingness to adapt his style to please his colleagues.
   b. great oratorical skills.
   c. first-hand experience with slavery.
   d. charm and good looks.

10. In the video, Professor James Stewart says that the relationship between William Lloyd Garrison and Frederick Douglass encompassed "one of the great magic moments in democracy" because
   a. the 1st Amendment was used to protect their rights to publish newspapers.
   b. people of different races spoke honestly and directly to each other.
   c. both successfully lobbied Congress to lift the gag rule in the South.
   d. they agree on using the existing political parties to bring about change.

11. The Seneca Falls Convention and the Declaration of Sentiments
   a. rejected the admonition given years earlier by Abigail Adams.
   b. called for the rejection of organized religion.
   c. marked the beginning of an independent women's rights movement.
   d. had little effect on subsequent efforts by women to achieve equality.

12. The social reform movements of the 1830s through the 1850s teach us that to bring about social change in America you must do all of the following EXCEPT
   a. agitate.
   b. reach across racial divides.
   c. have a vision.
   d. engage in violence.

Short Answer   Your answers should specifically address the points indicated in one or two paragraphs.

1. What do the Shakers and the Mormons illustrate about cultural life in the first half of the nineteenth century?

2. How and why was the women's rights movement of the 1840s connected to the religious and abolitionist movements of the era?

3. How and why did the abolition movement become more radical in the 1830s and 1840s? Why is it important that it did?

Essay Question   Your response should be several paragraphs long. Your answer should elaborate on the points indicated in a manner that expresses understanding of the material.

1. How and why did social reform movements, especially those relating to abolition and women's rights, emerge and develop out of the religious and cultural ferment of the early and mid-nineteenth century? What effects did these movements have on shaping America? What did that era teach us about social change?

ANSWER KEY

Multiple Choice

1. a; medium; video segment 1
2. b; medium; pp. 343–345; video segment 2
3. c; easy; video segment 2
4. d; medium; video segment 2
5. a; medium; pp. 387–389; video segment 2
6. c; easy; p. 344; video segment 3
7. b; medium; pp. 347–349; video segment 4
8. d; medium; pp. 347–349; video segment 4
9. a; medium; pp. 347–349; video segment 4
10. b; difficult; pp. 347–349; video segment 4
11. c; medium; p. 380; document, video segment 5
12. d; medium; pp. 338–349, 377–382, 387–389; video segments1-6

Short Answer

1. medium; pp. 387–389; video segment 2
   - What cultural changes encouraged the development of new religions?
   - How and why did each group arrange its community as it did?
   - What was the significance of each group?

2. medium; pp. 344–349, 380–382; video segments 1, 3, 4
   - How and why did religion help some women get out of their normal sphere?
   - What roles did women play in the abolition movement? How were they treated?
   - What connections did women make between slaves and their own status?

3. medium; pp. 347–349, 380–382; video segment 4
   - What characterized the antislavery movement before the 1830s?
   - Why was immediate emancipation considered radical?
   - Why was defining slavery as a sin important?
   - How did the abolitionists challenge the United States to live up to its principles?

Essay

1. medium; pp. 338–349, 377–382, 387–389; video segments 1–6
   - Consider the economic, social, and political changes occurring at the time.
   - Why did evangelical religious enthusiasm spread relatively quickly?
   - Why and how did people think they could perfect society?
   - How does temperance, moral reform, care for the insane, etc., have a moral basis?
   - How does abolition appear radical? How does it define slavery?
   - What factors influenced women to become organized in their own behalf?
   - What were the long-term effects of these movements?
   - What does it take to bring about social change?

LESSON 18: MOVING WESTWARD

Multiple Choice   Choose the letter of the best answer.

1. In the video, Professor David Gutierrez reminds us that the dark side of "manifest destiny" included elements of
   a. racism.
   b. continentalism.
   c. capitalism.
   d. socialism.

2. In the video, historian Chet Orloff observes that the Oregon Trail experience
   a. most often ended in failure.
   b. reinforced the idea of moving west to start over again.
   c. actually benefited the Indian peoples in the region.
   d. was extremely dangerous when Britain had claims to the area.

3. In the video, Professor Ernesto Chavez observes that, during the mid-1840s, a popular sentiment in the United States Congress was that
   a. America should go to war with Britain.
   b. immigration policies should be tightened.
   c. Mexico and its people were inferior to the United States.
   d. California should be admitted as a free state.

4. Texas was not annexed to the United States between 1836-1845 primarily because
   a. residents there rejected invitations to join.
   b. independence led to prosperity there.
   c. Britain threatened war if that occurred.
   d. slavery was practiced there.

5. In the video, Professor David Gutierrez points out that, from the Mexican point of view, the U.S.-Mexican War resulted from
   a. American agression.
   b. Mexican government incompetence.
   c. American unwillingness to pay for California.
   d. economic interests of Mexico's elite.

6. In the video, Professor Robert Johannsen points out that one reason American military efforts in the U.S.-Mexican War had support at home was because most Americans
   a. advocated the expansion of slavery.
   b. saw the war as a fight between a republic and a dictatorship.
   c. wanted to settle in the Southwest.
   d. desired easier access to the California gold fields.

7. All of the following were reasons the United States defeated Mexico in the U.S.-Mexican War EXCEPT
   a. American forces were better equipped.
   b. Mexico's internal divisions made governing that country difficult.
   c. Mexico's population didn't really care who won.
   d. American military leadership was better.

8. Among the terms of the Treaty of Guadalupe Hidalgo was the provision that
   a. Mexican landowners would be given fifteen million dollars.
   b. Indian peoples in the Southwest would be placed on reservations.
   c. a transcontinental railroad would be built from Texas to California.
   d. Mexicans who stayed in the United States would be citizens after one year.

9. One of the long-term consequences of the U.S.-Mexican War was that
   a. Mexico became more dependent on the United States.
   b. Americans felt guilty about exploiting Mexico.
   c. Mexico seized American property within its borders.
   d. American businesses entered a free-trade relationship with Mexico.

10. A significant consequence of the U.S.-Mexican War was
    a. short-term economic gain for Mexico.
    b. the United States now had another significant ethnic group within its borders.
    c. Mexican nationals who stayed in the United States lost citizenship rights.
    d. Indian peoples in the Southwest lost tribal identity.

11. In reference to Mexican-American identity in the United States in 1848, Professor David Gutierrez observes that
    a. the population was too small to have any recognition.
    b. the role of the Catholic Church declined.
    c. it would take years of juxtaposition with other cultures for distinction to develop.
    d. assimilation was extremely rapid.

12. In the video, Professor Eric Foner observes that, during the 1840s, the abolition and women's movements were
    a. uniting in their support for the Republican Party.
    b. convincing states to support equal rights amendments.
    c. losing ground to more radical political groups.
    d. demanding that freedom be a universal entitlement.

Short Answer   Your answers should specifically address the points indicated in one or two paragraphs.

1. Define the term *manifest destiny*. How is this concept linked to earlier "missionary" ideas in American history? How was the term an "intellectual shield" for American expansionism?

2. Why were the disputes between Britain and the United States in the Oregon Country settled peacefully? How were they settled?

3. Do you think President James K. Polk provoked war with Mexico in 1846 or was he defending U.S. territory at the time? Explain.

4. How did the United States' annexation of the Southwest affect Mexicans who had been living in that region?

Essay Question   Your response should be several paragraphs long. Your answer should elaborate on the points indicated in a manner that expresses understanding of the material.

1. Describe and explain how the United States acquired each major piece of new territory between 1801 and 1848. What were the consequences of this geographic expansion?

2. How and why did the meaning of freedom in America change in the period from 1801 to 1848? How did American Indians, women, and African Americans fit into the spectrum of American freedom and identity? In what way was a Mexican American identity present?

ANSWER KEY

Multiple Choice

1. a; medium; pp. 382–384; video segment 1
2. b; medium; pp. 384–387; video segment 2
3. c; medium; p. 394; video segments 2, 3
4. d; medium; pp. 389–391; video segment 3
5. a; easy; pp. 394–395; video segment 4
6. b; medium; pp. 395–399; video segment 4
7. c; medium; pp. 395–399; video segment 4
8. d; medium; comprehensive, lessons 13-18
9. a; difficult; pp. 399–402; video segment 4
10. b; medium; comprehensive, lessons 13–18
11. c; medium; comprehensive, lessons 13–18
12. d; medium; comprehensive, lessons 13–18

Short Answer

1. difficult; pp. 382–384; video segment 1
    - What noble ideas are being spread across the continent?
    - How does it connect to the Puritan mission and the Revolutionary ideals?
    - How would the idea help avert criticism of expansionism?

2. easy; pp. 384–387, 394; video segments 2, 3
    - What else was concerning the United States at the same time?
    - What attitudes did the Americans have toward the British?
    - Where was the boundary drawn? Why there?

3. medium; pp. 394–395; video segment 4
    - What was the incident that sparked the war?
    - Take a stand on the actions taken.
    - Explain your position.

4. medium; pp. 399–402; video segment 4
    - What did the Treaty of Guadalupe Hidalgo say about these people?
    - What happened to the property rights involved?
    - What sort of cultural adaptation occurred in the short term?

Essay

1. medium; comprehensive, lessons 13–18
   - Consider the Louisiana Purchase and the Adams-Onis Treaty. What areas were acquired? How did Oregon become part of the United States?
   - How and why was Texas annexed?
   - What territories were acquired in the Mexican Cession?
   - Consider the positive and negative effects.

2. difficult; comprehensive, Lessons 13–18; video segment 5
   - Consider how the free-labor concept emerged during this time.
   - Did political freedom change for white men?
   - How did the status of American Indians change? How could they maintain an identity?
   - How were women challenging limits on their freedom?
   - How did the status of African Americans deny freedom? What was their identity?
   - What occurred to affect Mexican Americans?

LESSON 19:
CRISIS AND COMPROMISE

Multiple Choice   Choose the letter of the best answer.

1. By 1850, one of the essential differences between the North and South was based upon
   a. rich versus poor.
   b. corn versus cotton.
   c. Whigs versus Democrats.
   d. free labor versus slave labor.

2. In 1850, New York City was
   a. a hotbed of abolitionist activity.
   b. losing business to Albany.
   c. closely involved with the well-being of the South.
   d. the eastern terminus for the transcontinental railroad.

3. By 1850, Charleston was characterized by all of the following EXCEPT
   a. open discussion of the slavery issue.
   b. laws preventing free black seamen from being in the city.
   c. having a small elite of urban blacks.
   d. being proud of its appearance.

4. By 1850, St. Louis was
   a. lobbying for approval of funding for a transcontinental railroad.
   b. ideally located for trade both east and west.
   c. largely removed from the slavery issue.
   d. suffering from an economic depression.

5. In referring to Santa Fe in 1850, Professor Deena Gonzalez uses the story of Gertrudes Barcelo to illustrate
   a. opportunities available in a time of transition.
   b. discrimination against women of Mexican origin.
   c. resistance to the United States takeover.
   d. attempts to destroy the pueblo people.

6. In Oregon in 1850,
   a. overland trade with the east was booming.
   b. free blacks were welcomed.
   c. relations between white settlers and Indian peoples were strained.
   d. the border dispute with Britain remained contentious.

7. In 1850, San Francisco
   a. became the capital of California.
   b. was experiencing a population boom.
   c. served as a model for efficient city government.
   d. banned the entry of Asians.

8. Southerners feared the admission of California as a free state because they
   a. wanted to use San Francisco as a slave-trading center.
   b. believed in upholding the terms of the Missouri Compromise.
   c. knew Mexican Americans were in positions of power there.
   d. would lose the balance of power in the U.S. Senate.

9. In the video, Professor James Roark observes Stephen Douglas' genius during the debates on the Compromise of 1850 was illustrated by his
   a. willingness to challenge John C. Calhoun.
   b. foresight in tabling discussion on the slave trade issue.
   c. insistence that fugitive slaves be protected.
   d. ability to gain majority approval on each piece of legislation.

10. In the video, Professor James Roark states the view that, for white southerners, the real test of the Compromise of 1850 would be determined by
    a. the spread of slaves into New Mexico.
    b. efforts to curb abolitionist activities in the South.
    c. northern willingness to abide by the Fugitive Slave Act.
    d. the success of the Democrats in the 1852 presidential election.

11. In the video, Professor Michael Holt supports the view that the Compromise of 1850
    a. conceded too much to the South.
    b. averted a civil war for a decade.
    c. should have balanced California's admission with a slave state.
    d. left too many issues unresolved.

Short Answer   Your answers should specifically address the points indicated in one or two paragraphs.

1. Why and how was New York state somewhat divided on the issue of slavery in 1850?

2. How did the views of David Wilmot, John C. Calhoun, and Lewis Cass articulate three distinct positions on the issue of slavery in the territories? Why did each take the position that he did?

Essay Question   Your response should be several paragraphs long. Your answer should elaborate on the points indicated in a manner that expresses understanding of the material.

1. Describe and explain the background, issues, terms, and consequences of the Compromise of 1850.

ANSWER KEY

Multiple Choice

1. d; medium; video segment 1
2. c; medium; pp. 400–401; video segment 2
3. a; medium; pp. 400–401; document; video segment 2
4. b; medium; pp. 400–401; document; video segment 2
5. a; difficult; pp. 400–401; document; video segment 2
6. c; medium; pp. 400–401; document; video segment 2
7. b; easy; pp. 400–401; document; video segment 2
8. d; medium; pp. 454–455; video segments 2, 3
9. d; medium; pp. 454–456; document, video segment 3
10. c; medium; video segment 4
11. b; medium; video segment 4

Short Answer

1. medium; pp. 400–401; document, video segment 2
    - What was going on in upstate New York regarding slavery?
    - Why did New York City have less enthusiasm for abolition?

2. medium; pp. 451–453
    - Who was Wilmot? Why did he want to keep slavery out of the territories? How did he propose to do that?
    - Who was Calhoun? On what basis did he think that slaves could not be kept out of the territories? Why is there some irony in his position?
    - Who was Cass? What did "popular sovereignty" mean? Why was it a middle ground?

Essay

1. difficult; pp. 400–401, 450–457; document; video segments 1–4
    - Background: How had the issue of slavery in the territories been dealt with previously? What prompted the "Great Debate" in 1850?
    - Issues: Why was California's admission as a free state important? What should be done with the other territory acquired from Mexico? What was the border dispute between Texas and New Mexico? Why were fugitive slaves in general and the slave trade in Washington, D.C., issues?
    - Terms: What agreement was reached on the above issues?
    - Consequences: What did each side gain or lose? What was the poison pill in the agreement? Why was it important?

LESSON 20:
IRREPRESSIBLE CONFLICTS

Multiple Choice   Choose the letter of the best answer.

1. In the video, Professor Paul Finkelman observes that, ironically, enforcing the Fugitive Slave Law of 1850 meant
   a. southerners opposed states' rights.
   b. abolitionists advocated adhering to federal law.
   c. free blacks were guaranteed constitutional rights.
   d. federal marshals could not cross state lines.

2. The case of Anthony Burns illustrated that
   a. firm resistance could protect fugitive slaves.
   b. President Franklin Pierce would enforce the Fugitive Slave Law.
   c. William Lloyd Garrison would support the Constitution.
   d. free blacks would receive federal protection.

3. As a result of the Kansas-Nebraska Act, Indian peoples in that region
   a. gained popular sovereignty rights.
   b. engaged in another frontier war.
   c. banned slavery on their reservations.
   d. ceded more land and moved.

4. In the video, Professor Paul Finkelman states that the Dred Scott decision affirmed that
   a. popular sovereignty would prevail in Kansas.
   b. African Americans had rights as citizens.
   c. the Constitution was proslavery.
   d. the Supreme Court was objective and non-partisan.

5. In the video, Professor Richard Blackett observes that the events of the mid-1850s
   a. radicalized many Northerners.
   b. illustrated the weakness of the abolitionists.
   c. solidified Democratic Party unity.
   d. all of the above.

Short Answer   Your answers should specifically address the points indicated in one or two paragraphs.

1.   What role did violence play in shaping public opinion and public policy in the period of 1850 to 1857? Describe two examples to support your answer.

2.   Why did Stephen Douglas support the concept of popular sovereignty? Why did popular sovereignty fail in Kansas?

3.   Why did the national party system break down in the 1850s? What was important about that?

Essay Question   Your response should be several paragraphs long. Your answer should elaborate on the points indicated in a manner that expresses understanding of the material.

1.   Describe and explain how and why the conflicts surrounding the Fugitive Slave Act of 1850, the Kansas-Nebraska Act, and the *Dred Scott* decision threatened the national unity of the United States of America.

ANSWER KEY

Multiple Choice

1.   a; difficult; pp. 456–459; documents, video segment 2
2.   b; medium; video segment 2
3.   d; medium; pp. 463–464; video segment 4
4.   c; medium; pp. 475–476; video segment 6
5.   a; difficult; pp. 456–476; video segments 1–7

Short Answer

1.   medium; pp. 456–459, 469–474; video segments 2, 4
   - Consider how violent action sharpened the growing division over slavery.
   - How much violence was used in resisting the Fugitive Slave law? What happened in Boston in particular?
   - What types of violence were associated with "Bleeding Kansas"? What were the effects?

2.   difficult; pp. 463–464, 472–474; video segment 4
   - Consider Douglas' party, the interests he represented, and his goals.
   - Why would popular sovereignty be attractive?
   - Explain what happened in Kansas that led to failure of the concept there.

3.   medium; pp. 464–469; video segments 4, 5
   - Why did the Whig Party practically disappear during the decade?
   - What area and positions did the Republican Party represent?
   - What stresses were being placed on the Democratic Party?
   - What happens when sectional interests are paramount?

Essay

1. difficult; pp. 456–476; video segments 1–7
    - Why did the Fugitive Slave Act heighten tensions? How was it resisted? How were sectional interests affected?
    - Why was the Kansas-Nebraska Act so controversial? What happened as a result?
    - What did the *Dred Scott* decision say? What choices were left for those opposed to the expansion of slavery?
    - Consider how the Compromise of 1850 was breaking down. What was dividing the nation?

LESSON 21:
THE UNION COLLAPSES

Multiple Choice   Choose the letter of the best answer.

1. Abraham Lincoln's "House Divided" speech was important because it
   a. stated his opposition to secession in vivid language.
   b. helped him emerge as a national opponent to Stephen Douglas.
   c. foreshadowed his position fortifying Fort Sumter.
   d. enabled him to gain the presidential nomination on the first ballot.

2. Abraham Lincoln's "Cooper Union" speech was important because it was
   a. well received in New York.
   b. delivered in the stronghold of another major Republican.
   c. credited with making Lincoln many people's second choice for his party's presidential nomination.
   d. all of the above.

3. John Brown organized a raid on Harpers Ferry in 1859 in order to
   a. lead a secessionist movement in the South.
   b. challenge Robert E. Lee's command of the military.
   c. incite a slave rebellion in Virginia.
   d. help Abraham Lincoln become president.

4. John Brown became a symbolic threat to southerners because they
   a. believed their own propaganda about the man.
   b. had proof that Lincoln supported him.
   c. refused to support any act of treason.
   d. thought he was a Christ-like figure.

5. In the video, several historians state the view that
   a. better political leadership could have avoided the Civil War.
   b. greater freedom for blacks in the South was inevitable.
   c. some kind of conflict between the sections seemed certain to happen.
   d. stronger efforts should have been made to compromise the issues in 1861.

Short Answer   Your answers should specifically address the points indicated in one or two paragraphs.

1. Explain Abraham Lincoln's views on slavery prior to the outbreak of the Civil War.

2. Explain why the Lincoln-Douglas debates were significant in 1858 and in 1860.

3. Why would Abraham Lincoln give some credit to Mathew Brady for his victory in the 1860 election? What does this say about elections in general?

4. Do you think it is fair to say that John Brown fired the "first shots" of the Civil War at Harpers Ferry in 1859? Why or why not?

5. Why did Abraham Lincoln win the presidential election of 1860?

Essay Question   Your response should be several paragraphs long. Your answer should elaborate on the points indicated in a manner that expresses understanding of the material.

1. How and why had the United States moved to the brink of a Civil War between 1858 and 1861? Was the Civil War inevitable?

2. Looking at the period from 1850 to 1861, analyze the key developments that led to the failure of compromise.

3. During the winter of 1860–1861, seven southern states seceded from the Union. Explain the development of this idea and process from the 1780s to 1861.

ANSWER KEY

Multiple Choice

1. b; medium; video segment 2
2. d; difficult; video segment 2
3. c; medium; video segment 2
4. a; medium; pp. 480-481; document; video segment 4
5. c; medium; p. 486; video segment 6

Short Answer

1. medium; pp. 365–366, 476–477, 479; video segment 2
    - How did his family background and work experience affect his outlook?
    - What did his membership in the Whig and then Republican parties mean in this regard?
    - Why was he so opposed to the *Dred Scott* decision and popular sovereignty?

2. medium; pp. 479, 483–484; document; video segments 2, 5
    - What was Lincoln trying to accomplish in the debates?
    - What was important about the Freeport Doctrine?
    - What happened as a result of the debates in 1858?
    - How is the Illinois senate race connected to the presidential election in 1860?

3. medium; pp. 483–484; video segment 5
    - Who is Mathew Brady and what did he do?
    - What effect did Brady's action have on the election?
    - How important is image in elections? Why is it important?

4. medium; pp. 448–450, 480–481; document, video segment 4
    *   What exactly did Brown do?
    *   What were the reactions from the North and the South to Brown's actions and his hanging?
    *   What is your opinion? Why do you hold that view?

5. easy; pp. 480–484; video segment 5
    *   Why was Lincoln a strong candidate? Who were his opponents?
    *   What issues attracted voters to Lincoln?
    *   What sort of campaign did Lincoln undertake? What did he have to do to win?
    *   What do the election results demonstrate about our electoral system?

Essay

1. medium; pp. 448–450, 458–459, 477–484; video segments 2–5
    *   What was the significance of the Lincoln-Douglas debates?
    *   What role did John Brown's raid and execution have on emotions and beliefs?
    *   What was the importance of the 1860 presidential election?
    *   Why was secession a threat to the United States?

2. difficult; Comprehensive of Lessons 20, 21
    *   What was the most controversial part of the Compromise of 1850? What issues did this arouse?
    *   What role did the abolitionists play in the 1850s?
    *   Why was the Kansas-Nebraska Act so significant?
    *   What effect did "Bleeding Kansas" have on the nation?
    *   What was the significance of the *Dred Scott* decision?
    *   Why were the Lincoln-Douglas debates important?
    *   Why were the actions of John Brown critical?
    *   Why did the presidential election of 1860 lead to a secession movement?

3. difficult; Comprehensive of Lessons 20, 21
    *   Was the Constitution a compact between states or a compact between the people of all the states?
    *   How did the Virginia and Kentucky Resolutions affect the concept of states' rights?
    *   Why did the nullification crisis of the 1830s escalate the development of secessionist thought?
    *   How and why did the leaders of the secessionist movement finally proceed to act in 1860–1861?

LESSON 22:
AND THE WAR CAME

Multiple Choice   Choose the letter of the best answer.

1. At the time of his inauguration, President Abraham Lincoln's choices regarding Fort Sumter included all of the following EXCEPT
   a. pull out the troops stationed there.
   b. ask Great Britain to mediate the dispute.
   c. send in armed reinforcements.
   d. supply the fort with provisions.

2. In the video, Professor James McPherson refers to Lincoln's choice of action regarding Fort Sumter as a
   a. miscalculation.
   b. stroke of genius.
   c. recognition of Southern claims.
   d. provocation to Great Britain.

3. Major Robert Anderson surrendered Fort Sumter in April 1861 because he
   a. supported the Confederacy.
   b. mistrusted Lincoln's motives.
   c. had no chance to survive otherwise.
   d. wanted to initiate a wider war.

4. In the video, Professor James McPherson maintains that the border states of Maryland, Kentucky, and Missouri were
   a. critical to eventual northern victory.
   b. likely to join the Confederacy in 1862.
   c. on the verge of outlawing slavery prior to the attack on Fort Sumter.
   d. certain to be sites for major battles in the Civil War.

5. In the video, Professor Gary Gallagher states that the key to victory in the Civil War for each side was
   a. conquering the other's territory.
   b. gaining diplomatic recognition from Great Britain.
   c. establishing an effective railway system.
   d. maintaining the support of the civilian population.

6. According to historian James McPherson, both General Robert E. Lee and General Ulysses S. Grant were
   a. not afraid of failure.
   b. unwilling to take risks.
   c. overrated.
   d. brilliant in their pre-Civil War careers.

7. General George McClellan was a disappointment to President Lincoln because he
   a. did not train troops well.
   b. failed at of West Point.
   c. was afraid to risk failure.
   d. tried to split the Republican Party.

8. The Battle of Shiloh was important because
   a. the South maintained control of northern Mississippi.
   b. Generals Lee and Grant had faced off for the first time.
   c. the North gained control of the Mississippi River.
   d. it indicated that the war was going to be costly.

Short Answer   Your answers should specifically address the points indicated in one or two paragraphs.

1. Do you think that President Abraham Lincoln forced the South to fire the first shots of the Civil War? Why or why not?

2. Why did Southerners generally avoid saying that they were fighting the war to maintain slavery? What were the effects of taking this position?

3. What did the South have to do to win the war? What did the North have to do?

4. Compare and contrast the military leadership of Generals Ulysses S. Grant and Robert E. Lee.

Essay Question   Your response should be several paragraphs long. Your answer should elaborate on the points indicated in a manner that expresses understanding of the material.

1. Describe and explain the advantages and disadvantages of each side at the beginning of the Civil War. How did the major battles fought in 1861–1862 illustrate each side's strengths and weaknesses? What was the status of the war at the end of 1862?

ANSWER KEY

Multiple Choice

1. b; medium; pp. 494-495; video segment 2
2. b; medium; pp. 494-495; video segment 2
3. c; medium; video segment 2
4. a; medium; pp. 496-497; video segment 3
5. d; medium; pp. 498-500; video segment 3
6. a; medium; video segment 4
7. c; easy; pp. 502-504; video segment 5
8. d; medium; pp. 504-506; video segment 5

Short Answer

1. easy; pp. 494–495; video segment 2
   - What did Lincoln do?
   - What choices did the South have?
   - Take a position and defend it.

2. difficult; pp. 497–498; video segment 3
   - What reasons did they give for fighting?
   - To what extent was their way of life dependent on slavery?
   - How would this appeal to non-slaveholders?
   - Would this make the cause more noble?
   - How would this affect southern attitudes after the war?

3. medium; pp. 498–500; video segment 3
   - Explain the advantages, challenges, and strategy of each side.
   - Consider the importance of maintaining civilian support.

4. medium; video segment 4
   - What was Grant's greatest talent as a commander?
   - What was Lee's greatest talent?
   - What quality of leadership did they both have in common?

Essay

1. medium; pp. 495–506; documents; video segments 3, 4, 5
   - Consider resources, geography, and civilian and military leadership.
   - Consider the battles of Bull Run, Forts Henry and Donelson, Shiloh, Antietam, and Fredericksburg.
   - Evaluate the relative positions of each side at this point in the war.

LESSON 23: HOME FRONTS

Multiple Choice   Choose the letter of the best answer.

1. In the video, Professor James Oliver Horton points out that the Emancipation Proclamation
   a. freed all slaves in the United States.
   b. reflected President Lincoln's racist views.
   c. focused the war on the South's attempt to preserve slavery.
   d. appeased the non-slaveholding Southerners.

2. The military involvement of the 54th Massachusetts regiment in the Civil War indicated that black troops
   a. were poorly trained.
   b. needed black officers.
   c. avoided most combat situations.
   d. could be courageous under fire.

3. Augusta County, Virginia, was typical of the southern home front during the Civil War in the respect that
   a. prices remained relatively stable.
   b. wheat production dominated the economy.
   c. white residents supported the union.
   d. slavery began to disintegrate during the war.

4. Franklin County, Pennsylvania, was typical of much of the northern home front during the Civil War in all of the following ways EXCEPT
   a. confederate troops moved across its soil.
   b. businesses prospered.
   c. families worried about military casualties.
   d. blacks fleeing the South passed through.

5. "Digital history" opens up new opportunities for
   a. students to become historians.
   b. universities to offer fewer classes.
   c. businesses to alter records.
   d. libraries to restrict access to sources.

Short Answer   Your answers should specifically address the points indicated in one or two paragraphs.

1.   How was the Civil War a "rich man's war and a poor man's fight" on both sides? Do you think this is typical of most wars? Why or why not?

2.   How did Augusta County, Virginia, and Franklin County, Pennsylvania, illustrate the issues of the home fronts during the Civil War?

Essay Question   Your response should be several paragraphs long. Your answer should elaborate on the points indicated in a manner that expresses understanding of the material.

1.   Slavery was the fundamental issue leading to the outbreak of the Civil War and remained a key issue during the war. Explain the background, purpose, and results of the Emancipation Proclamation. How was slavery disintegrating during the war? How did the use of black troops alter the course of the war? What did all of these wartime developments indicate about the future of slavery in the United States?

2.   Compare and contrast the home fronts of the North and South during the Civil War. In your answer, be sure to address how the war affected the economy, politics, and society of both sections. How did the developments on the home fronts affect the eventual outcome of the war?

ANSWER KEY

Multiple Choice

1.   c; medium; pp. 509-510; video segment 2
2.   d; medium; pp. 510-511; video segment 2
3.   d; medium; video segment 4
4.   a; medium; video segment 3
5.   a; medium; video segment 5

Short Answer

1.   medium; pp. 513–515, 519–522; video segments 3, 4
     - Consider who was in a position to benefit from the Civil War.
     - Describe how conscription was handled in the war. Who could be exempt?
     - From what you know, how does the Civil War compare to other wars in this regard?

2.   medium; video segments 3, 4
     - How was the economy affected by the war in these areas?
     - To what extent was physical damage due to battles (or the threat of fighting) a factor?
     - Consider how slavery was disintegrating in Augusta County and the experience of Franklin County with refugees.
     - How were families most affected?

Essay

1.   difficult; pp. 507–522; video segments 2–4, 6
   - Consider the pressures Lincoln faced prior to the Proclamation.
   - Clarify the purpose of the document. What exactly did it do?
   - How did the Proclamation transform the nature of war?
   - How did slaves take their own initiatives toward emancipation in areas in rebellion?
   - How important were black troops? How did they get involved in the fighting?
   - What expectations were raised? Could slavery survive if the Union won?

2.   medium; pp. 507–522; video segments 2–4, 6
   - Consider the economic challenges and opportunities of both sides.
   - How could the North maintain a two-party system? How much power could and did Lincoln exercise? How did the South's emphasis on states' rights affect their war effort?
   - How did class issues surface? How was the race issue addressed?
   - Consider how and why the North was able to marshal its resources and maintain the war.
   - How could the South sustain the support of the civilian population?

LESSON 24:
UNION PRESERVED, FREEDOM SECURED

Multiple Choice   Choose the letter of the best answer.

1. Vicksburg, Mississippi, was an important military objective for the Union because seizing it would allow the Union to
   a. stop the export of cotton.
   b. divide the Confederacy.
   c. force General Lee to surrender.
   d. implement the Emancipation Proclamation in that area.

2. The Union gained control of most of the Mississippi River in the battle of
   a. Gettysburg.
   b. Antietam.
   c. Vicksburg.
   d. Shiloh.

3. General Grant and the Union forces won the battle of Vicksburg by
   a. attacking from the east.
   b. laying siege to the city.
   c. running gunboats past Confederate fortifications.
   d. all of the above.

4. General Robert E. Lee invaded Pennsylvania in June of 1863 for all of the following reasons EXCEPT to
   a. take the war out of Virginia.
   b. gather food and fodder.
   c. engage Grant's army in a final showdown.
   d. shatter northern civilian morale.

5. One of the main reasons the Union forces won at Gettysburg was because
   a. General Meade fought a skillful battle.
   b. southern soldiers lost their courage.
   c. northern troops gave up their defensive positions.
   d. Lee failed to attack the center of Union strength.

6. As a result of the Battle of Gettysburg, the South
   a. lost control of the Mississippi River.
   b. suffered 28,000 casualties.
   c. suffered the loss of an important railroad center.
   d. decided to sue for peace.

7. In the Gettysburg Address, President Abraham Lincoln
   a. framed the Civil War as a test of American principles.
   b. called for the immediate emancipation of all slaves.
   c. recognized the values of the Confederacy.
   d. promoted General Meade to commander of all Union forces.

8. President Lincoln made Ulysses S. Grant General-in-Chief of Union forces in March 1864 because
   a. Lincoln did not want Grant to be a presidential candidate.
   b. General Meade had been killed the previous year at Gettysburg.
   c. Grant had proven to be a winner.
   d. General Lee was once again threatening to invade Pennsylvania.

9. The strategy employed by the Union forces in 1864–1865 was one of
   a. coordinated offensives.
   b. passive resistance.
   c. massive retaliation.
   d. aggressive defense.

10. The purpose of General William T. Sherman's march from Atlanta to the sea was to
   a. trap the Confederate army at Savannah.
   b. escape a Confederate attack.
   c. demoralize the civilian population.
   d. link up with Grant's forces.

11. Ulysses S. Grant's military successes were the result of his
   a. ability to win battles with small, mobile forces.
   b. extreme doggedness in sustaining huge Union casualties to force Confederate surrender.
   c. superior tactical skills.
   d. close consultation with Lincoln in working out military strategy.

12. All of the following were reasons why death rates were so high in the Civil War EXCEPT
   a. antiquated military strategies.
   b. callous doctors and nurses.
   c. rapid spread of disease.
   d. lack of medical knowledge.

13. The death toll from the Civil War was
   a. almost equal to the death total from all wars in which the United States has engaged.
   b. significantly smaller than the death toll of U.S. personnel in World War II.
   c. relatively light compared to U.S. casualties in Vietnam.
   d. grossly overstated by journalists covering the war.

14. All of the following contributed to Lincoln's reelection in 1864 EXCEPT
   a. massive voter registration of northern blacks.
   b. Union military victory on the eve of the election.
   c. the Democratic candidate's stance on the war issue
   d. Andrew Johnson's selection as Lincoln's running mate

15. In March of 1865, as the Confederacy was close to defeat, Jefferson Davis proposed the final desperate strategy of
    a. paying German mercenaries to fight against the North.
    b. using women in combat.
    c. assassinating Lincoln.
    d. having slaves become soldiers.

Short Answer   Your answers should specifically address the points indicated in one or two paragraphs.

1. Describe and explain the significance of the battles of Vicksburg and Gettysburg. How did the results of each battle shape the course of the Civil War?

2. How did Abraham Lincoln give meaning to the Civil War in the Gettysburg Address? What were the main ideas that he expressed? Why does that speech live on in American memory?

3. Describe and explain the major features of the Union's military strategy after Gettysburg. How did Generals Sherman, Sheridan, and Grant implement that strategy?

Essay Question   Your response should be several paragraphs long. Your answer should elaborate on the points indicated in a manner that expresses understanding of the material.

1. Describe and explain why the North won and the South lost the Civil War. In your answer, be sure to consider both the civilian and military aspects of the war.

2. Why is Abraham Lincoln considered to be the nation's greatest president? In your answer, be sure to analyze the essence of the Lincoln legacy and consider how he lives on in American memory.

3. How did the Civil War fundamentally transform America? In your answer, consider why some refer to the war as the "Second American Revolution" and how the Civil War lives on in American memory.

ANSWER KEY

Multiple Choice

1. b; medium; p. 523
2. c; easy; p. 523
3. d; difficult; p. 523
4. c; medium; pp. 522-523; video segment 2
5. a; medium; pp. 522-523; video segment 2
6. b; easy; pp. 522-523; video segment 2
7. a; medium; document; video segment 3
8. c; medium; document; video segment 3
9. a; easy; document; video segment 3
10. c; medium; pp. 524-525, 528; video segment 4
11. b; difficult; pp. 524-525, 528; video segment 4
12. b; medium; pp. 524-525, 528, 531; video segment 3
13. a; medium; pp. 524-525, 528, 531; video segment 3
14. a; medium; pp. 526-528
15. d; medium; pp. 528-530; video segment 4

Short Answer

1. medium; pp. 523–524; video segment 2
   - How were Grant and the Union forces able to attack Vicksburg, place it under siege, and eventually force it to surrender?
   - How did the victory at Vicksburg give the Union a strategic advantage?
   - What advantages did the North have in the battle of Gettysburg?
   - Why was the Union victory at Gettysburg a tremendous morale boost for the North?
   - How did the Union victories at Vicksburg and Gettysburg alter the course of the Civil War?

2. medium; document; video segment 3
   - How did the Gettysburg Address explain the significance of the battle at Gettysburg from the northern perspective?
   - How did Lincoln bring forward the ideals of the Declaration of Independence?
   - How did Lincoln add the element of a "new birth of freedom," and what did that mean?
   - How was "freedom" given a more inclusive definition?
   - What is your opinion on why the Gettysburg Address lives on in American memory?

3. medium; p. 523–528, 531; video segment 4
   - How did the Union plan to conquer the South?
   - What did General Sherman do to destroy the South's ability and willingness to fight?
   - What role did General Sheridan play in Union victory?
   - Why was General Grant able to push through to victory?

Essay

1. medium; pp. 493–531; video segments 4, 5, 6
   - How and why was the Union able to capitalize on its advantages?
   - How and why was the Confederacy not able to defend its claimed territory?
   - How important was President Lincoln to the Union cause?
   - What is your assessment of the most significant factors in the outcome?

2. medium; pp. 493–531; video segment 6
   - What factors determine presidential greatness?
   - How important was Lincoln's role during the Civil War?
   - What were Lincoln's strongest personal qualities?
   - How was Lincoln able to transform the nature of the Civil War?
   - What is your assessment of Lincoln's legacy, and how do he and that legacy live on?

3. medium; p. 532; video segment 6
   - How did the war alter the economic and political landscape of America?
   - How did the war affect African Americans?
   - What aspects of the war do you consider to be revolutionary?
   - Why does the Civil War have an enduring place in our national memory?

LESSON 25: RECONSTRUCTING THE NATION

Multiple Choice   Choose the letter of the best answer.

1. In the video, Professor Richard Blackett observes that for black Americans the Reconstruction era began as a period of
   a. despair.
   b. hope.
   c. fear.
   d. prosperity.

2. The 13th Amendment to the Constitution
   a. guaranteed equal protection of the laws.
   b. defined citizenship.
   c. abolished slavery.
   d. protected voting rights.

3. In the video, Professor Michael Perman observes that land was not redistributed to ex-slaves because
   a. that would have kept the South in turmoil for years.
   b. General Sherman promised to restore property to slaveholders.
   c. land was of little value because of the war.
   d. most ex-slaves moved north.

4. Voting by African Americans in the South during the first few years of Reconstruction was facilitated by all of the following EXCEPT
   a. union leagues.
   b. the Republican Party.
   c. churches.
   d. the Democratic Party.

5. Prince Rivers exemplifies a
   a. competent black politician during Reconstruction.
   b. White Redeemer who reclaimed political power by 1876.
   c. sharecropper who entered a debt cycle in the 1870s.
   d. corrupt Republican politician who move South after the war.

6. In the video, Professors Perman and Brundage indicate that northerners eventually gave up on reconstruction because of all the following reasons EXCEPT
   a. the whole project was very difficult to implement.
   b. whites in the South were militantly hostile.
   c. black politicians were too corrupt.
   d. expectations of northern whites were not being met by blacks.

7. In the video, historians observe that the South won the battle of history because
   a. black intellectuals were biased.
   b. influential southern historians projected Reconstruction as a total failure.
   c. northern historians neglected to study the period.
   d. southern scholars were better writers.

Short Answer Your answers should specifically address the points indicated in one or two paragraphs.

1. What did "freedom" mean to African Americans in 1865? How did ex-slaves begin to exercise freedom?

2. Why was freedom "contested territory" in the South during reconstruction? How was it contested?

3. What are the key provisions of the Thirteenth, Fourteenth, and Fifteenth Amendments? To what extent did these amendments bring about a "Constitutional revolution"?

4. How and why did sharecropping emerge during reconstruction? What were the short- and long-term consequences of this arrangement?

5. Why did the Ku Klux Klan emerge in the late 1860s? How did their terrorist activities affect the course of reconstruction?

6. Explain the following statement: "By 1870, Northerners had begun a retreat from the ideals of reconstruction."

7. Explain this statement: "The North won the war, but the South won the peace."

Essay Question Your response should be several paragraphs long. Your answer should elaborate on the points indicated in a manner that expresses understanding of the material.

1. In 1865, former Union General Carl Schurz referred to the Civil War as a "revolution but half accomplished." During the subsequent twelve years, the American people grappled with serious economic, social, and political issues. Describe and explain how these major issues were resolved. In what ways was the revolution still only half accomplished by 1877? What did that mean for the future of America?

ANSWER KEY

Multiple Choice

1. b; easy; pp. 536-538; video segment 1
2. c; easy; vide segment 2
3. a; difficult; pp. 540, 560-562; video segment 3
4. d; medium; pp. 551-552; video segment 5
5. a; medium; pp. 555-557, 560; video segment 5
6. c; difficult; pp. 564-565; video segment 7
7. b; difficult; pp. 536-573; video segments 1-8

Short Answer

1. medium; pp. 541–545; video segment 3
   - Consider elements of personal freedom that had not been possible before, e.g., regarding mobility, family, expression, religion, education, etc.
   - How did slaves pursue economic freedom?

2. medium; pp. 546–549, 556–559, 565–567; video segments 3, 5
   - Consider why black codes were passed and what they tried to do.
   - What happened regarding land and labor?
   - What motivated the Ku Klux Klan and other terrorist groups? How effective were they?

3. medium; pp. 549–551, 553–557, 560; video segments 2, 4–6
   - How did these amendments affect slavery, citizenship and equal rights, and voting?
   - What fundamental changes did this mean for the American people?

4. medium; pp. 540, 560–562; video segment 3
   - Consider the needs of landowners and laborers.
   - How did this system address those needs?
   - Were there benefits of the system?
   - What was the major fault with this system?

5. medium; pp. 556–559; video segment 5
   - Who joined the Klan? What were their motives?
   - What effect did the Klan have on black participation in politics?
   - How did Klan activity affect Northerners and reconstruction policies?

6. medium; pp. 564–565; video segment 7
   - Why would a shift in attitude set in?
   - How did the Grant administration indicate a different direction in northern policies and emphasis?
   - What role did racial prejudice play?

7. medium; pp. 536–573; video segments 1–8
   - How had the South successfully resisted northern efforts to reshape their society?
   - Who was in power in the South by 1877? What did that mean for African Americans?
   - Who told the story of Reconstruction for generations?

Essay

1. medium; pp. 536–573; video segments 1–8
   - What were the major economic issues involving land and labor?
   - How was freedom for blacks going to be protected? How would equality be expanded?
   - How would black participation in the political process proceed?
   - How did resolution of these issues take place? What was the status of the ex-Confederate states by 1877? What was the status of the ex-slaves?
   - Do you think a golden opportunity was missed by the American people during Reconstruction? What issues were postponed for later generations?

LESSON 26:
LOOKING BACKWARD,
LOOKING FORWARD

Multiple Choice   Choose the letter of the best answer.

1. All of the following were innovations featured at the Centennial Exhibition in 1876 EXCEPT
   a. radio.
   b. telephone.
   c. dishwashing machine.
   d. 1,500-horsepower engine.

2. By 1876, New York City was characterized by
   a. public ownership of all utilities.
   b. clear divisions between the living conditions of the rich and poor.
   c. isolation from economic development in the West.
   d. political corruption that sealed Samuel Tildon's presidential election victory.

3. In 1876, all of the following characterized San Francisco EXCEPT
   a. busy seaport.
   b. sophisticated culture.
   c. heavy damage from an earthquake.
   d. high percentage of foreign-born residents.

4. In 1876, Portland, Oregon, was characterized by
   a. a strong Catholic missionary impulse.
   b. a sophisticated culture.
   c. the second busiest seaport in the country.
   d. single white male laborers.

5. In 1876, Mexican Americans in the Santa Fe region were
   a. suffering an erosion of status.
   b. dominating local politics.
   c. benefiting from trade with the East.
   d. receiving compensation for lands taken after the war.

6. By the mid-1870s, Charleston, South Carolina, was experiencing
   a. continued oppression by carpetbaggers.
   b. some resurgence in business.
   c. serious strikes by labor unions.
   d. renewed talk of secession.

7. In the video, Professor James O. Horton observes that in regard to African Americans in 1876,
   a. they had less freedom than in 1776.
   b. constitutional amendments had no positive effect.
   c. the federal government seemed less willing to protect rights.
   d. most of them had moved out of the South.

8. The Thomas Jefferson-Sally Hemings relationship
   a. was fabricated by a fringe group of writers.
   b. shows the compassion Jefferson had for his slaves.
   c. was widely accepted by early twentieth century historians.
   d. illustrates that America has been more of a mixed-race place than previously acknowledged.

9. In the video, Professor James O. Horton points out that
   a. the advantages of race may be defined differently in different eras.
   b. DNA testing is not a reliable historical source.
   c. race relations need to be determined by state law.
   d. biological differences make mixing of the races imprudent.

Short Answer   Your answers should specifically address the points indicated in one or two paragraphs.

1. Why was Chicago displacing St. Louis as the commercial center of the Midwest by 1876?

2. In what ways did American Indians enjoy less freedom in 1876 than in 1776?

3. Why were women still told in the 1870s that different treatment was really privilege?

4. How and why has race been a social construction in America?

Essay Question   Your response should be several paragraphs long. Your answer should elaborate on the points indicated in a manner that expresses understanding of the material.

1. We have examined the development of the cities of New York, Charleston, St. Louis, Santa Fe, San Francisco, and Portland. How and why had these cities changed between the time of their founding and 1876? How would you characterize each city in 1876?

2. How and why had the story of American freedom changed from the colonial period to 1876? How and why was freedom limited? Why is the story of freedom unfinished?

3. Who is an American? What does being an American mean? How and why did American identity develop and change from the colonial period to 1876?

4. The idea of equality has been a core principle of the United States since 1776. How and why was the United States pushed to uphold this idea between 1776 and 1876? What was the status of equality in America in 1876?

ANSWER KEY

Multiple Choice
1. a; easy; video segment 1
2. b; medium; video segment 2
3. c; medium; video segment 2
4. d; medium; video segment 2
5. a; medium; video segment 2
6. b; medium; video segment 2

7. c; difficult; video segment 3
8. d; medium; video segment 4
9. a; difficult; video segment 4

Short Answer

1. easy; video segment 2
    - What effect were railroads having on commerce?
    - Why had St. Louis been slow to support railroad construction?

2. medium; video segment 3
    - In what geographic area did Indians have freedom in 1776?
    - How and why had they lost territory during the century?
    - What was their status in 1876?

3. difficult; video segment 3
    - What rights were denied women in 1876?
    - Why did men fear granting women equal rights?
    - How did the "privilege" argument try to dispel women's demands?

4. medium; video segment 4
    - To whose advantage did racial definitions go?
    - Are there any biological reasons or natural law reasons to draw racial distinctions?

Essay

1. medium; video segments 2; Lessons 2, 3, 5, 11, 19
    - Consider the role of geography in relation to each city.
    - How did population growth affect the cities? Who tended to settle there?
    - What sort of economic growth had taken place?
    - What is the status of each city in 1876?

2. medium; video segments 1-5; Lessons 6, 12, 18
    - Who was free in colonial America? How was freedom expressed?
    - How did the revolutionary period universalize and democratize freedom?
    - What role did manifest destiny have on freedom?
    - What was the free-labor ideal?
    - How did freedom change for minorities?
    - How do you think the boundaries of freedom will change in the future?

3. difficult; video segments 1-5; Lessons 6, 12, 18
    - To what extent did American identity apply to all people living in America?
    - Did a distinctive American identity emerge in colonial America?
    - How did the Declaration of Independence and the Constitution affect American identity?
    - How did the Civil War result in a definition of citizenship?
    - Who was excluded from the full rights of citizenship in 1876?

4. difficult; video segments 1-5; Lessons 6, 12, 18
    - What did equality mean in 1776?
    - How did society give meaning to equality?
    - Who was excluded from equal rights and opportunities? How did they try to be included?
    - Who was still excluded from equality in 1876? Why?